ALSO BY BARRY STRAUSS

Masters of Command: Alexander, Hannibal,
Caesar, and the Genius of Leadership

The Spartacus War

The Trojan War: A New History

The Battle of Salamis: The Naval Encounter That
Saved Greece—and Western Civilization

What If? The World's Foremost Military Historians
Imagine What Might Have Been
(contributor)

Western Civilization: The Continuing Experiment
(with Thomas F. X. Noble and others)

War and Democracy: A Comparative Study of the
Korean War and the Peloponnesian War
(with David McCann, co-editor)

Rowing Against the Current: Learning to Scull at Forty

Fathers and Sons in Athens: Ideology and Society
in the Era of the Peloponnesian War

Hegemonic Rivalry: From Thucydides to the Nuclear Age
(with Richard Ned Lebow, co-editor)

The Anatomy of Error: Ancient Military Disasters
and Their Lessons for Modern Strategists
(with Josiah Ober)

Athens After the Peloponnesian War:
Class, Faction and Policy, 403–386 B.C.

The
DEATH
of
CAESAR

The Story of History's
Most Famous Assassination

BARRY STRAUSS

SIMON & SCHUSTER

New York   London   Toronto   Sydney   New Delhi

Simon & Schuster
1230 Avenue of the Americas
New York, NY 10020

First Simon & Schuster hardcover edition March 2015

SIMON & SCHUSTER and colophon are registered
trademarks of Simon & Schuster, Inc.

For information about special discounts for bulk purchases,
please contact Simon & Schuster Special Sales at
1-866-506-1949 or business@simonandschuster.com.

The Simon & Schuster Speakers Bureau can bring authors to your live event.
For more information or to book an event, contact the Simon & Schuster Speakers
Bureau at 1-866-248-3049 or visit our website at www.simonspeakers.com.

Interior design by Ruth Lee-Mui
Maps by Jeffrey L. Ward
Jacket design by Michael Accordino
Jacket image courtesy private collection of David Xavier Kenney
Spine photograph: Statue of Julius Caesar © Ruth Eastham & Max Paoli/Getty Images

Manufactured in the United States of America

10 9 8 7 6 5 4 3

Library of Congress Cataloging-in-Publication Data is available.

ISBN 978-1-4516-6879-7
ISBN 978-1-4516-6882-7 (ebook)

To Marcia

Contents

Part Three

THE ROAD BACK

Author's Note

Ancient names are spelled following the style of the standard reference work, *The Oxford Classical Dictionary*, 3rd ed. (Oxford: Oxford University Press, 1999).

Translations from the Greek or Latin are my own, unless otherwise noted.

Chronology

September 28, 48	Death of Pompey
Autumn 48	Caesar Meets Cleopatra
April 46	Death of Cato
September 21–October 2, 46	Caesar celebrates four triumphs
September 26, 46	Temple of Mother Venus dedicated
March 17, 45	Battle of Munda
August 45	Caesar, Antony, Decimus, and Octavian travel together
September 13, 45	Caesar amends will in favor of Octavian
October 45	Caesar's fifth triumph
December 31, 45	Caesar appoints one-day consul
January 26, 44	"I am Caesar, not Rex"
January–February 44	Caesar becomes Dictator in Perpetuity
February 15, 44	Lupercalia; Caesar rejects diadem
March 15, 44 B.C.	Caesar assassinated
March 17, 44	Amnesty for assassins
	Caesar's acts confirmed
March 20, 44	Caesar's funeral
June 7, 44	Antium Conference
August 44	Brutus and Cassius leave Italy
April 14, 43	Battle of Forum Gallorum
April 21, 43	Battle of Mutina
August 19, 43	Octavian's first consulship
September 43	Death of Decimus
November 27, 43	Second Triumvirate Established
December 7, 43	Death of Cicero
October 3, 42	First Battle of Philippi
	Death of Cassius
October 23, 42	Second Battle of Philippi
	Death of Brutus
35	Death of Sextus Pompey
September 2, 31	Battle of Actium

August 1, 30	Antony commits suicide
August 12, 30	Cleopatra commits suicide
30	Egypt becomes Roman province
August 18, 29	Temple of Deified Julius dedicated
January 16, 27	Octavian receives name Augustus

Cast of Characters

CAESAR'S MEN

CAESAR (Gaius Julius Caesar), 100–44 B.C. Brilliant politician, general, and writer, he was eventually Dictator in Perpetuity. The most polarizing figure of the age, he made many Romans fear that he wanted to become king and harm their interests, and so they decided to assassinate him. Age in 44 B.C.—fifty-five.*

OCTAVIAN (Gaius Julius Caesar Octavianus, born Gaius Octavius, later Imperator Caesar divi Filius and, finally, Augustus), 63 B.C.–A.D. 14. Caesar's brilliant and ruthless grandnephew and heir made his way through the dangerous political waters of the age to become Augustus, Rome's first emperor. Age in 44 B.C.—eighteen on the Ides of March.

MARK ANTONY (Marcus Antonius), ca. 83–30 B.C. One of Caesar's best generals, he was a cagey politician who defeated the assassins, became

* Age in 44 B.C. stated if known or at least roughly known.

Cleopatra's lover and one of the two most powerful men in the Roman Empire, only to be defeated by Octavian. Age in 44 B.C.—thirty-nine.

LEPIDUS (Marcus Aemilius Lepidus), ca. 89–12 B.C. One of Caesar's generals, a loyalist, he commanded a legion in Rome at the time of Caesar's assassination. He was Chief Priest and eventually one of the three triumvirs but he was squeezed out by Antony and Octavian. Age in 44 B.C.—forty-five.

THE MAIN CONSPIRATORS

BRUTUS (Marcus Junius Brutus), ca. 85–42 B.C. Brutus's name, eloquence, and reputation for ethical behavior made him the most famous of the assassins and their public face. On the less positive side, he had a penchant for betrayal and he squeezed money out of provincials. He wanted to kill Caesar without launching a revolution or disturbing the peace—an impossible ambition. Age in 44 B.C.—forty.

CASSIUS (Gaius Cassius Longinus), ca. 86–42 B.C. Perhaps the man who hatched the conspiracy, Cassius was a military man and a supporter of Pompey, who only reluctantly accepted Caesar before finally turning on him. He advocated harsher measures than his brother-in-law, Brutus. Age in 44 B.C.—forty-one.

DECIMUS (Decimus Junius Brutus Albinus), ca. 81–43 B.C. Often forgotten, Decimus was the third leader of the conspiracy against Caesar. A brilliant young general from a noble family, he rose in Gaul under Caesar and then turned on him, either out of republican principle or thwarted ambition, or both. He fought Antony in Italy and Gaul, was betrayed and executed. Age in 44 B.C.—thirty-seven.

TREBONIUS (Gaius Trebonius), ca. 90–43 B.C. One of Caesar's leading generals, he played a prominent role in the conspiracy against him and was later treacherously murdered. Age in 44 B.C.—forty-six.

CASCA (Publius Servilius Casca), died 42 B.C.? He struck the first blow against Caesar on the Ides of March. He served as People's Tribune in 43 B.C. and then went east and fought under Brutus at Philippi, where he probably died either in battle or by suicide afterward.

GAIUS CASCA (Gaius Servilius Casca). Brother of Publius, struck Caesar in the ribs, which might have been the fatal blow.

CIMBER (Lucius Tillius Cimber), died 42 B.C.? Caesar liked his officer, Cimber, even though Cimber was known as a brawler and a drinker. But Cimber betrayed Caesar and signaled the start of the attack on the Ides of March by pulling the toga from Caesar's shoulders. As governor of Bithynia, he supported Brutus and Cassius. He fought at Philippi, where he probably died.

PONTIUS AQUILA, died 43 B.C. People's Tribune who refused to stand during Caesar's triumph in 45 B.C. and so offended the dictator. He might be the same Pontius Aquila whose estate was confiscated by Caesar. He served under Decimus in the fighting of 43 B.C. and fell in battle.

THE WOMEN

SERVILIA (Servilia Caepio), born ca. 100 B.C.–died after 42 B.C. Mother of Brutus, mother-in-law of Cassius and Lepidus, half-sister of Cato, and mistress of Caesar, the noble Servilia was one of the most well-connected and powerful women of Rome. Could anyone have been more conflicted over the plot that killed Caesar? Age in 44 B.C.—about fifty-five.

CLEOPATRA (Cleopatra VII Philopator, Queen of Egypt), 69–30 B.C. The legendary queen was the lover of two of the most powerful Romans of the era, first Julius Caesar and then Mark Antony. Age in 44 B.C.—twenty-five.

JUNIA TERTIA, died A.D. 22. Daughter of Servilia, wife of Cassius, and, some said, mistress of Caesar.

CALPURNIA (Calpurnia Pisonis). Caesar's third and last wife, she was the daughter of a noble political family. She tried in vain to stop Caesar from going to the Senate on the Ides of March. Age in 44 B.C.—thirty-three.

FULVIA (Fulvia Flacca), ca. 75–40 B.C. Married to the politicians Clodius, Curio, and finally to Mark Antony, she was one of the most able women of the era. She may have stage-managed Antony's role in Caesar's funeral and she recruited an army in 41 B.C. Age in 44 B.C.—about thirty.

PORCIA (aka Portia, full name: Porcia Catonis), died 42 B.C. Daughter of Cato, Porcia married her cousin Brutus after the death of her first husband, the staunch conservative Bibulus. Perhaps she helped turn Brutus against Caesar. In any case, he let her into the secret of the conspiracy. Age in 44 B.C.—about twenty-five.

ATIA, died 43–42 B.C. Caesar's niece and mother of Octavian, the future Augustus, she sent news to her son abroad about the terrible events of the Ides of March.

SEMPRONIA (Sempronia Tuditana). Mother of Decimus, Sempronia had a reputation for brains, beauty, adultery, and revolutionary politics. She supported Catiline in 63 B.C. and invited his Gallic allies into her home.

PAULA (Paula Valeria), wife of Decimus. Tongues wagged when in 50 B.C. she divorced her previous husband on the very day he was due home from military service abroad in order to marry Decimus. She remained loyal to him until his death.

FRIENDS OF THE CONSPIRATORS

CICERO (Marcus Tullius Cicero), 106–42 B.C. The greatest orator and political theorist of the age, he supported Pompey in the Civil War but remained on good terms with Caesar. He then supported the assassins, moved heaven and earth to fight Antony, gambled on an alliance with Octavian, and lost. He was executed in 42 B.C. Age in 44 B.C.—sixty-two.

DOLABELLA (Publius Cornelius Dolabella), 70–43 B.C. A turncoat, Dolabella supported Pompey, switched to Caesar, then favored the conspirators, and then defected to Antony in return for a prominent command in the East. After treacherously murdering Trebonius, he was defeated by the armies of Cassius and committed suicide.

CINNA (Lucius Cornelius Cinna). A praetor in 44 B.C. and Caesar's former brother-in-law, he ostentatiously supported the assassins in public, which infuriated many people.

OTHERS (NEUTRALS, UNCOMMITTED PARTIES, DIFFERENT GENERATION)

CATO THE YOUNGER (Marcus Porcius Cato), 95–46 B.C. A prominent senator and a follower of Stoic philosophy, he was Caesar's archenemy. He committed suicide rather than surrender to Caesar, an act that galvanized opposition to the dictator.

POMPEY (Cnaeus Pompeius Magnus), 106–48 B.C. Second only to Caesar as a Roman general and statesman in the mid-first century B.C., he changed from Caesar's ally and son-in-law to his leading opponent—and the result was civil war.

CNAEUS POMPEY (Cnaeus Pompeius), ca. 75–45 B.C. Older son of Pompey, he was defeated by Caesar at the Battle of Munda.

SEXTUS POMPEY (Sextus Pompeius Magnus Pius), 67–35 B.C. The younger son of Pompey, he led the naval opposition to Octavian and Antony.

LABIENUS (Titus Labienus), died 45 B.C. Caesar's right-hand man in Gaul, he supported Pompey in the Civil War and fought against Caesar to the bitter end.

ATTICUS (Titus Pomponius Atticus), 110–32 B.C. Banker, Roman knight, friend, and correspondent of Cicero, and well-connected politically. Age in 44 B.C.—sixty-six.

DEIOTARUS (King of Galatia), ca. 107–ca. 40 B.C. This wily and violent political survivor switched his support for Roman factions several times. He was accused of plotting in 47 B.C. to assassinate Caesar. Age in 44 B.C.— about sixty-three.

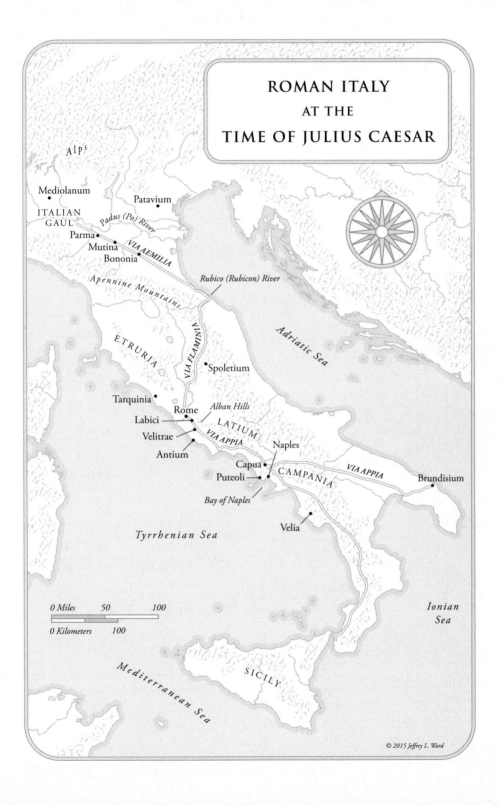

ROMAN ITALY
AT THE
TIME OF JULIUS CAESAR

Alps

Mediolanum

Patavium

ITALIAN
GAUL

Padus (Po) River

Parma

Mutina

Bononia

VIA AEMILIA

Apennine Mountains

Rubico (Rubicon) River

ETRURIA

VIA FLAMINIA

Adriatic Sea

Spoletium

Tarquinia

Rome

Alban Hills

Labici

LATIUM

Velitrae

VIA APPIA

Antium

Naples

Capua

CAMPANIA

VIA APPIA

Puteoli

Brundisium

Bay of Naples

Tyrrhenian Sea

Velia

Ionian
Sea

0 Miles   50   100

0 Kilometers   100

Mediterranean Sea

SICILY

© 2015 Jeffrey L. Ward

IRELAND

BRITAIN

Atlantic

Ocean

Rhenus (Rhine) R.

Sabis R.
★ Sabis

GERMANY

Danuvius (Danube) R.

BRITTANY
Veneti ★

Alesia ★

Vesontio ●

Jura Mountains

Alps

● Aventicum

ITALIAN
GAUL

GAUL

Mediolanum

● Cularo

Rhodanus (Rhone) R.

Padus (Po) R.

LIGURIA

Mutina ★

Pyrenees Mountains

Narbo ●

★
Massilia

Rubico (Rubicon) R.

ETRURIA

Ad

Rome ●   ITA

LUSITANIA

HISPANIA

Balearic Islands

SARDINIA

Napl

Corduba ●
★ Munda

Mediterranean Sea

Pillars of Hercules

Utica ●

SIC

Carthage ●

NUMIDIA

MAURETANIA

AFRICA

0 Miles   200   400

0 Kilometers   400

LIBYA

© 2015 Jeffrey L. Ward

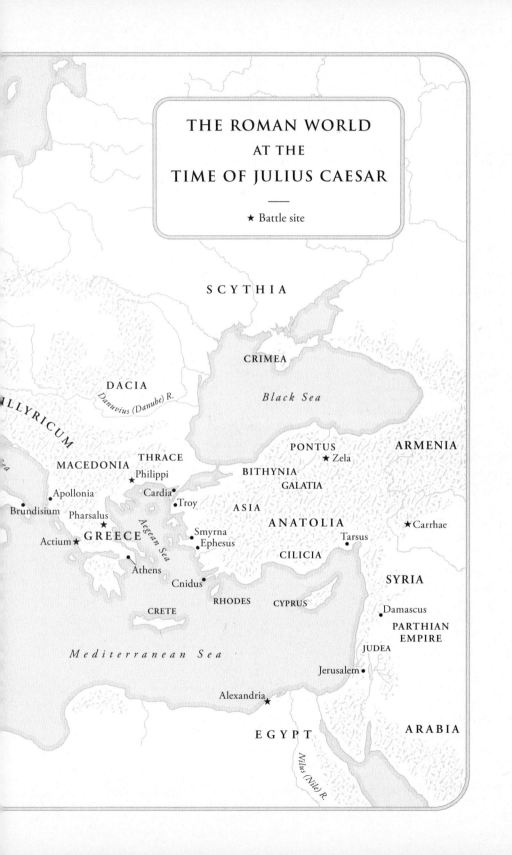

THE ROMAN WORLD
AT THE
TIME OF JULIUS CAESAR

—

★ Battle site

SCYTHIA

CRIMEA

DACIA

Danuvius (Danube) R.

Black Sea

ILLYRICUM

PONTUS   ARMENIA
★ Zela

MACEDONIA   THRACE   BITHYNIA
            Philippi   GALATIA
Apollonia ★ Cardia
                  •Troy   ASIA
Brundisium Pharsalus   ANATOLIA   ★Carrhae
            ★
Actium★ GREECE   Smyrna   Tarsus
                          •Ephesus
            Aegean Sea   CILICIA
        Athens   SYRIA
            Cnidus•
                  RHODES   CYPRUS   •Damascus
        CRETE   PARTHIAN
                                        EMPIRE
                                    JUDEA
Mediterranean Sea
                          Jerusalem •

        Alexandria
                ★
        EGYPT   ARABIA

        Nilus (Nile) R.

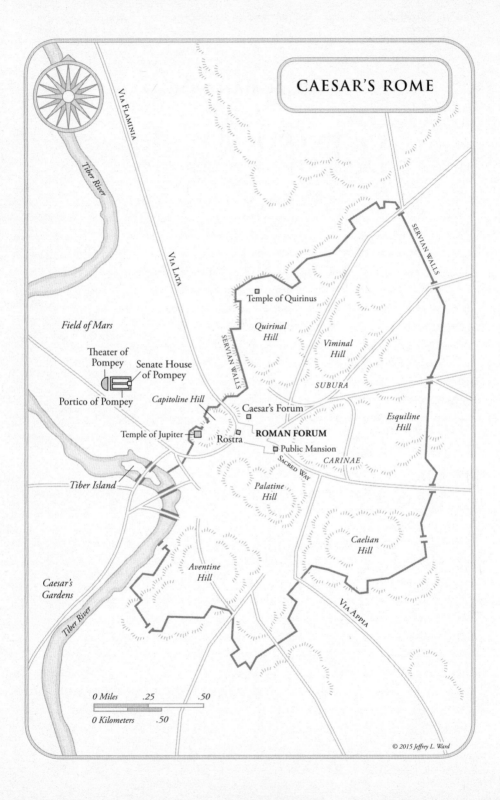

CAESAR'S ROME

Via Flaminia

Tiber River

Field of Mars

Via Lata

Temple of Quirinus

Quirinal Hill

Viminal Hill

SERVIAN WALLS

Theater of Pompey

Senate House of Pompey

SUBURA

Portico of Pompey

Capitoline Hill

Caesar's Forum

Temple of Jupiter

Rostra

ROMAN FORUM

Esquiline Hill

Public Mansion

CARINAE

Tiber Island

SACRED WAY

Palatine Hill

Caesar's Gardens

Caelian Hill

Aventine Hill

Tiber River

Via Appia

0 Miles   .25   .50

0 Kilometers   .50

© 2015 Jeffrey L. Ward

Part One

RETURN

to

ROME

1

RIDING WITH CAESAR

IN AUGUST 45 B.C., SEVEN MONTHS BEFORE THE IDES OF MARCH, A procession entered the city of Mediolanum, modern Milan, in the hot and steamy northern Italian plain. Two chariots led the march. In the first stood Dictator Gaius Julius Caesar, glowing with his victory over rebel forces in Hispania (Spain).

In the position of honor beside Caesar was Marcus Antonius—better known today as Mark Antony. He was Caesar's candidate to be one of Rome's two consuls next year, the highest-ranking public officials after the dictator. Behind them came Caesar's protégé, Decimus, fresh from a term as governor of Gaul (roughly, France). Beside him was Gaius Octavius, better known as Octavian. At the age of only seventeen, Caesar's grandnephew Octavian was already a man to be reckoned with.

The four men had met in southern Gaul and traveled together over the Alps. They took the Via Domitia, an old road full of doom and destiny—Hannibal's invasion route and, according to myth, Hercules' road to Spain.

Caesar was heading for Rome. For the second time in little over a year,

3

he was planning to enter the capital in triumph, proclaiming military victory and an end to the civil war that began four years earlier, at the start of 49 B.C. But it was not easy to end the war, because its roots went deep. It was in fact the second civil war to tear Rome apart in Caesar's lifetime. Each war reflected the overwhelming problems that beset Rome, from poverty in Italy to oppression in the provinces, from the purblind selfishness and reactionary politics of the old nobility to the appeal of a charismatic dictator for getting things done. And behind it all lay the dawning and uncomfortable reality that the real power in Rome lay not with the Senate or the people but with the army.

Dark-eyed and silver-tongued, sensual and violent, Caesar possessed supreme practical ability. He used it to change the world, driven by his love for Rome and his lust for domination. Caesar's armies killed or enslaved millions, many of them women and children. Yet after these bloodbaths he pardoned his enemies at home and abroad. These overtures of goodwill raised suspicions—could the conqueror be a conciliator?—but most had no choice but to acquiesce.

Of all the Romans in his entourage, Caesar chose these three men— Antony, Decimus, and Octavian—for places of honor on his reentry to Italy. Why? And why would one of them betray him within seven months? And why, after Caesar's death, were the three men able to raise armies and turn on each other in a new war that retraced their route from northern Italy into southern Gaul?

Consider how each of these men came to Caesar in the years before 45 B.C.

THE RISE OF DECIMUS

Decimus Junius Brutus Albinus, to use his full name, was a close friend of Caesar. They had worked together for at least a decade, beginning in 56 B.C. In that year, when Decimus was about twenty-five years of age, he made a sensation as Caesar's admiral in Gaul. He won the Battle of the Atlantic, which conquered Brittany and opened the door to the invasion of England.

First impressions are important and, in this case, accurate. War, Gaul, and Caesar were Decimus's trademarks. He was speedy, vigorous, resourceful, and he loved to fight. He was proud, competitive, and eager for fame. Like other ambitious men of his class, he won elected office in Rome, but the capital and its corridors of power never captivated him as the Gallic frontier did.

Decimus was born on April 21, around 81 B.C. He came from a noble family that claimed descent from the founder of the Roman republic, Lucius Junius Brutus. Decimus's grandfather was a great general and statesman but his father was no soldier and his mother was a flirt who dallied with revolution and adultery and perhaps with Caesar, who seduced many of the married noble ladies in Rome. A great historian suggested that Decimus was Caesar's illegitimate son. Intriguing as this theory is, it is not supported by the evidence.

In any case, young Decimus found his way to Caesar's staff. The military suited Decimus. By hitching his wagon to Caesar's bright star he restored his family's name for armed might. He was Caesar's man as much as any Roman was.

We don't know what Decimus looked like. He might have been attractive like his mother, a well-known beauty, and as tall as one of the Gauls whom he once impersonated. The dozen of Decimus's letters that survive mix the coarse atmosphere of the camp with the formal politeness and self-assurance of a Roman noble. Elegant at times, his prose also includes clumsy phrases like, "just take the bit between your teeth and start talking." Perhaps some of the roughness of his gladiators—Decimus owned a troupe—rubbed off on him but, if so, it didn't stop him from trading pleasantries with Rome's greatest orator, Marcus Tullius Cicero.

In Gaul, Decimus joined the greatest military adventure of his generation. It took Caesar only eight years (58–50 B.C.) to conquer the big, populous, warlike region that the Romans called "Long-Haired Gaul," after the flowing tresses of its people—an area that comprised most of France, all of Belgium, part of the Netherlands, and a sliver of Germany (the Provence region of France was already a Roman province). (He also invaded Britain.) With its gold, agricultural produce, and potential slaves, Gaul made Caesar the richest man in Rome. He shared the wealth with officers like Decimus.

After his victory at sea off Brittany in 56 B.C., Decimus next appears in 52 B.C., when a great Gallic revolt almost broke Roman rule. Decimus took part in the most dramatic day of the war at the siege of Alesia (in today's Burgundy). As Caesar tells the story, Decimus began the countercharge against a Gallic offensive and Caesar followed, conspicuous in his reddish purple cloak. The enemy collapsed and the war was over except for mopping-up operations the following year.

In 50 B.C. Decimus was back in Rome for his first elective office—quaestor, a financial official. That same year, in April, Decimus married Paula Valeria, who came from a noble family. There was scandal here to wink at because in order to marry Decimus she divorced her previous husband, a prominent man, on the very day he was scheduled to come back from service in a province abroad.

A year after Decimus and Paula married, in 49 B.C., civil war broke out between Caesar and his oligarchic opponents. They considered him a power-hungry, populist demagogue who threatened their way of life. He found them narrow-minded reactionaries who insulted his honor—and no one paid more attention to honor than a Roman noble.

Caesar's chief opponents were Pompey and Cato. Pompey the Great—Cnaeus Pompeius Magnus—was no ideologue; in fact, he was Caesar's former political ally and son-in-law. A conqueror whose career took him to Hispania, Roman Asia (modern Turkey), and the Levant, Pompey was Rome's greatest living general until Caesar. Marcus Porcius Cato, also known as Cato the Younger, was a prominent senator, loyal to the old-fashioned notion of a free state guided by a wise and wealthy elite. Rigid and doctrinaire, he was mocked for thinking that Rome was the Republic of Plato when others regarded it as the Sewer of Romulus. He was Caesar's archenemy.

Most of Decimus's family tended to sympathize with Pompey and Cato, and his wife's brothers fought for them. As an adult, Decimus was adopted into the family of Postumius Albinus, a patrician clan that claimed an ancestor opposed to Rome's kings, and his adoptive family had conservative leanings, too. Yet Decimus remained in Caesar's camp. It was probably early in 49 B.C. that Decimus issued coins celebrating his victories in Gaul, his loyalty, his sense of duty and spirit of unity—all propaganda themes of Caesar's in the civil war.

That same year Caesar named Decimus admiral for the siege of the city of Massilia (Marseille), an important seaport and naval base on Gaul's Mediterranean coast that supported Caesar's enemies. In the six-month struggle that followed, Decimus destroyed Massilia's fleet. He won Caesar's praise for his vigor, spirit, oratorical skill, foresight, and speed in combat. He gave Caesar's cause a propaganda boost because until then, Pompey had monopolized naval glory.

Caesar now returned to Italy and then turned east for a showdown with Pompey. He left Decimus in Massilia to serve as governor of Gaul through 45 B.C. as his deputy. Decimus then acquired additional military renown by defeating the rebellious Bellovaci, said to be Gaul's best warriors.

Decimus seems as hard as the country in which he spent much of his adult life. He was one of those Romans—they were rare, but probably less rare than the sources admit—who took on the manners and customs of the barbarians he fought. He spoke the Gaulish language, which few Romans did, and he knew the country well enough to be able to put on Gallic clothes and pass as a local.

Around July 45 B.C. Decimus met Caesar in southern Gaul on his way back from Hispania. There Decimus no doubt rendered his accounts of the province that he had governed in the dictator's absence. That Caesar was well pleased with Decimus is clear from the position of honor that Caesar gave him on the return to Italy.

After more than a decade in Caesar's service, Decimus came home rich, a hero, and on the rise. He was about to take office as one of the praetors (high judicial officials) in Rome for the rest of 45 B.C. Caesar had chosen him as governor-designate of Italian Gaul (that is, roughly, northern Italy) for 44 B.C. and consul-designate for 42 B.C.

In short, Decimus was well on his way to restoring his family's fame. There was only one hitch. Decimus's father and grandfather held office by the free choice of the Roman people and at the command of the Senate. Decimus did everything on Caesar's say-so. That accorded poorly with the cherished ideal of every Roman noble, *dignitas*. It's a difficult word to translate. In addition to "dignity," it means "worth," "prestige," and "honor." Perhaps the best single translation is "rank."

The question now for Decimus was whether he would be satisfied to remain in Caesar's shadow or whether he would insist on being his own man.

MARK ANTONY

As Caesar entered Mediolanum on his return homeward, Mark Antony stood beside him in his chariot. Antony looked the part of a hero. Born on January 14, ca. 83 B.C., he was in the prime of life. He was handsome, strong, and athletic. He wore a beard in imitation of Hercules, the demigod whom his family claimed as an ancestor. The Romans connected Hercules with Hispania, which gave symbolic significance to Antony's presence. His personality conveyed vigor. He was gregarious, intelligent, and self-assured. He drank lustily and in public and endeared himself to his soldiers by eating with them. If Caesar's health had declined at all over the years, as some say, then the robust presence of Antony would prove reassuring.

Antony came from a senatorial family. His father's people, the Antonii, tended to be moderate conservatives, but Antony's mother, Julia, was Julius Caesar's third cousin. Perhaps that was his ticket to Caesar's staff in Gaul, which Antony joined in 54 B.C.

As a youth, Antony had cut a wide swath in Rome, where he became notorious for drinking, womanizing, racking up debts, and keeping bad company. By his mid-twenties, Antony was over his wild ways. He studied oratory in Greece and distinguished himself as a cavalry commander in the East between 58 B.C. and 55 B.C. Already in his earliest armed encounter, he was the first man on the wall during a siege, and he went on in numerous battles to display courage and win victories.

Antony's early service for Caesar in Gaul is unrecorded, but it was probably impressive because Caesar sent him back to Rome in 53 B.C. to run for quaestor—an election that he won. He then returned to Gaul as one of Caesar's generals and, like Decimus, left with a record full of promise.

Also like Decimus, Antony held elective office in Rome in 50 B.C. As one of the ten People's Tribunes, elected each year to represent ordinary people's interests, Antony played a role in that year's fateful clash between Caesar and his opponents in the Senate. Led by Cato, the Senate stripped Caesar of his governorship of Gaul and denied him the chance to run for a second consulship. Caesar feared that, if he returned to Rome, he would be put on trial and unfairly convicted by his enemies. Antony tried to stop the Senate from its moves against Caesar, but he was rebuffed and fled Rome for Caesar's camp.

Antony emerged in the Civil War with Pompey as Caesar's best general and an indispensable political operative. He received such key assignments as organizing the defense of Italy, bringing Caesar's legions across an enemy-infested Adriatic Sea, and linking up with Caesar in Roman Macedonia. Antony played his most important role at the Battle of Pharsalus in central Greece on August 9, 48 B.C., when he commanded Caesar's left flank in the decisive battle against Pompey. When Caesar's veterans broke Pompey's ranks, Antony's cavalry chased the fleeing enemy.

It was a sudden and terrible defeat for Caesar's enemies. They still had cards to play—hundreds of warships, thousands of soldiers, major allies, and plenty of money. But with the sight of thousands of Pompey's dead soldiers at the end of the Battle of Pharsalus, you could almost hear the sound of the political tide turning in the Sewer of Romulus.

While he spent the next year in the East, winning allies, raising money, conquering rebels, and wooing a new mistress, Caesar sent Antony back to Rome. There Antony arranged for Caesar to be dictator for the year and for himself to be Master of the Horse (Magister Equitum), as a dictator's second-in-command was called. This was Caesar's second dictatorship.

It dismayed lovers of liberty. Meanwhile, traditionalists took offense at Antony's rowdy and degenerate lifestyle, which he resumed with abandon. The sources speak of wild nights, public hangovers, vomiting in the Forum, and chariots pulled by lions. It was hard to miss his affair with an actress and ex-slave with the stage name of Cytheris, "Venus's Girl," since she and Antony traveled together in public in a litter.

Both civil and military politics in Rome slipped out of Antony's hands. When proponents of debt relief and rent control turned violent, Antony sent troops into the Forum and blood flowed—the troops killed eight hundred men. Meanwhile, some of Caesar's veteran legions, now back in Italy, mutinied for pay and demobilization.

The situation called for Caesar's firm hand, and he returned to Rome in the fall. He put down the mutiny and agreed to reduce rents, although he refused to cancel debts. As for Antony, Caesar always knew how to turn people's weaknesses to his advantage. After speaking against Antony in the Senate, Caesar turned around and gave him a new assignment.

It was a job that most Romans would have turned down, but not Antony. He lacked political finesse, but he didn't mind getting his hands dirty and he was loyal. Caesar gave Antony the job of selling all of Pompey's confiscated assets to various private bidders. Pompey was the second-richest man in Rome, surpassed only by Caesar. Antony was a *sector*, literally, a "cutter," that is, someone who bought confiscated property at a public auction and sold it off piecemeal at a profit. The Romans considered that an ignoble profession, not suitable for a man of Antony's birth. It was not only a dirty business but a dangerous one because in 47 B.C. Pompey's allies and sons were still armed and at large. A soldier like Antony would surely prefer to win glory in the campaigns in Africa and Spain. Instead, he stayed in Rome through early 45 B.C. raising the money through his sales that Caesar needed to pay his troops. Antony was constantly short of funds and no doubt Caesar allowed him to skim a little off the top for himself.

Antony now mended his ways once more by marrying again after a divorce, this time choosing a twice-widowed noblewoman, Fulvia. Of all the powerful women of the era, Fulvia is in a class of her own. She alone once wore a sword and recruited an army, which earned her the back-handed compliment of having her name inscribed on her enemy's sling bullets along with rude references to her body parts. But she did most of her fighting with words. A populist through and through, Fulvia married three politicians in turn: the street-fighting demagogue Clodius, Curio—a People's Tribune who supported Caesar—and finally and most fatefully, Antony. Antony's enemies claimed that Fulvia controlled him, which is not true. But this strong woman probably stiffened his spine and she almost certainly shared with Antony the political skills learned from her two earlier husbands.

When Antony joined Caesar on his return to Italy in August 45 B.C., he was back in the dictator's favor. As he stood beside Caesar and entered Mediolanum, basking in the public's acclaim, Antony might have imagined a glorious future. But obstacles lay on the road ahead.

OCTAVIAN

The third man in Caesar's entourage was Octavian. He was born on September 23, 63 B.C. A good twenty years younger than Antony or Decimus, he projected an authority beyond his years. If Antony was Hercules then Octavian was a short-statured Apollo: very handsome, bright-eyed, and with slightly curly blond hair. Only the bad teeth and indifferent hair grooming betrayed the reality of a man who scorned appearances and cut to the heart of things. It was an inner strength that compensated for a less than herculean physique.

Neither Antony nor Decimus had been with Caesar in Hispania but Octavian had. He arrived too late for the fighting, however, because a serious illness kept him bedridden. Octavian was never the healthiest of men. When he recovered he and his companions reached Caesar in Hispania after a shipwreck and a dangerous trip through hostile country, which earned the dictator's admiration—a quality that only increased as he spent time with the clever and talented young man. Caesar now gave his grandnephew the honor of sharing his carriage in Hispania. It was not the first time that

Caesar showed his esteem for Octavian, but then again, the youth had long showed promise.

In 51 B.C., at the age of only twelve, Octavian gave the funeral oration for his grandmother Julia—Caesar's sister—on the Speaker's Platform in Rome. Soon after turning fifteen in 48 B.C. he was elected as one of Rome's highest-ranking priests. One of his responsibilities was temporarily serving as chief magistrate, and he made quite a sight at his age sitting on the tribunal in the Forum and handing out judgments. In 46 B.C. Caesar returned to Rome and celebrated a series of triumphs for his victories in Gaul and the civil war. In one of them, he allowed Octavian to follow behind his triumphal chariot (presumably on horseback), wearing an officer's insignia, even though Octavian had not even taken part in the campaign. Since this honor usually went to the sons of a triumphing general, it suggested that Caesar thought of his seventeen-year-old grandnephew as practically his son. It was an interesting choice.

Unlike Antony, Decimus, or Caesar himself, Octavian was not the pure product of the old Roman nobility. Octavian was of noble descent only on his mother's side—his mother, Atia, was the daughter of Caesar's sister Julia. Octavian's father, Gaius Octavius, came from a wealthy but not quite top-tier background; from a family of Roman knights, that is, a social order of Romans who were wealthy but not senators. Gaius Octavius was his family's first senator. The Octavii came from Velitrae (modern Velletri), a small and insignificant place in the Alban Hills outside Rome, an origin offering plenty of material for snobs to look down at. Gaius Octavius had a successful military and political career cut short by his death in 59 B.C. around the age of forty.

Yet young Octavian had something special about him. He was Caesar's blood relative, but other qualities recommended Octavian to Caesar. Octavian's cousins Quintus Pedius and Lucius Pinarius were also descended from Caesar's sister Julia, but they did not inspire the same esteem. Young Octavian no doubt already showed signs of the intelligence, the ambition, the fingertip feel for politics, the strategic vision, and the ruthlessness—in short, the genius—that would eventually take him to the height of power.

THE FOUR HORSEMEN

The four men in the chariots entering Mediolanum were not united. Three of them wanted Caesar's favor but only one could be the favorite. Antony was about to become consul with Caesar's blessing. Decimus was about to become a praetor in Rome and had Caesar's nod for another important governorship next and then, two years later, the consulship. But Octavian would shortly get an equally high office and even better access to the sources of power.

How did Antony and Decimus react to the sudden rise of a young rival? We can only guess. Romans had little respect for youth and less for relatively low birth, so maybe they underestimated him. Yet experienced men like Antony and Decimus certainly noticed Octavian's place in Caesar's entourage. Octavian could be charming, but Decimus might well have recognized his chariot-mate's coldblooded ambition. Decimus claimed descent from the founder of the Republic, but the grandson of a local politician Velitrae was muscling him out in the eyes of the man who ran Rome. Jealousy might be too strong a term, but Decimus was a Roman, and honor mattered to him.

Cicero alleged that Antony was behind an assassination attempt on Caesar in 46 B.C. That sounds like a Roman orator's usual slander but an event in 45 B.C. is more plausible. According to Cicero, when Antony went to southern Gaul to meet Caesar that summer 45 B.C., he heard a colleague's cautious suggestion about assassinating the dictator. Antony was not interested, but neither did he report the danger to Caesar as a loyal friend would. Instead, Antony kept it to himself.

As the victory parade entered Mediolanum, the men projected unity but behind the veneer they were jostling for power. The dictator could not afford to ignore this but he did. For now, he had dozens of men to see, prominent Romans who had hurried northward to greet him. No one among them was more important or more paradoxical than Marcus Junius Brutus (not to be confused with Decimus Brutus). In a few short years Brutus had gone from Caesar's enemy to his friend and deputy. Always in the background was the figure that united them: Servilia, Brutus's mother and Caesar's former mistress.

2

THE BEST MEN

BRUTUS

In August 45 B.C. Caesar met in the city of Mediolanum with Marcus Junius Brutus, his chosen governor of Italian Gaul for the previous year. In 45 B.C. the province had rotated to another man and Brutus had returned to Rome, but now he made the trek back to northern Italy to report to his chief.

Coming under the dictator's inspection could only have been a daunting prospect, even if at fifty-five Caesar was beginning to show his age. He was subject to dizzy spells, possibly a symptom of the epilepsy that brought him infrequent seizures. He was balding. After nearly fifteen years of war, his face was creased and his cheeks sunken. Yet Caesar still was cunning and dangerous. He personified talent, strategy, memory, literature, prudence, meticulousness, reasoning, and hard work, as a contemporary said.

Still, Brutus was not easily cowed. At forty, he was in the prime of life. He was proud, talented, sober, high-minded, and probably a little vain.

At the very least, Brutus had leading-man looks. A coin and a marble bust, identified as Brutus's portrait, show the man's intelligence, his forceful personality, and his regular, classical features. He appears as vigorous, determined-looking, and mature. He had a thick, curly head of hair, a pronounced brow, deep-set eyes, a straight nose, thick lips, a jutting chin, and a muscular neck. Brutus might have sweated a bit before Caesar because, unlike Antony, Decimus, or Octavian, he was not one of Caesar's longtime supporters but a rehabilitated enemy. Brutus was an example of Caesar's policy of clemency—forgiving his opponents and sometimes even rewarding them with public office.

By entrusting Italian Gaul to Brutus, Caesar showed his confidence in the man. It was a strategic province, the very place where in 49 B.C. Caesar had launched his march on Rome in the Civil War, and the governor's job came with command of two legions. It was essential not to give the governorship to an ambitious man yet it couldn't go to an incompetent or a vulture, either. The province's inhabitants were Caesar's supporters because many of them owed their recent Roman citizenship to him—most other Italians were already Roman citizens—and so they had to be treated well. A capable but unthreatening administrator was called for. Brutus was the solution.

Unlike Antony or Decimus or Caesar himself, Brutus was no general. A civilian through and through, he deferred to Roman constitutional norms. Rome had no written constitution but it was set in the ways of its government—ways that meant everything to a man like Brutus but much less to those outside the charmed circle of privilege. Although Brutus was a philosopher, he was also a man of the world. He believed in the Republic, in liberty, in arranging favors for friends, and in getting ahead. Caesar could do business with a man like this. Brutus turned out to be an excellent governor—the rare Roman who did not fleece the locals. Instead, in gratitude, they put up a statue of him in Mediolanum.

Brutus was probably not thrilled with his appointment. As lieutenant governor (quaestor) in Cilicia (southern Turkey) in 53 B.C., he extorted money from the locals and lined his purse. In Italian Gaul, his wings were clipped. Since Caesar embraced a policy of making alliances with provincial elites, it was harder to steal from them. And Caesar had men to keep an eye on governors, especially in important places like Italian Gaul. No more looting the locals for Brutus. Caesar had other ways of rewarding those who served him but that depended on Caesar's goodwill and not on the independence that a Roman noble cherished.

Caesar and Brutus traveled together through Italian Gaul, possibly conferring about which lands in the prosperous province to hand over to Caesar's veterans. The dictator praised Brutus for a job well done and promised him a bright future. Caesar said he would make Brutus urban praetor (Rome's chief judge) for 44 B.C. and one of the two consuls for 41 B.C. Aside from the dictator the consuls were the highest officials in Rome. Politician that he was, Caesar perhaps made other promises, too. During the Civil War years Caesar had grabbed powers for himself and, now that peace was back, the optimists hoped he would return them to the Senate and the people of Rome. It cost Caesar nothing to encourage such hopes, which might explain why Brutus said afterward that he thought Caesar was going over to their side—the side of the elite that traditionally ran Rome and clung to a narrow and conservative vision of the public good, a group that liked to call themselves the *optimates,* or "Best Men."

Rome had no political parties but its politicians tended to divide into two groups. The alternative to the *optimates* or "Best Men" was the *populares,* or "Populists." Both groups were led by elites and courted the votes of ordinary people, often by offering welfare benefits.

The Best Men represented inherited privilege. They believed that a tiny elite, centered on the Roman nobility, should continue to govern the empire and its 50 million people, just as it had governed the city of Rome for centuries. In their view only a very few men had the birth, the breeding, the wealth, and the virtue to keep Rome great and free. They had little interest in sharing their privileges even with the upper classes of Italy or the empire, much less the masses.

The Populists stood for change. They championed the poor, the landless, the foreigners, the noncitizens, nobles who were trapped in debt, and men throughout Italy who were rich but not noble—a group known as Roman knights or equestrians—and who sought admission to the Senate.

The Senate was an exclusive club. Its members served for life and jealously guarded their privileges. They came mostly from a few prominent families. They had each served in one of Rome's top political offices, most of which had a one-year term, sometimes followed by service abroad, and then leading to a lifetime in the Senate. Although the Best Men dominated the Senate, Populists too were represented there.

Caesar was not one of the Best Men. Quite the opposite—he was Rome's greatest Populist, who put together a broad new coalition that rode to power on popular consent and his legionaries' swords.

The Romans called their political system the Republic, Latin for "commonwealth." Whether it would still be a republic when Caesar was through was the question of the day for the Best Men.

CICERO

If the Republic had a voice in 45 B.C., it was Cicero. It was, however, a muted voice, since few people dared to oppose Caesar in public. A former consul and a leader of the Best Men, in 49 B.C. Cicero supported Pompey in the Civil War and afterward made his peace with Caesar. Now sixty years old, Cicero withdrew from most political life and devoted himself primarily to philosophy. Ancient portrait busts depict him as aging but vigorous and wrinkled, with a prominent chin, aquiline nose, and receding hairline.

Cicero didn't trust Caesar. In private, he called him a king. Cicero thought Brutus's optimism about Caesar and the Best Men was ridiculous.

"Where would he find them?" Cicero asked rhetorically. "He'd have to hang himself," because after the bloodbath of the Civil War, few Best Men were left alive. Brutus was one of them, or so Cicero had thought, but Brutus disappointed him. "As for Brutus," Cicero added, "he knows on which side his bread is buttered."

It was easy for Cicero to be skeptical of Caesar when Caesar was several hundred miles away. It was difficult to resist Caesar when sitting in the same room, as Brutus had to do. Cicero, who knew this, disparaged Caesar in private but praised him in public. Caesar was one of Rome's most powerful speakers and a charmer to boot. When Cicero wrote that Caesar "speaks Latin the most eloquently of nearly all the orators," Caesar returned the compliment by calling Cicero "almost the pioneer and inventor of eloquence." He went further, saying of Cicero that "it was a greater thing to have advanced the frontiers of the Roman genius than to have done the same with the frontiers of the Roman empire." Caesar would not have spoken as warmly about Cicero's politics, but politics was close to Cicero's heart.

In an outpouring of philosophical writing between 46 and 44 B.C. Cicero offered a brilliant description of republican ideals. Cicero grieved for the Republic but he recognized that it might not survive. The Romans were practical people, after all. In 46 B.C. he wrote a correspondent that the Republic was in ruins, at the mercy of force instead of justice. "Liberty," wrote Cicero, "has been lost." But later that year Cicero wrote a friend that he saw hopeful signs that Caesar was trying to set up "some sort of a constitutional system" in Rome. And Cicero sympathized with Brutus for paying court to Caesar. "What else can he do?" Cicero asked.

Whether or not Cicero liked Brutus, he recognized Brutus's talent and his prominence. In *Brutus* (46 B.C.), Cicero paid Brutus what he considered to be the highest compliment. He said that Brutus was making such progress in his young career that he could become a great orator in the Forum. In other words, Brutus could have become like Cicero in his heyday. Cicero laid it on thick, despite his private doubts about Brutus's oratory. As for why Brutus never reached the oratorical heights, the answer was easy: Caesar had a chilling effect on free speech. Flattery replaced frankness, for example, in a speech that Cicero himself gave in 46 B.C. The orator did all he could to flatter Caesar and the "immortal fame" achieved by his "godlike courage." Cicero wrote to a friend afterward that the day seemed so beautiful to him that he almost thought he caught a glimpse of a reviving republic.

But it was hard to stay optimistic in the new Rome. Cicero muttered darkly about Greek history and its rich store of examples of how wise men bore *regna* (singular, *regnum*)—monarchy—and *rex*—king. These were words of abuse in Rome. In Roman eyes, monarchy had a suggestion of arbitrary power, tyranny, and even enslavement. A king was the enemy of free, constitutional government.

Brutus's ancestors were famous for driving the last king from Rome long ago, but instead of standing up to Caesar, Brutus actually seemed to believe the dictator's rubbish. So Cicero complained, but he should have known by now that Brutus had a way of believing what was convenient for himself. In a lifetime of flip-flops, Brutus displayed a stunning flexibility. Perhaps Brutus's upbringing explains his inconsistency.

SERVILIA

Brutus's mother, Servilia, was one of the most powerful women in Rome. She was the talented, attractive, and ambitious daughter of a prominent patrician clan. She was born with important connections and made it her business to acquire new ones. None mattered more than her son and her lover.

In 77 B.C., eight-year-old Brutus lost his father. The man, also named Marcus Junius Brutus, was one of the leaders of a revolt opposed by Pompey. After holding out under siege Brutus's father finally surrendered, only to be treacherously killed. Pompey either gave the order or did nothing to stop it. In either case, the dead man's family blamed and despised Pompey.

The education of young Brutus fell into Servilia's hands. Roman women married young, and Servilia was a teenager (ca. 85 B.C.) when she had Brutus. In her early twenties when her husband was murdered, Servilia married another important politician. But he didn't have her heart.

Skilled in the art of attracting powerful men, she saved for herself the most powerful of them all—Caesar. As one writer says:

> But before all other women Caesar loved Servilia, the mother of Marcus
> Brutus, for whom during his first consulship [59 B.C.] he bought a pearl
> costing six million sesterces [that is, nearly 7,000 times the annual wages

of one of Caesar's legionaries, or the equivalent of hundreds of millions of dollars in today's terms].

Servilia served as Caesar's confidante and at times his agent in delicate political negotiations as well as his eyes and ears in Rome while the conqueror was abroad. Later, Caesar moved on to other amours. As for Servilia, she had a knack for inserting herself into important situations and she did her best to take charge. She cultivated connections with financiers and political operators.

A formidable woman in an era of formidable women, Servilia wielded political power behind the scenes. This "very knowing and careful lady," as Cicero described her, sometimes found herself at home surrounded by eminent men seeking her advice; she could influence the writing of legislation. No one appears to have found that unusual.

Her main interest, however, was her children. She married her three daughters to up-and-coming politicians. As for her son, Brutus—her "every care begins and ends with you," said a correspondent to Brutus when he was a grown man, and it was surely true from his childhood on. Servilia devoted herself to his career, beginning with having him adopted into her own family. The major male role model in young Brutus's life was his uncle and his mother's half brother, Cato—a man who was also Caesar's archenemy.

Brutus, it seemed, spent half his life living up to Cato's unyielding expectations and the other half living them down. And then, a year before Brutus met Caesar in 45 B.C., Cato was gone. But Cato's ghost seemed only to grow more solid every day, with his disapproving glare hovering over all Rome and zeroing in on Brutus's tender heart, a lifeless uncle who spoke more loudly to his ward now than he ever had in the flesh.

CATO

Brilliant, eloquent, ambitious, patriotic, and a crank, Cato was an original. He was an elitist who looked down on the masses. Yet Cato also defended freedom of speech, constitutional procedure, civic duty and service, honest administration, and the enlightened pursuit of the public interest.

Like Caesar, Cato impressed contemporaries as lofty and persuasive. Unlike Caesar, he was austere. A follower of Stoic philosophy, Cato showed his contempt for luxury by traveling on foot instead of in the litters favored by people of his class. Cato sometimes walked Rome's cobbled streets barefoot. A surviving portrait bust gives him a serious, pensive, and faraway look.

Cato believed in a republic that was stern, virtuous, and free. Its public officials would look for guidance to the Senate, a place of open debate among the noblest, wisest, and most experienced men in Rome.

Cato believed that Caesar cared only about power and glory and that he would destroy republican liberty in order to advance his career. An angry Cato once called Caesar a drunkard but he knew better. "Caesar," Cato later said, "is the only man to try to overturn the Republic while sober." His criticism of Caesar backfired once and embarrassed Cato at a tense Senate meeting. Someone passed Caesar a letter and Cato, smelling conspiracy, demanded to read it. It turned out to be a passionate note from his half sister Servilia.

Brutus shared Cato's hostility to any man who monopolized political power. Freedom, they believed, required sharing power. Like his distant cousin Decimus, Brutus claimed descent from Lucius Junius Brutus, who expelled the last king from Rome in 509 B.C. and founded the Republic. On his mother's side, Brutus's ancestor was Gaius Servilius Ahala, who in 439 B.C. killed a would-be tyrant. To proclaim his heritage, Brutus displayed a family tree in the reception room (*tablinum*) of his house, a complement to the beeswax ancestor masks that every noble family kept in a cherished place at home.

Unlike the unintellectual Antony or Decimus, Brutus shared his uncle Cato's passion for philosophy and perhaps also shared some of his uncle's distrust of Servilia's lover, Caesar. Brutus could hardly have ignored the rumor that he was Caesar's illegitimate son. It was almost certainly false, since Caesar was fifteen at the time of Brutus's birth in 85 B.C. Ironically, it might have been a useful rumor to help a young man get ahead, even if Brutus bristled at the idea of illegitimacy.

Having learned how to steer between Cato and Servilia, Brutus developed a taste for compromise but also, as it turned out, a talent for betrayal.

CHANGING SIDES

Young Brutus's career went well. As lieutenant governor in 53 B.C. Brutus lent money to the people of one city in Cyprus at the steep annual interest rate of 48 percent. When they refused to pay, Brutus's enforcer, backed up by armed horsemen, locked the town councilmen in their council house until five of them starved to death. When Cicero found out about this, he was shocked.

Civil war broke out four years later in 49 B.C. Cato led the diehards who insisted that Caesar was so dangerous a threat to the Republic that no compromise was possible. Although Brutus blamed Pompey for the death of his father, he took his side, following both republican principle and Cato. During the following military campaign, Brutus took part in the Battle of Pharsalus in 48 B.C., the great showdown with Caesar. Pompey managed to escape from Pharsalus, and so, in a manner of speaking, did Brutus. According to one report, Brutus slipped out of Pompey's camp, which was under siege after the defeat, and made his way through marshes to a nearby city. There he wrote to Caesar.

Brutus probably knew that Caesar had proclaimed a policy of clemency. He pardoned his enemies, which was a stunning reversal of Rome's previous dictator, Lucius Cornelius Sulla. Under Sulla's brutal rule (82–80 B.C.), the dictator's foes were executed and their property confiscated. Caesar now demonstrated that he was not Sulla. Brutus wanted more than a pardon; he wanted to prosper and he did.

There were stories that Caesar gave orders at Pharsalus to spare Brutus and that he did so as a favor to Servilia. Caesar was not sentimental, so, if the story is true, it must have been a political move. The powerful Servilia was an excellent friend and a dangerous enemy. There are references also to Caesar's supposed fear that Brutus was his son. That was surely untrue but Caesar surely knew the gossip and did not want even the suspicion of having killed his own child.

And then there was Caesar's opinion of Brutus. Cicero heard years later from one of Caesar's close friends that Caesar was in the habit of saying of Brutus, "What this man wants, is a major problem, but whatever he wants he wants very much." Here Caesar captures the personality of a man who was important and determined but hard to pin down.

Brutus's greatest value to Caesar was as a symbol. Cato's nephew and a popular man in Rome, where he had a reputation for honesty, Brutus was the first great name of the Roman nobility to join Caesar. Perhaps Brutus reasoned that he had done his duty by fighting at Pharsalus and, with Caesar's victory, it was time to accept reality. No die-hard he.

Caesar gave Brutus a warm welcome. Plutarch claims that the two men took a walk together. They were alone and Caesar asked where Pompey was headed. Brutus said he did not know but he reasoned that Egypt was probably Pompey's destination because of his allies there. Caesar was convinced, says Plutarch, and so he dropped everything and headed to Egypt.

Caesar tells a different story in the *Commentaries on the Civil War*, his classic version of events that combines history with propaganda. He had to tread lightly about the unsavory facts of a conflict in which he was killing fellow Romans. Caesar says that he headed east to Ephesus (in modern Turkey) before he got the news that Pompey had been seen in Cyprus, which made Caesar conclude that Pompey's destination was Egypt. Only then did Caesar make for Egypt. But Caesar never mentions Brutus in his *Commentaries*. Perhaps Caesar decided to draw the veil on the story of Brutus's betrayal of Pompey or perhaps Caesar considered Brutus's information too tentative for him to rush off to Egypt.

Cicero too made his peace with Caesar, but many of the Senate's grandees fought on. They still had men and money and the Mediterranean's most powerful fleet. The leaders went to the Roman province of Africa (modern Tunisia), where they could count on allied support. Pompey went to Egypt but was murdered as he stepped ashore.

It took Caesar another year before he dealt with his enemies in Roman Africa, but when he did, in April 46 B.C. he crushed them in battle. Caesar then marched west to Utica (west of modern Tunis), a seaport and the capital of the province. The town was under the command of Cato, the last holdout in North Africa. Caesar relished the great symbolic victory of Cato's surrender. He wanted Cato to accept Caesar's clemency.

But Cato refused. He considered Caesar a tyrant. Mercy from him, said Cato, was harder to bear than death. Cato decided to commit suicide. He told his son that he had been raised in liberty and freedom of speech, and he was too old now to learn slavery. Alone at night, Cato took a dagger and ripped out his intestines, only to have his supporters discover him and have a doctor stitch him back up. Cato finally tore out the stitches and died.

When Caesar found out, he is supposed to have said, "O Cato, I begrudge you your death; for you begrudged me the sparing of your life." Cato's suicide spoiled Caesar's story. Still, a simple and effective means of damage control lay at hand—silence. Today we think of the Romans as people who admired noble suicides, but that only came later. In 46 B.C., suicide was frowned on: even Brutus disapproved of his uncle Cato's act as unholy and unmanly. But Caesar made a big misstep.

When he returned to Rome in the summer of 46 B.C., Caesar got permission from the Senate to celebrate four triumphs in a row. This allowed him to one-up Pompey, who was famous for celebrating three triumphs in three separate years. Pompey's last triumph, held in 61 B.C. for his eastern victories, was especially grand. Caesar's, of course, were even more lavish.

Since celebrating the death of Roman citizens was improper, Caesar had to gloss over the Civil War in his triumphs. Instead he highlighted his victories over the Gauls and over other foreign enemies. The crowd enjoyed such unscripted moments as his soldiers mockingly chanting, "Romans, watch your wives, see the bald adulterer's back home."

Triumphal parades included inscribed placards. Caesar took care not to post the names of any Roman citizens. Yet Caesar allowed paintings to be displayed in the parade that depicted the suicides of three leading Roman generals after their defeat in Africa. One of them showed Cato "tearing himself apart like a wild animal." The crowd groaned in response. By criticizing Cato's death, Caesar gave the memory of his archenemy new life.

That was just the beginning. The following months witnessed a pamphlet war over Cato. Brutus commissioned Cicero to write *Cato*, a short work in praise of his late uncle. Although aware that it would surely offend Caesar and his friends, Cicero took the job. He considered Cato a great man who had predicted the future with remarkable clarity. Although the piece does not survive, it is clear that it exalted Cato, whom Cicero called elsewhere "first in manly courage among all peoples." Elite opinion followed. For some reason Brutus was unhappy with Cicero's work so he too wrote a short tribute called *Cato*. Caesar replied with *Anti-Cato*. Caesar attacked Cato as greedy, drunk, and a lecher.

Yet while his uncle and mentor Cato had killed himself with a dagger in North Africa rather than surrender to Caesar, Brutus was enjoying the benefits of the dictator's clemency in the cities of the north Italian plain. Eventually, Brutus would have to face the contradictions in his own behavior.

PORCIA

The summer of 45 B.C. was a trying time for Brutus's mother, Servilia, even though she had a new estate near Naples to enjoy. It was confiscated from a supporter of Pompey, and it ended up in her hands either as a gift or by purchase at a good price. Evidently, Servilia still had a place in Caesar's heart or in his calculations. In any case, she felt no qualms about profiting at the expense of one of his enemies.

But Servilia had a new daughter-in-law to deal with. Brutus divorced his wife, Claudia, and took a new bride, Porcia. She was his cousin and the daughter of his late uncle, Cato. She was also the widow of Bibulus, a bitter enemy of Caesar, who had died two years earlier.

Porcia was a woman to contend with. When she was young, a famous orator wanted to take her from Bibulus to produce an heir. The orator was an older man, an admirer of Cato and eager to breed from the best stock. He even offered to give Porcia back to Bibulus after she produced an heir, if Bibulus loved her. But Cato, who had authority in the matter, refused. Instead, he gave the orator his own wife!

But Porcia was formidable as well as desirable. If the story is true, Porcia once stabbed herself deeply in the thigh in order to prove her worth to Brutus. It seems that she was indeed a child of Cato. Porcia was just the sort of woman to prove attractive to the son of the strong Servilia.

Nor is it difficult to understand Servilia's distress. In the summer of 45 B.C., Servilia and Porcia were not getting along even though Brutus tried to do right by both. Why the two women were at odds is not recorded but Brutus's allegiance to Caesar was surely an issue. There is no reason to doubt that the Brutus-Porcia marriage was a love match, but many Romans would have regarded Brutus's marriage as a slap to Caesar. One thing is certain. The son of Servilia might get taken in by Caesar's smooth talk, but the daughter of Cato would never fall for it.

3

DECISION IN A VILLA

CAESAR RETURNED TO ITALY FROM HISPANIA IN AUGUST 45 B.C. but he took his time reaching Rome. He didn't enter the city until October, when he celebrated a triumph. In the meantime, he went to his villa about twenty miles south of the city, near Labici. There he could wake up in a bedroom whose floor was paved with a delicate, carpetlike mosaic of opaque glass tiles, with plant motifs and depicting a vase full of flowers, all framed by a meander-pattern cornice. He could do business while strolling shaded porticos amid luxurious yellow marble.

An area of fertile volcanic soil, Labici was famous in antiquity for its fruit and vegetables and its vintage wine. Caesar enjoyed the cool peace of the Alban Hills, the same hills where, still today, people go to flee the searing summer heat of Rome. But if the vexing politics of the capital city gave Caesar an added reason for postponing his return, it would be understandable.

Rome was full of people who demanded that Caesar restore the political system as it was before the Civil War. Caesar had other ideas. They thought in terms of the city, while he thought in terms of the empire. As he once wrote, once the Civil War was over, people could look forward to the tranquility of Italy, peace in the provinces, and the security of the empire. Caesar looked far beyond the walls of the Senate House or the corners of the Roman Forum—in fact, he was building a new Senate House and a new Forum. He expressed scorn for the Republic that so many of his contemporaries held sacred. Finally, Caesar had a desire for power. He was already Dictator for Ten Years, a title given him by the Senate in 46 B.C. and he held a host of other honors. We can't reconstruct precisely what he had in mind for the future. Caesar never expressed that clearly and perhaps his plans were still developing. One thing, though, is certain: Caesar's vision of Rome's future was incompatible with the Roman Republic's past. Either Caesar or the Republic could survive, but not both.

A CLASH OF VISIONS

Now that the Civil War was over, Rome's senators were ready to take back the power that they considered rightfully theirs. The way they saw it, after five years of war, tens of thousands of men killed, cities sacked, libraries burned, and money spent on carnage, it was the hour of the men in the long robes. The senators had known victorious generals breathing fire before, demanding primacy or dictatorship and, sometimes, cutting off a few heads. They had seen it all and they were confident that it meant nothing.

The Roman nobility were so impressed by their collective authority that they couldn't imagine anyone going beyond it. They trusted in their ability to co-opt even the strongest opposition, to make it part of the Republic again. They had tamed Pompey and they were sure they could do the same to Caesar. Even now, in spite of everything, they told themselves Caesar wanted nothing but the Republic. In letters dictated to slaves, at drinking parties, or in walks in their gardens with the murmur of water in the fountains in the background, they all stated the same confident conclusion. But Caesar cheated them.

Caesar had no intention of playing the senators' game. Cato understood that, Cicero sometimes did, but most people denied it. Caesar's charm masked the truth. He forgave his enemies and even appointed them to Rome's top offices. He had a smile for nearly everyone. He wrote personal letters even during military campaigns. He gave lavish gifts. It was a very good act but it was only an act.

Caesar had outgrown the city of Rome and its petty quarrels. He could afford to appoint his enemies as praetors and consuls because those jobs no longer mattered. Real power now lay with Caesar's circle of friends. He no longer cared about the Senate. His challenge was in not making that obvious.

A year earlier, in 46 B.C., when he had returned to Rome from North Africa, Caesar was tactful. Now in 45 B.C., after a hard struggle in Hispania, Caesar was less willing to compromise. The war had come down to a do-or-die battle at Munda (near modern Seville) on March 17, 45 B.C. and the enemy almost pulled off a victory. Caesar had to plead with his men to do their part and his life was in danger at one point. In the end, his army won in a rout, but before that it was close.

The experience might have shaken Caesar or merely confirmed his darkest thoughts. In either case, Hispania seems to have left him more focused and less patient, more sensitive to life's fragility and less willing to consult with outsiders.

In principle, the Civil War was over, but there were still military rumblings on the empire's fringes and political unrest in Rome. Syria was in revolt.

In short order, Sextus Pompey—the younger of the two sons of Pompey, he survived defeat—would come out of the mountains and reemerge as a military threat in Hispania. Meanwhile, back in Rome, neither senators nor ordinary citizens accepted the idea of a long-term dictatorship. They still expected Caesar to give them back the Republic, albeit with him in a dominant position.

Most of Rome's elite still loved their Republic. Cicero said that nothing in the world was comparable to it. Sallust, a great historian, advised Caesar, around 46 B.C., to "strengthen the Republic for the future, not in arms only and against the enemy, but also in the kindly arts of peace, a task far, far thornier."

Even the urban plebs (as the Romans called the common people of the city of Rome) found something to love in the Republic. Poor people did not hold public office but they did get to vote. Elections brought attention and gifts from the candidates, who were usually wealthy. A hotly contested election often yielded welfare benefits for the poor.

Caesar disagreed. The man with wit and grace enough to turn so many married heads in Rome, the dandy whom Cicero once refused to take seriously because he paid too much attention to his hairstyle, that same Caesar could sometimes be as direct as a dagger thrust. He is said to have called the Republic "a nothing, a mere name without form or substance." The remark comes from a pamphlet by an enemy of Caesar. It may be fiction but it sounds like Caesar's stinging wit.

The old guard said that they wanted Rome to be a government of laws and not men. Caesar would have none of it, judging the old guard fraudulent, deluded, or both. He believed that only his genius offered the people of the empire peace and prosperity. To understand why he reached that conclusion, we need to understand who Caesar was.

BECOMING JULIUS CAESAR

Caesar had come a long way. He had gone from a childhood in the Subura slums of Rome to the Royal Residence off the Forum, where he lived as Rome's Chief Priest, having won election to that high office at a young age; from running and hiding in the hills of Central Italy and fighting malaria and a death sentence from the dictator Sulla to running a campaign against Rome's hereditary enemy and winning a battle in the hills of Anatolia so dazzling that Caesar could only describe it with the famous phrase, VENI VIDI VICI, "I came, I saw, I conquered"; from winning, at the age of twenty, Rome's second-highest military honor and the right to a standing ovation from senators whenever he entered the room, to lording it over the

defeated rebel chieftain of Gaul lying at his feet; from carrying out three
marriages and countless bedroom amours with Rome's leading political
wives to conducting an affair with a queen descended from one of Alexander the Great's generals. In earlier years, Caesar had been a reforming consul
who fought and beat the Senate; a political broker who considered no one
his equal except Rome's then-greatest general, Pompey, and Rome's then-
richest man, Marcus Licinius Crassus. By 45 B.C. Caesar outstripped them
both; became a conqueror on three continents; and wrote military commentaries destined to last as literary classics for two thousand years. Caesar
was both genius and demon, excelling at politics, war, and writing—a triple
crown that no one has ever worn as well.

Caesar lived in a society in which modesty was not a virtue. He was
what Aristotle called a great-souled man—one with high-flying ambitions
and no small opinion of himself. He believed in his intelligence, versatility, and efficacy. He lacked neither courage nor nerve, and his appetite for
self-promotion was limitless. As he saw it, he was a political virtuoso with a
common touch. He was the man who did everything in the crisis of battle
and saved his army again and again. He was stern, fair, and prudent with
the enemy, and infinitely merciful to the people of Rome. He stated approv-
ingly a belief that "the imperator Gaius Caesar deserved well of the republic
after all his achievements."

His whole life experience, no doubt starting at his mother's knee, had
taught Caesar that he deserved to be the first man in Rome. He was confident that he could lead the people and he had little use for the Senate. He
considered the latter an obstacle to his vision of a new and greater Rome: a
rebuilt city worthy of an empire, a reimagined empire that treated its inhabitants as citizens rather than subjects, and a reformed state that considered
the masses as contributors to the public good rather than as stumbling
blocks in the way of a noble elite.

As consul in 59 B.C., Caesar ran over the objections of the Senate and
passed two land laws that provided relief to the poor. He also passed one of
the first laws to protect the people of the empire from abuses by provincial
governors. The Senate opposed Caesar but he simply bypassed it and had

the laws approved by the people in their legislative assemblies. This was legal but against all custom.

Caesar had little patience for custom or for the Senate. He was a refuge for the poor and proud of it, and he despised the Senate's absolute refusal to make the slightest concession to their needs. He promoted men who horrified the snobs of the Senate—Roman knights, Italians, new citizens from Gaul or Hispania, even sons of freedmen, not to mention young members of the nobility who were in debt or had committed crimes. He made no apologies—in fact, he once said that if it took thugs and murderers to defend his dignitas (that is, his honor), he would gladly reward them with high public office. Nor did Caesar hesitate to use force against his elite enemies. He had Cato thrown out of the Senate and imprisoned after a blustery debate and he had his fellow consul, one of the Best Men, assaulted in public after he tried to stop enactment of one of the land laws.

All his life Caesar loved risk and embraced violence. There was the time he made a dangerous crossing of the Adriatic in a small boat with a few friends and slaves and just a military dagger strapped to his thigh, under his tunic, to use if he met pirates—young Caesar was in a hurry to get back to Rome. Or the time that he marched his army into a trap on the River Sabis in Gaul, without taking the proper precautions, and almost saw his forces overwhelmed by a well-prepared enemy. Caesar won anyhow by rallying his men all over the battlefield, by fighting close to the front himself, and by relying on a superb second-in-command, Titus Labienus. He presented the near disaster as a famous victory in his *Commentaries*, although he downplayed the contribution of his Number Two.

Caesar took his most famous risk in 49 B.C., when he crossed the Rubicon. This small river marked the boundary between Italian Gaul and Italy proper. It was illegal for a general to bring his army into Italy without the Senate's approval. Yet Caesar did so on a January night in 49 B.C. (November 50 B.C. by our calendar).

Nowadays, "crossing the Rubicon" means making a difficult decision with no way back. So it was with Caesar. He defied the Senate and broke the law. It was the beginning of five years of civil war. Led by Cato and

Pompey, Caesar's enemies in the Senate had demanded that he give up his command and return to Rome as a private citizen. Realizing that would spell the end of his political career if not his life, Caesar refused. Addressing his soldiers, he said that his enemies were in charge of the Senate and threatened both the liberty of the Roman people and his dignitas. The men pledged their support to their commander. And so Caesar decided to risk everything on civil war. He crossed the Rubicon and marched for Rome.

No politician could stop Caesar, nor could any army defeat him. For nearly a decade the people of Gaul treated him like a king. Take one small example, the surrender of Vercingetorix at Alesia, where the Gallic leader threw himself and his best armor at Caesar's feet after Caesar circled him on his horse. Having tasted such hard-won dominion, Caesar had no interest in turning it over to the petty, bitter politicians in Rome who, as he saw it, forced him into civil war in spite of all his services to his country.

But anyone with the least taste for romance can't help but think that the biggest influence moving Caesar to take even more power was his mistress, the queen of Egypt.

CLEOPATRA

Caesar met Cleopatra in 48 B.C. when he went to Egypt in pursuit of Pompey. Pompey had been assassinated when he stepped ashore, betrayed by his supposed friend Egypt's King Ptolemy XIII. Caesar had no use for Ptolemy. He had robbed Caesar of Pompey's surrender and besides, the king refused to fund Caesar's troops. But Caesar found a willing ally in Ptolemy's sister, Cleopatra. She gladly offered to pay in exchange for support for her claim to the throne.

She was smuggled into the palace in Alexandria, covered, as one story has it, in bed linens, then unrolled in front of Caesar. Cleopatra had great physical presence. She was short and vigorous—she could ride a horse and hunt. If we can judge by her coins, she was not conventionally pretty—she had a prominent chin, a large mouth, and a rugged nose, but the coins might give her exaggerated masculine features to make her look kingly.

Certainly, Cleopatra was clever, cunning, and seductive. She represented glamour—she was Egypt, a land of antiquity and elegance. She was glory because she was descended from Alexander the Great's marshal, Ptolemy I. She was youth; Cleopatra was twenty-one, Caesar was fifty-two. Within a month of their meeting, she was pregnant.

When Caesar and Cleopatra were together, the parties often went on until first light. They cruised together on the Nile on her state barge. Accompanied by more than four hundred ships, they pushed south nearly all the way to Ethiopia, past majestic temples and exotic flora and fauna. It was a journey of exploration and adventure as well as romance.

By spring 47 B.C., after hard fighting in Alexandria and the Nile Delta, Caesar was master of Egypt. And Cleopatra was mistress of Caesar, or so the legend has it. They were two power politicians, not fools for love. Sound political reasoning urged Caesar to prefer Cleopatra to Ptolemy—she was weaker. Ptolemy had strong popular support in Alexandria; Cleopatra needed Rome. She would make a loyal client as ruler of Egypt.

Yet the bright young queen might have had an impact on Caesar even so. What did he think, for example, if she asked him why he wasn't a god? After all, she was a goddess and every king or queen of Egypt was divine. Alexander the Great was a god, and so, for that matter, were other rulers of the Greek East. Why not Caesar? Why, for that matter, wasn't he a king? By praising his forceful behavior in Alexandria, Cleopatra might have reinforced Caesar's desire to be done with the tiresome grandees of the Senate and the constitutional trivialities that they hid behind to protect their privileges. And her connection to Alexander could remind Caesar that there were new worlds to conquer in the East.

In summer 47 B.C., after Caesar's departure from Egypt, Cleopatra had a son. She named him Ptolemy XV Caesar, but he was known as "Caesarion" or Little Caesar. She claimed that Caesar was the father. It's hard to know how Caesar responded, if at all, because the subject is encrusted with later propaganda battles. A Roman source says that "certain Greek writers" claimed that Caesarion looked and walked like Caesar.

Caesar was probably not a doting father, but it's easy to imagine the boy stirring his soul. Twenty years earlier, when he was thirty-three, Caesar had lamented the fact that Alexander the Great was already dead at his age while Caesar had not yet achieved anything of note. Now, he was a great conqueror, and Caesarion linked him genetically with one of Alexander's generals. Still, even if Caesar did accept the boy as his own, he certainly never thought of making a half Egyptian, born out of wedlock, his heir in Rome.

We are on firmer grounds imagining that Alexandria impressed Caesar. The great city would have impressed anyone. It was about as populous as Rome and immensely grander. Founded by Alexander the Great, it was the showplace of the Ptolemaic dynasty. Beginning with its famous lighthouse, which rose to a height of about 350 feet on an island north of town, Alexandria's architecture bedazzled. The Palace District, the ports, the colonnades, the Museum, the great Library, the tombs of the Ptolemies and of Alexander the Great, the wide boulevards on a grid plan, the play of marble and granite—it all captivated a visitor. Alexandria outshone Rome. No wonder Caesar put so much emphasis afterward on building a bigger and better Rome.

Caesar did not forget Cleopatra when he left Alexandria in 47 B.C. The next year, back in Rome, he included a gilded statue of the queen as part of his new forum. The statue was a slap in the face to Roman traditionalists.

But Caesar wasn't thinking of them. He knew that most of the Senate and nearly all the ex-consuls (consulars, as they were called) had opposed him in the Civil War. What mattered to Caesar were a few trusted loyalists as well as his allies in the new elites of Italy and the provinces, the urban plebs, and, above all, the army. Let the Best Men grumble in spite of all he did to conciliate them. Caesar's men would treat him as he deserved, he who was his country's best hope.

CAESAR'S MEN

Not only did the war in Gaul make Caesar one of history's greatest conquerors; it also let him build a state within a state. There was, first and foremost, his army.

Other Roman generals before Caesar used their men's loyalty as a political tool but no one did it better. It was clear at the time and it still shines through on the pages of Caesar's *Commentaries*. The emotional heart of that work is not the senior officers but the centurions, the Roman equivalent of a captain. Caesar depicts their bravery, self-sacrifice, and professionalism. They repaid him in Rome, as political allies and more. His centurions even lent Caesar money before he crossed the Rubicon and started the Civil War in 49 B.C.

Centurions were not poor. They probably came from the upper middle class—and, if not, they were paid well enough to end up there. By contrast, ordinary soldiers were very poor and they simply loved their chief. Not that Caesar responded sentimentally. Power, he once said, depended on only two things: soldiers and money. Caesar paid his men and worked magic with them. He cultivated a reputation for endurance and sharing the soldiers' sacrifices. He shared his men's risks, too. At the start of one engagement, for instance, he sent the officers' horses away to make clear that it was a matter of do or die. He sent his own horse away first.

Whether it was the little things, like leaving his hair and beard unshaven as a sign of mourning for heavy casualties, or the big ones, like giving out wages, loot, and land, Caesar took care of it all. The upshot was to make Caesar's men "absolutely attached to him and absolutely steadfast." What was said of Rome's legendary founder, Romulus, could be said of Caesar, too:

> He was more pleasing to the masses than to the Senate but it was in the hearts of the soldiers that he was the most popular by far.

When they marched in Caesar's triumphs in 46 B.C. his soldiers, wearing military dress including proudly displayed decorations, shouted for joy and sang bawdy songs about Caesar's sexual exploits. They also called out together, "If you do right, you will be punished, but if wrong, you will be king." What they meant of course was that Caesar broke the law as consul and began a civil war, and yet dodged punishment and ended up on top.

It's said that Caesar was delighted to know that he and his men understood each other. But he didn't leave the show of sympathy to mere words.

Caesar gave his soldiers big cash bonuses at the triumphs. Each of his veterans got a lump sum of 6,000 denarii—more than twenty-five times a legionary's annual wage of 225 denarii. Centurions received double this amount while military tribunes (colonels) and cavalry commanders received four times—stupendous bonuses made possible only by Caesar's enormous wealth, won in the spoils of war.

It was a taste of things to come. The soldiers were the real power in Rome. In less than three years that would be obvious to everyone. For now, it was still possible to believe that the soldiers bowed their heads to the political authorities.

Caesar counted on the support of the urban plebs and he made payments to them, too. The soldiers had no interest in sharing their wealth so they rioted in protest—and were crushed by him in turn. More than a quarter of a million male citizens were each eligible for 100 denarii. Then there were rent rebates, both in Rome and the rest of Italy—a boon to the poor. Caesar was not yet ready to agree with what, centuries later, the Roman emperor Septimius Severus told his sons on his deathbed: "Make the soldiers rich and pay no attention to anyone else." Caesar knew that without the support of his legions, he couldn't rule at all, but without the support of the people, he couldn't rule in peace. So he had three of the rioting soldiers killed, two by ritual execution, and he displayed their heads outside his office.

In addition to the soldiers and the urban plebs, Caesar built a new elite. Starting in Gaul he put together a team of advisors that included politicians, administrators, lawyers, propagandists, fixers, and bankers. They served as his gatekeepers, troubleshooters, spies, and hatchet men. Almost none of them came from Rome's nobility; some were not even born Roman citizens; most came from the ranks of the upper classes of Italy, who were Roman citizens but by and large excluded from high office.

The two most powerful of Caesar's new elite were Gaius Oppius, a Roman knight, and Lucius Cornelius Balbus, a new citizen from Hispania. In the know and usually tight-lipped, they worked behind the scenes and served as Caesar's eyes and ears. Balbus and Oppius were chiefs of staff, ministers of communications, and secretaries of the treasury combined. They pulled many strings in Rome. Cicero complained that Balbus was drawing up decrees and signing Cicero's name to them without ever consulting him. In the old days, sighed Cicero, he was virtually helmsman on the Republic's ship of state, but now he barely had a place in the hold.

It was virtually impossible to see Caesar without going through them, as Cicero discovered to his displeasure. The process was not only wearisome but an affront to one's dignitas—to think of the social inferiors with whom he had to rub shoulders! It would seem that Caesar himself recognized how unpopular his gatekeepers made him. Caesar supposedly said that if a man like Cicero had to wait to see him, then everyone, including Cicero, must have really hated him. Evidently Caesar felt that as unfortunate as this was, there was no alternative.

CAESAR'S REFORMS

While Caesar stayed in his villa at Labici, waiting to enter the capital, he might have considered how much he had already changed Rome. The year before he had passed a dazzling series of laws that advanced the country in everything from the grain dole to the calendar and from the countryside to new colonies abroad.

To the urban plebs he brought handouts, entertainment, and debt relief—but not enough to hurt the wealthy. To his supporters in the provinces he brought Roman citizenship. To leading Roman knights he opened up public offices and seats in the Senate, which he eventually expanded from 600 to 900. A few of Caesar's new senators were citizens who came from Italian Gaul and probably even from Gaul across the Alps. To the former supporters of Pompey he offered pardons and promotions. He used his massive wealth to purchase new friends including senators who got low- or no-interest loans as well as freedmen and even slaves who had influence with their masters.

Caesar offered land for his veterans and grain for the urban poor, but with a sting—he reduced the number of those on the grain dole and began plans to move large numbers of the city's poor to new colonies abroad. Eighty thousand colonists were settled by the time of his death. He helped debtors by decreeing that land be valued at pre–Civil War prices, but he refused to forgive people's debts altogether, which reassured creditors. At the same time he encouraged the immigration of doctors and teachers to Rome.

Caesar limited the term of provincial governors to two years—he didn't want anyone else using his province as a springboard to supreme power as he had used Gaul. He increased the number of public officials, which both responded to the press of public business and gave jobs to his friends. But his most important administrative reform by far concerned the calendar. Rome's lunar calendar, based on a year of about 354 days, was out of sync with the seasons. Caesar put through an epoch-making reform—the solar calendar of 365 days plus leap year that is still in use today by most of the world (with a few adjustments in the 1700s A.D.). The new calendar started on January 1, 45 B.C.

As for the capital city, Caesar replaced republican austerity with imperial pomp and sealed it with a dynasty's stamp. And at the center of everything, dictator and nearly demigod, stood Caesar.

CITY OF MARBLE

Caesar followed his triumphs in Rome in September 46 B.C. with a series of spectacular public banquets and games, including gladiatorial games dedicated to his daughter, Julia, nine years after her death. It was the first such event held in honor of a daughter. Even more unusual, the games were combined with those for the inauguration of a new temple, the Temple of Venus Genetrix—Mother Venus, which was dedicated on September 26. This was major, and in fact, it marked nothing less than the start of a monumental rebuilding of the heart of Rome. As in other things, Caesar was following in Pompey's footsteps.

Pompey built a spectacular new complex as a memorial of his triumph of 61 B.C. and his success in the East. Pompey had freed the sea of pirates, defeated the terrible rebel King Mithradates of Pontus, and won the Republic a new and glittering set of provinces and protectorates. The new complex consisted of two interconnected parts, the Portico of Pompey and the Theater of Pompey. The Romans sometimes referred to the whole thing as Pompey's Works. Although its outline can be traced in today's street plan—and even in the footprints of some of the buildings—little of the structure survives. Still, the complex was every bit as iconic in its day as the Colosseum would be later.

Pompey's Works included Rome's first permanent theater, what was in effect Rome's first public park, a temple to Venus the Victorious (Pompey's personal goddess of Victory), art galleries, shops, government offices, and a new Senate House, including a statue of Pompey. The whole thing was a gigantic monument to an overbearing general who threatened to suffocate the liberty of the Republic by his ego and ambition.

From its dedication in 55 B.C., Pompey's Works was immensely popular. A year later Caesar launched a big new project of his own, the Forum Julium, or Caesar's Forum. Like the Portico of Pompey, it was to be a colonnaded, rectangular space with a temple to Venus, but Caesar dedicated his temple to "Mother Venus" because Venus was founder both of Caesar's family and the Roman people, so the change from Victorious to Mother did double duty.

In front of the Temple of Mother Venus stood a statue of Caesar on horseback in a conquering pose made famous by Alexander the Great. Adjacent to the Forum there would be a new Senate House, the Julian Senate House (Curia Julia), named for Julius Caesar's family, the Julii.

Unlike Pompey's Works, Caesar's Forum did not include a theater, but Caesar planned to build one relatively close by (eventually, it became the Theater of Marcellus, completed under Augustus and still partially standing). Nor was there a park but, as we shall see, Caesar had a plan to outdo Pompey on that score. Best of all, and unlike Pompey's Works, Caesar's Forum had a central location in Rome, adjacent to the Roman Forum. Pompey's Works was located in the Field of Mars, about half a mile away, on the low-lying plain between the republican city walls and the bend of the River Tiber. Caesar planted his flag practically in the center of Roman power. The real estate alone cost a fortune, nearly enough to fund Rome's armies for a generation.

The Temple housed a statue of Venus by Arcesilaus, a prominent Greek sculptor in Rome. Other decorations in the temple—all gifts to the goddess—included priceless paintings, engraved gems, and a breastplate of British pearls. Finally there was that gilded statue of Cleopatra.

Caesar's new Forum and Senate House were just the beginning. He ordered a complete overhaul of Rome's most important political real estate, the Assembly Place, located in front of the Senate House. There would be a new assembly space, a new Speaker's Platform, and, just beyond it to the east, a new judicial complex, the Julian Court Building, also named after Caesar's family. He arranged for the construction in the Field of Mars of a huge marble colonnade to be used for elections—called the Julian Enclosure. It all represented an unfriendly takeover of the Republic's most hallowed ground by one family. Ironically, although Caesar expanded the spaces for public speeches and elections, he made them irrelevant. Behind the scenes, the dictator pulled the strings and decided who would or wouldn't hold office.

There was more. Caesar planned a great new Temple of Mars, the war god, and a library to rival the famous Library of Alexandria. To end the problem of the city's frequent floods, he ordered the River Tiber to be diverted from the center of Rome. He also planned a major port for the mouth of the Tiber at Ostia, located about twenty miles southwest of Rome.

It is tempting to imagine Caesar and Cleopatra planning such projects together as a way of bringing Rome up to the grandeur of Alexandria—of making it a city worthy of Caesar. Then again, public works projects represented jobs for the poor and contracts to be awarded strategically; both were ways for Caesar to increase his support.

WHAT CAESAR WANTED

Even as Dictator for Ten Years, even with an expanded Senate, a redesigned Forum, a frightened silence in the public square, and an enormous ebb and flow of population, Caesar still lacked legitimacy. Most Romans expected the Republic to continue much as it had before. Yet Caesar's actions spoke louder than any words. They made it clear that the dictator wanted power to flow to him and his friends and away from the traditional institutions of the Senate and the people.

Caesar could justify his actions by pointing to the need for reform and the unyielding rigidity of the old guard. Such words would fall on deaf ears. Neither the Senate nor the people were ready to give up their ancient liberties. Caesar could not convince them; he could merely accustom them to change as it accumulated. Because Rome was still a republic he could never obtain the appreciation that he considered worthy of his dignitas and his achievements.

It would take more than one lifetime to change Rome. And Caesar might have wondered just how much lifetime he had left.

There are those who think he was depressed. "I have lived long enough for nature or glory," said Caesar repeatedly in 46 B.C. Some of his friends thought that he had no wish to live longer because his health was poorer than it had been. There are accounts of fainting spells and night terrors towards the close of his life—symptoms, perhaps, of his epilepsy.

Caesar was an epileptic but he was also a politician, so he carefully managed information about his health. He did have occasional seizures, possibly with related dizziness or fainting, but some of the incidents mentioned in the sources look suspicious and might be merely excuses to cover up missteps in the Forum or battlefield lapses. Overall, Caesar's health was good. Indeed he planned another major military campaign.

Yet even Caesar knew he was mortal. He also knew that he did not have a legitimate heir, a son to continue his legacy in Rome.

OCTAVIAN

In his villa at Labici, Caesar revised his will. It was the Ides of September—September 13, 45 B.C. The key to the document was that, after Caesar's death, he would adopt Gaius Octavius—Octavian—and give the boy his name—Caesar. He also made Octavian heir to three-quarters of his fortune.

Earlier that summer Caesar gave Antony a privileged position in the return to Italy and he gave Decimus a position equal to Octavian's. There may be truth to the rumor that Antony hoped to be adopted by Caesar. Decimus sat in the second carriage and he already was adopted (by another man), but where there's a will there's a way and he too might have hoped to get the nod. But Caesar chose Octavian.

We can reject as slander Antony's charge that Octavian sold his body to Caesar, but that still leaves the question of why Caesar chose as he did. Perhaps the old fox sensed that Octavian's blood ran even colder than Antony's, and if so, surely Caesar approved. As events would soon show, young Octavian was brilliant, shrewd, ambitious, audacious, and utterly ruthless, and so a man after Caesar's heart. Octavian knew how to turn on the charm and that too surely impressed Caesar, perhaps even worked its magic on him. Besides, Antony, the man Caesar chose to do his financial dirty work, was not the man to be great Caesar's heir. Or was it also a matter of blood being thicker than water? Antony was a distant cousin of Caesar but Octavian was his grandnephew.

As for Decimus, he was not Caesar's kin. Decimus was a heroic battlefield commander but fell short as a strategist. Both Decimus and Antony were more closely tied to the old nobility than Octavian but neither could match his cunning. Antony and Decimus were mature men in their late thirties. Octavian was a month short of his eighteenth birthday. Yet in Caesar's eyes, Octavian was their equal if not their superior.

After Hispania, the topic of a son might well have occurred to Caesar. Pompey had been dead for three years and yet he still made war on Caesar via his sons. Caesar had no son except perhaps for Cleopatra's boy, the illegitimate Caesarion. Adopting Octavian was a solution.

Both legally and politically, this was complicated. In Rome, adopting an adult was standard practice but adopting by one's will was not. Octavian was not required to accept. In fact, Caesar left open the possibility of Octavian's rejection and named substitute heirs. Finally, Caesar was only in his mid-fifties. He might expect to live another two decades, by which point Octavian would be a mature man. Caesar also allowed for the possibility that he might yet have a legitimate son who would take precedence over Octavian. Still, the document was a remarkable vote of confidence in Caesar's young grandnephew.

The will was given over to the chief of the Vestal Virgins for safekeeping. Apparently, even in Rome, where little or nothing was sacred, this meant it was kept secret. But we have to wonder if any of the three men who shared the chariots that returned to Italy in 45 B.C.—Antony, Decimus, or Octavian himself—suspected Caesar's fateful choice.

4

CAESAR'S LAST TRIUMPH

At the beginning of October 45 b.c., after a long stay at his villa at Labici, Caesar finally entered Rome. It was his fifth triumph. This one marked his victory in Hispania and its theme was silver, symbol of Hispania's famous mineral wealth. It was even harder than in 46 b.c. to hide the fact that the war was a civil war—a fight against Romans rather than foreign foes—and so a triumph was offensive if not illegal. Still, Caesar was determined to mark the occasion, but it didn't go without incident.

As the dictator rode past the benches of the People's Tribunes in his triumphal chariot, nine of them stood in salute, but one tribune remained seated. Ten People's Tribunes were elected each year, in principle to represent ordinary people, but they sometimes came from the Best Men. The seated tribune was Lucius Pontius Aquila, who had supported Pompey in the Civil War. This Pontius was possibly a friend of Cicero. He might have been the same Pontius who lost his estate near Naples (it became Servilia's property) and if so, he had a personal grudge against Caesar.

Caesar was furious. "Ask me for the Republic back, Tribune Aquila!"

he cried. Nor was that all. For days, whenever Caesar promised something in public, he added sarcastically, "That is, if Pontius Aquila will let me." Surely, not everyone appreciated the joke. Ordinary Romans considered the People's Tribunes their champions.

Caesar capped his Spanish triumph with a public banquet for the people of Rome. Then, four days later, he gave them an unprecedented second feast. He said that he wanted to make up for cutting corners in the first meal. Caesar was a politician, though, and it might be that he felt the public's anger about the People's Tribune and he wanted to make amends. Having killed Romans in Hispania, he now fed other Romans.

Caesar threw open his new estate to the public to hold the banquets. Not to be confused with Caesar's villa at Labici about twenty miles south of Rome, this estate was called the *horti Caesaris*—Caesar's Gardens. The Gardens were located about a mile southeast of the Tiber Island, on the hills overlooking the west bank of the river, near Rome but outside it. It was one of those pleasure palaces that the grandees of Rome built on the hills in and around the city; estates that took in the summer breezes and avoided the bogs where the malarial mosquitos bred. Caesar's Gardens contained great halls and expansive colonnades as well as a park, all decorated with fine sculpture and paintings. There might have been a shrine to Dionysius—in those days a favorite god of Egypt. There was certainly a stunning view of the great city across the river as well as a dock for private access to it.

But Caesar's Gardens were more than just a stately home and its grounds. Caesar planned to use the colonnade as a backdrop for political theater. It worked only too well—it backfired, actually—during one of the post-triumph feasts. Caesar stood in an open space between the columns and took the salute of the crowd. Unfortunately, a man known as Herophilus or Amatius stood practically beside him in the next open space and got almost an equally enthusiastic reception. Herophilus claimed to be the grandson of the great Marius, making him a favorite of the poor. Gaius Marius (ca. 157–86 B.C.), Sulla's archrival, was a great general and Populist. He was married to Caesar's aunt, his father's sister Julia. Marius impersonators or his alleged descendants kept turning up in Rome.

Nothing survives of Caesar's Gardens today and we have only a general sense of their location. Two statues were found in Rome that may well come from them. Both are Roman copies of Greek originals. They illustrate the classical themes of the power of the gods and the fickleness of fate.

Both are of the highest-quality marble—Pentelic marble—from outside Athens. One shows the god Apollo. He is sitting on a rock in his shrine at Delphi, at the spot that the Greeks thought marked the center of the world. The fragmentary piece shows the god's imposing body turned toward the viewer. He might originally have held a scepter in his right hand. The second statue shows a son of Niobe. The boy is leaning on the ground in a dramatic pose, his body facing the viewer, his head turned upward and sideways in a look of fear and emotion. According to myth, Niobe had fourteen children, all healthy, but she bragged about them and insulted the gods. In retaliation, the gods sent Apollo and his sister Artemis, who struck the children dead in a matter of minutes. Niobe and her husband soon died as well in grief and anger.

Did the statues remind Caesar that he too was just human, regardless of what his flatterers said? Or were they just two more beautiful trophies?

FROM DICTATOR TO GOD

Caesar spent six months in Rome, from early October 45 B.C. to mid-March 44 B.C. It was his longest stay in the city in fifteen years, but it was less a return than a respite. He already decided to go east at the start of spring to command the war against Parthia just as he went west a year before to command the war in Hispania. What then was the purpose of his time in Rome? To settle things, wrote Cicero, "They say he [Caesar] wouldn't go against the Parthians unless matters were settled in Rome." Precisely what "settled" means is unclear, but by the end of 45 B.C., no one could mistake Caesar for a friend of the Republic.

It was irregular enough that he was sole consul instead of one of the usual two consuls, but then he stepped down in September. He remained dictator for ten years and in fact, the Senate reaffirmed that position. Still, Caesar insisted that two of his staunchest generals be appointed suffect (that is, supplemental) consuls for the rest of the year—Gaius Trebonius and Gaius Fabius. He did not bother with a vote. Later, people booed Fabius when he entered the theater because he lacked the legitimacy of an elected official. It showed that people resented how Caesar took away their power as voters.

The last straw seemed to come on December 31, 45 B.C.—New Year's Eve. Fabius died suddenly. Caesar made his old comrade-in-arms, Gaius Caninius Rebilus, suffect consul for the rest of the year—that is, for less than twenty-four hours. Caesar was hurrying along the prizes of Civil War, as the historian Tacitus wrote many years later. At the time, Cicero joked that Caninius was so very vigilant that he never closed his eyes while consul, but this was bitter humor from the pen of a conservative. Cicero also wrote that it was hard to hold back the tears. There were, he said, innumerable other things of this kind going on in those days.

All this, however, was just a prologue. The main act took place in late January or early February of 44 B.C. when the Senate named Caesar DICTATOR IN PERPETUO—that is, Dictator in Perpetuity. The new title was important both for what it was and what it wasn't.

The issue wasn't power, as Caesar already had massive powers. No one held high office without his approval even if technically he lacked a veto. He controlled the army and the treasury. He could be consul if he chose.

The issue wasn't formal monarchy, either. Caesar kept proclaiming that he wasn't a king. It's credible enough that he didn't aspire to the title *rex*, as he said. The hated title was more trouble than it was worth. But a dictator for life was virtually a king, as people understood in antiquity. Shortly after the Ides of March, Cicero wrote, "We should actually call King the man whom we in fact had as king." Asinius Pollio, a supporter of Caesar and later a great historian, wrote in 43 B.C. that he loved Caesar but he knew that with him Rome suffered unrestricted rule where everything was in the power of one man.

The issue was the future. Once Caesar was Dictator in Perpetuity, there was no turning back. Not even Sulla held such a title. On the contrary, Sulla stepped down and ended his life in retirement. Caesar let people know what he thought of that in a witticism, "Sulla didn't know his ABCs when he laid down his dictatorship," meaning that Sulla didn't know the basic rules of politics. The source of the quotation is an enemy of Caesar, it is true, so it might be made up, but it bears the sharp mark of Caesar's intelligence.

Another sign that Caesar's dictatorship was here to stay is the oath that the Senate voted to swear. Every senator promised to maintain Caesar's safety and to consider him sacrosanct—that is, to threaten the death penalty to anyone who harmed him.

Kings have heirs. The public did not know that Caesar had chosen his grandnephew Octavian as his heir, but they did learn that Caesar named him as the dictator's formal second-in-command, the Master of the Horse, for most of the next year. The appointment would begin on March 18, 44 B.C., when both Caesar and Marcus Aemilius Lepidus, one of Caesar's generals and the current Master of the Horse, were scheduled to leave Rome on their respective military campaigns for the rest of 44 B.C. This was an astonishing honor for an eighteen-year-old, especially considering the Romans' distrust of youth. Combine this with the provisions of Caesar's will and it becomes clear that the Dictator in Perpetuity planned for a successor. You might as well have tolled all the bells in Rome for the death of the Republic.

The cascade of new honors, though only details, shows just how low some Romans were willing to bow before the new realities of power.

The Senate wasted no time in flattering Caesar once news of the victory at Munda reached Rome on April 20, 45 B.C. The senators called for fifty days of Thanksgiving—ten more than they granted the previous year for Caesar's victory in North Africa. They made April 21 an annual day of commemoration, with races to be held in the circus. They called Caesar *Pater Patriae*, or "Father of the Fatherland." They gave Caesar the title of *liberator* and authorized the building of a Temple of Liberty. They also allowed him to use the title of *imperator* permanently—previous generals used it only temporarily. Imperator, or "commander," was a title given to a general by his troops after an especially great victory. The Senate also allowed Caesar to wear the purple and gold of a triumph on all formal occasions as well as a laurel wreath–symbol of the king of the gods, Jupiter. People joked that this was Caesar's favorite honor because it allowed him to cover up his receding hairline—he was vain about going bald.

The Senate of Cato and men like him would never sink so low, but those men were gone. The Civil War had killed them. Cicero was the last lion of the Senate and he was in semiretirement. Besides, he was not about to roar at Caesar. There were, it seems, no big senatorial cats left.

So the flattery sweepstakes now escalated with the commissioning of new statues. Take, for example, Quirinus. He was one of the many obscure gods whom the Romans worshipped. Originally perhaps a local deity, by Caesar's day Quirinus was taken to represent the hero Romulus, legendary founder of Rome, after Romulus became a god. So it was decided to erect a statue of Caesar in the Temple of Quirinus on the Quirinal Hill with the inscription "To the undefeated god." Symbolically this made Caesar almost the second founder of Rome. Cicero registered a private protest by writing wittily to a friend that it was better to have Caesar share a temple with the god Quirinus than with the goddess Salvation. Why? If Caesar was like Quirinus there was hope of getting rid of him, since tradition stated that the senators killed the original Quirinus—Romulus—in order to stop him from becoming a tyrant.

Another statue of Caesar was placed on the Capitoline Hill next to the statues of the seven kings of Rome and an eighth statue, of the man who drove out the last king and established the Roman Republic in the traditional founding date of 509 B.C. That eighth man was Lucius Junius Brutus, whom Brutus and Decimus each claimed as an ancestor. Yet another statue of Caesar was carried in the procession that opened the games celebrating Munda in July 45 B.C. behind a statue of Victory. This third statue of Caesar was made of ivory, an honor usually reserved for the gods.

The placement, processional use, and material of the statues—at least one was made of ivory—came close to calling Caesar a god. The inscription on the statue in the Temple of Quirinus made no bones about it. One wonders if Caesar erased it as he erased the inscription calling him a "demigod" the year before. Some people did object. According to Cicero, no one applauded Caesar's statue in the summer procession—the "odious" procession, as he called it.

Never mind. By early 44 B.C., the Senate took the final steps. They made Caesar an official god of the Roman state. He would have his own temple, priest, sacred couch for his image, and name—Divus Julius, the Deified Julius. None of this was put into effect while Caesar was alive.

It's not clear which, if any of these honors came on Caesar's initiative. By making Caesar a god, the Senate was possibly trying to win support among the many inhabitants of Rome who came from the Greek East and who might appreciate the gesture.

CLEOPATRA IN ROME

Not long after Caesar threw open his gardens across the Tiber to the public, he closed them again for the exclusive use of Cleopatra. It was Cleopatra's second visit to Rome, which she had visited the previous year as well. It was not unusual for foreign rulers to come to the city on diplomatic business. Cleopatra's father, Ptolemy XII, did so in his day. But, diplomat or not, Cleopatra was also Caesar's mistress and she had the added incentive of conceiving another child by him.

As a busy head of state, Cleopatra surely spent much of her time in Rome in the traditional business of visiting kings and queens—that is, networking with important people. They gave each other gifts. Cleopatra brought bangles from Egypt while the Romans offered information and access.

Mark Antony came to see her. Perhaps that lit the spark that later flamed into one of history's most passionate love affairs. Cicero came to see her, too, but love was not on his mind—far from it. He received a promise of some choice books from Egypt's famous royal collection. But he never got them.

"I hate the Queen," Cicero wrote in spring 44 B.C. He was probably not alone in that sentiment. Romans distrusted foreigners, especially Greeks and powerful women. Her royal presence only fueled the rumors that

Caesar wanted to be a king himself or that Caesar planned to move permanently from Rome to Alexandria, the city of his mistress, or to Troy, the city of his mythic ancestor Aeneas. They also said he would take the wealth of the empire with him, drain Italy of its manpower, and leave the city of Rome in the hands of his friends.

CAESAR TURNS EAST

Caesar wanted to settle things in Rome first before embarking for Parthia. He said he was concerned about his laws being disregarded. But Caesar spent too little time in Rome for us to think that he was seriously worried about this. More likely he found politics in Rome frustrating and dull compared to his favorite arena—war. And perhaps Caesar thought a breathing space would make the Romans used to his rule. In fact, if the men he left behind fell short of his standards, people might even long for his return.

He was gathering a huge army, one so big that plans were in motion by fall 45 B.C. at the latest. It would be the largest force that Caesar ever commanded—16 legions, or 80,000 infantrymen if full strength and 10,000 cavalrymen. Six of the legions, along with auxiliary troops, were to winter near Apollonia (in modern Albania) at the western end of the Via Egnatia, the Roman road that ran eastward to the Hellespont. Caesar planned to leave Rome for his new war on March 18, 44 B.C.—the usual springtime start of the campaign season, and a year and a day after his victory at Munda.

At first glance, Caesar's Parthian Expedition looks like a matter of national security, but on closer look, it had explosive consequences in domestic politics. The national security argument focused on defending Rome's eastern frontier against a rival empire that had already invaded Roman Syria. Powerful Parthia stretched from eastern Iran to what is now eastern Turkey and Kurdistan. Parthia was the only border state that threatened Rome. Conquering Parthia would end the threat, yet the Romans split on party lines when it came to this war. The Populists were hawks and the Best Men were doves.

Crassus, with Caesar's encouragement, had attacked Parthia in 53 B.C. and lost. For Caesar, Parthia represented another grand military campaign, this time, as in Gaul, against foreigners rather than against fellow Romans, as in the Civil War. Victory in Gaul had made Caesar Dictator in Perpetuity; the victory in Parthia might make him king. No one who still believed in the Republic could face the new war with ease.

But the war was probably popular with ambitious young Roman men, both in the elite and the masses, for reverse reasons. Fighting in Gaul had made tens of thousands of men rich and powerful. The Parthian War offered the ambitious a new opportunity for the same success. They probably jumped at the chance.

One young Roman had more to gain from the war than anyone else—Octavian. In December 45 B.C., Caesar sent him to Apollonia, a major Roman military base, to spend the winter with the legions and a military tutor. The tutor would teach him the art of war, while the legions would let Octavian practice his political skills. It was a way of introducing Caesar's chosen heir to Caesar's soldiers. To anyone watching closely, it was another reason to fear the Parthian War.

In the Republic, opposition to the war would be aired in full in the Senate. There would be a no-holds-barred debate, set-piece speeches, accusations, boasts, divisions, votes, and repercussions. But now the dictator decided.

Caesar claimed that he already had enough glory, but maybe not. Maybe he wanted to end his military career fighting foreigners and not in a civil war. Because he had encouraged Crassus to attack Parthia in 53 B.C., Caesar might feel that now his dignitas demanded that he avenge the loss. He might want to avenge others who also fell at the decisive Battle of Carrhae—Crassus's son, Publius, who fought for Caesar as an officer in Gaul, as well as a unit of Gallic cavalrymen. He might want to eliminate the possibility of Parthian support for Pompey's son Sextus, who was still at large.

On his way to Parthia Caesar would have to deal with the situation in the Roman province of Syria. An able and dangerous man, Quintus Caecilius

Bassus took control there in 46 B.C. He was a supporter of Pompey and he promptly arranged for the murder of Caesar's cousin Sextus Caesar. When Caesar sent out a new governor the next year, Bassus defeated him. Now Caesar decided to deal with Bassus himself.

COMEDY IN A VILLA

Everybody who was anybody in Rome had a country villa. Actually, they often had several. Cicero, for instance, owned three villas on the Bay of Naples as well as another in Tusculum, in the Alban Hills. The Roman elite loved both locales. Cicero had a lovely Neapolitan villa outside Puteoli (the modern city of Puzzuoli near Naples) on the high ground of the eastern shore of Lake Lucrinus with a view of the sea.

He complained about his rich and apathetic neighbor, Lucius Marcius Philippus, whose huge estate included fishponds—to Cicero, the symbol of idle, irresponsible wealth. A former consul, Philippus was a schemer who although related to Caesar managed to get through the Civil War without choosing sides. He had Caesar's approval at the war's end. Philippus was married to Caesar's niece Atia and was stepfather to her son, Octavian. He was, in short, very well-connected.

It's no surprise that on the night of December 18, 45 B.C., Philippus received a visit from Caesar. It was the second night of the Saturnalia, the Roman winter festival. The dictator was no easy guest because he did not travel light—two thousand soldiers as well as additional staff accompanied Caesar, as Cicero claimed. It's possibly an exaggeration, but surely Caesar had a large number of men and the army crammed the estate. Cicero took note because Caesar was coming to his house the next day. To prepare, Cicero borrowed guards from a friend and pitched a camp for the soldiers. Cicero describes the whole thing in a breathless letter that he dashed off the same day to his friend Atticus, full of verbal shortcuts and Greek words, as if he couldn't wait to get the story out but wanted to make it pretty.

Cicero was probably glad to have Caesar's attention after a long year. In

February, Cicero's beloved daughter Tullia died after childbirth. Her son survived, as did his father, her former husband, Publius Cornelius Dolabella. The two had divorced a few months earlier after an unhappy marriage. Cicero was inconsolable, although many friends and colleagues sent their condolences. Caesar wrote from Hispania. A friend wrote archly that Tullia lived no longer than the Republic.

In May, Cicero drafted a letter to Caesar, sending it first to Balbus and Oppius. They asked for so many changes that Cicero thought better of it and gave up the idea. Now, he would actually speak to the great man.

On December 19, 44 B.C., after Caesar spent the morning working and taking a walk on the beach, he arrived at Cicero's. There followed a bath, no doubt including a massage and scrape-down, then an anointment with a thin layer of perfumed oil. Finally, Caesar sat down to a sumptuous meal and ate freely. Caesar engaged in his usual act of vomiting after dinner. Like many other elite Romans, Caesar followed a regular course of emetics to keep his weight down while indulging in gastronomy.

It was all very jovial and very disciplined. Cicero felt satisfied that he made a good impression after a serious but not crushing effort. Caesar seemed pleased. Yet Cicero noticed that Caesar did not change expression when he heard bad news about a supporter. Behind Caesar's smiling face was the man who had taken away Cicero's political power and sway. And behind Cicero's flattery and gratitude was the man who resented it intensely.

There was no talk of anything serious, said Cicero, but plenty of talk about literature. How did the former consul feel about that? "Not a guest to whom you would say, 'I'd love it if you'd come back to see me here.' Once was enough." After leaving Cicero's villa, Caesar's next stop was the estate of Dolabella. A demagogue who once tried to outbid Caesar for popular support, Dolabella had fought for Caesar in Africa and Hispania. The dictator planned to make use of him in the future. Now, Caesar's entourage passed Dolabella's villa nearby. While Caesar sat on his horse, the whole force of armed men lined up on either side of him in a salute to Dolabella.

Cicero ends his letter with this almost cinematic image of the reality of

Roman power. The orator who once steered the fate of nations from the well of the Senate was reduced to reporting about a man on horseback. The question was, would anyone take the horseman down?

THE THREE LAST STRAWS

Titus Livius was a teenager at the time of the Ides of March. A citizen of Patavium (modern Padua) in northern Italy, he was swept up in the civil wars of the era. But Livy, as he is better known, stayed alive and wrote one of the greatest histories of ancient Rome. Large parts of it survive today, but unfortunately we have only a capsule sketch of the chapters on Julius Caesar—a summary written later during the Roman Empire. Still, the summary includes an important analysis. It shows the enormous public relations challenge facing Caesar as he was about to take on a new role. His whole life, Caesar was a master manipulator and stage director. But the role of Dictator in Perpetuity required a new script. No Roman "rewrite man," no matter how skilled, could tell it without arousing resistance in some part of his audience.

The Senate granted Caesar the highest of honors, but they in turn generated a Roman politician's bad dream—*invidia*, that is, ill will. As Livy states, three incidents in December 45 B.C., January 44 B.C., and February 44 B.C. tipped the balance against Caesar in a crucial segment of public opinion. They were, it seems, the last straws as far as some Romans were concerned.

The first incident probably took place in December 45 B.C. or possibly early 44 B.C. The Senate was voting honor after honor to the dictator. Some said that his enemies jumped on the bandwagon in order to embarrass Caesar with an overload of distinctions. Only a few senators voted no. Eventually the Senate decided to present the honors to Caesar formally. They marched as one to Caesar's Forum. The consuls and praetors headed up the group followed by the other officials and the rest of the senators. Typically, attendance at a Senate meeting was low, but they might have numbered 100 to 200 of the 800–900 total Senate body. They were wearing their robes of office and no doubt made an impressive sight. A large crowd of ordinary people followed behind.

Caesar was sitting in front of the Temple of Mother Venus. Etiquette called for him to stand to greet the senators but he did not get up. Not only that, but he also made a joke about their news, saying his honors needed to be cut back rather than increased. By practically rejecting a gift and by refusing to recognize the senators' rank, Caesar insulted them—and, some said, insulted the Roman people as well. Why a man as shrewd as Caesar did this is not clear. Perhaps he wanted to test the limits of his power.

The sources are full of commentary about this incident. There are explanations for why Caesar might have insulted the senators, but no one knows for certain whether the insult was intentional. Some say that it was the main and deadliest cause of ill will against Caesar, others merely that it gave the future conspirators one of their chief excuses. It allowed Caesar's enemies to argue that he wanted to be addressed as a king.

The Romans often thought of their government as "the Senate and the Roman People," SENATUS POPULUSQUE ROMANUS, the famous SPQR. In the incident in the Forum Julium, Caesar gave the strong impression that he no longer cared about the Senate. Next he seemed to turn on the Roman people.

The second incident pitted Caesar against two of the People's Tribunes for 44 B.C., Gaius Epidius Marullus and Lucius Caesetius Flavus. One day in January 44 B.C., they found a diadem on the head of Caesar's statue on the Speaker's Platform in the Roman Forum. Some one—no one knew who—put it there. A diadem was the ancient Greek equivalent of a crown—far simpler, but still a symbol of royalty. It was an embroidered white silk ribbon that ended in a knot and two fringed strips. Marullus and Caesetius removed the diadem and said that, to his credit, Caesar had no need of such a thing. Caesar was angry even so. He suspected a put-up job—the tribunes arranged for the diadem to appear so that they could remove it and look good. Meanwhile, people would suspect him of wanting to be a king. Then, shortly afterward, on January 26, 44 B.C., matters escalated.

Caesar and his entourage were traveling the Appian Way after coming down the narrow path from the shrine of Jupiter Lattiaris on the Alban

Mount (now Monte Cavo), which rises above the crystalline waters of Lake Albanus, southeast of Rome. There, they celebrated the Feriae Latinae, the old, annual festival of the Latin-speaking peoples. Normally it was held in the spring but the dictator had moved it to January because of his planned departure for the Parthian War. As they traveled north they passed the town of Bovillae, where Caesar's family, the Julii, traced their roots to a time even before the founding of Rome.

The Senate granted Caesar the right to come back to Rome on horseback as if celebrating a minor triumph. So, people crowded around the mounted dictator as he reached the city's Appian Gate. Suddenly, someone in the crowd greeted him as king—rex. Others took up the cry. Caesar answered: "I am Caesar, not Rex." It was witty because, like the English word *king,* Rex was a family name as well as a royal title. Caesar's ancestors, in fact, included "Kings"—the Marcius Rex family. Caesar's wordplay suggested that someone merely had his name wrong. Cynics figured that the whole thing was staged, making it just another occasion for Caesar to show off his supposed republican sentiments.

The tribunes Marullus and Caesetius were not amused. They had the man who first cried "Rex" arrested. Now Caesar finally expressed his anger, accusing them of stirring up opposition to him. They in turn issued a declaration that they felt threatened in the exercise of their office. Caesar called a meeting of the Senate.

There were calls for the death penalty for the tribunes but he rejected that. He spoke more in sorrow than anger, he said. He wanted to grant his usual clemency but the issue, said Caesar, was his dignitas. So he insisted that the tribunes be removed from office and ousted from membership in the Senate. And so they were. As his parting shot, Caesar demanded that the tribune Caesetius's father disinherit his son, but the man refused and Caesar dropped the issue.

The removal of the tribunes should have ended the matter but some people accused Caesar of blaming the messengers—they said that he should have been angry at those who called him Rex rather than at the tribunes. Shortly afterward, elections were held to choose new consuls and some people voted for Marullus and Caesetius. That suggests resentment as well at Caesar's tendency to turn elections into rubber stamps.

The Roman plebs took their tribunes seriously as the champions of the common people. Caesar did too at one time. In 49 B.C., he said that one of the main reasons for crossing the Rubicon was to protect the People's Tribunes from abuse by the Senate. Now he put himself on the wrong side of public opinion. The result was to generate invidia—ill will—on the grounds that Caesar wanted to be king. But Caesar actually indulged in the finery of Rome's ancient kings such as high red boots and golden wreaths.

Which brings us to Livy's third incident, the celebration of the Lupercalia festival on February 15, 44 B.C. The incident in Caesar's Forum was unscripted, while the incident at the Appian Gate was either unscripted or veered out of control. The Lupercalia was definitely scripted, but who wrote the script and what it was are unclear.

The story is as follows. The Lupercalia was an annual festival associated with fertility. After a sacrifice, the priests, wearing only loin cloths, ran around central Rome and touched bystanders, especially women, with goatskin straps. The festival was associated with Romulus, mythical founder of Rome, which no doubt appealed to Caesar or anyone who saw him as Rome's second founder. Before February 15, the Senate set up a special association of priests in Caesar's honor in connection with the festival. Mark Antony was the Chief Priest, so he led the runners.

The Lupercalia was an annual celebration, but in 44 B.C. it was a festival like no other. The jaw-dropping main event saw Caesar offered a diadem and ostentatiously refusing it. Caesar was sitting in the Roman Forum on the Speaker's Platform, or Rostra.

The Speaker's Platform itself was an impressive new monument that was part of Caesar's redesign of Rome's civic center. The old Speaker's Platform stood for centuries before being demolished. *Rostra* means the Beaks, a name referring to the bronze-covered rams or "beaks" of captured warships with which it was decorated. The Speaker's Platform was the main place for addressing the Roman people and, accordingly, the old Speaker's Platform stood in a central position. When Caesar rebuilt Rome's civic space, he moved the new Speaker's Platform to a corner of the Roman Forum, a sign of what the dictator thought of public speakers.

Caesar's Speaker's Platform stood over 11 feet high and was more than 43 feet long. It had a curved front, probably extended on supports into a rectangular platform. Seven steps led up to the Speaker's Platform from the back, while the front faced the open space of the Forum. The whole thing was lined with marble. Four statues decorated the platform. Caesar restored the statues of Sulla and Pompey, each on horseback, which the people had earlier destroyed. In addition, two statues of Caesar were erected, one with his famous oak wreath—the Medal of Honor or Civic Crown—and the other with a grass-and-wildflower wreath, an even higher military honor. One of the two statues was on horseback. In short, the only images on the Speaker's Platform were two dictators and a domineering general and politician who was also Caesar's son-in-law. There were no champions of liberty like Brutus's ancestor, Lucius Junius Brutus.

It was here that Caesar sat on February 15 on the occasion of the Lupercalia. He was dressed in a triumphing general's purple toga as well as the high boots and long-sleeved tunic of a king of old. He wore a gold wreath and sat on a gilded chair. A large crowd had gathered.

After his run, Mark Antony climbed up to the Speaker's Platform and placed a diadem on Caesar's head, saying, "The People give this to you through me." A few applauded but most people responded with silence. Lepidus, newly appointed Master of the Horse, was there. His response was a groan and gloomy look. Caesar removed the diadem and Antony tried again, only to get the same response. Finally Caesar ordered it to be taken to the Capitoline Temple with the words "Jupiter alone of the Romans is King." This received an enthusiastic response.

To commemorate the event, Caesar had an entry made in the *fasti*, the official calendar of the Roman state, writing that "the Consul Mark Antony had offered the Kingship, by the People's command, to the Dictator in Perpetuity Gaius Caesar but Caesar had refused."

The sources buzz with speculation about who was behind the event and why. Some make Antony the prime mover and say that he surprised Caesar, either to flatter him or maybe even to embarrass him. Later on it was claimed that Antony was just trying to bring Caesar to his senses and to get him to give up any thoughts of kingship. Others give Caesar's enemies a central role. In this version, two opponents of Caesar came up to the Speaker's Platform and tried to get Caesar to accept the diadem. We'll never know the real story of the Lupercalia, but it is clear enough that Caesar had fences to mend with a public that feared his ambition.

Caesar still had many supporters. His loyal colleague Aulus Hirtius, for example, later insisted that Caesar was a *vir clarissimus*—a man of extraordinary brilliance—who made the Republic stronger. He and others called Caesar a great man. It was only the nobles and those "with claims to power" who found Caesar "unbearable," claimed one ancient supporter. Most people "gloried in his many great victories" and "admired someone who they thought was more than just a man." Yet, in the winter of 44 B.C., precisely what ordinary Romans thought was debatable. Caesar brought the urban plebs land and peace by ending the violent feuds of the nobles, while also enriching their lives with feasts and spectacles. Yet the urban plebs resented Caesar's attacks on the People's Tribunes and his undermining of elections. They probably had little regard for the new senators from Gaul. To some, it seemed that Caesar was losing the people.

At the time, many believed that Caesar's rejection of the crown at the Lupercalia was a way of trying to see if there was support for him to become king. They believed that he wanted to be king and they despised him for it.

Hatred is one of a ruler's greatest dangers, especially hatred from the common people. Hatred stirs conspiracies, while hatred by the people makes conspirators think they can get away with their plans. Caesar was about to test that principle.

In three months, Caesar had disrespected the Senate, dispensed with People's Tribunes, and flirted with monarchy. By February, the conspiracy that would bring Caesar down was being born. In fact, it might already have been alive.

Part Two

BLOOD

on the

STONES

5

THE BIRTH OF A PLOT

THE PLOT TO KILL CAESAR BEGAN WHEN GAIUS CASSIUS LONGINUS walked across town to visit his brother-in-law. He had not spoken to Marcus Junius Brutus in months, even though Cassius was married to Brutus's sister, because he was angry over losing a plum job to him. Now, however, Cassius needed Brutus. The conversation began with a friendly exchange and an agreement to reconcile. Then came a long and serious discussion. Finally, Cassius threw his arms around Brutus in embrace. And with that, the life of Julius Caesar lay in the balance. It was February 44 B.C.

Or so the best-known source tells the story. It is plausible, but, in truth, we don't know just how the conspiracy began or with whom. Shakespeare tells us that Brutus and Cassius were at the heart of it, but the Bard was only following one ancient tradition. Other sources state that three men, not two, headed the conspiracy—and that Decimus, in fact, stood beside Brutus and Cassius as its leaders. Our earliest in-depth source for the conspiracy even names Decimus first among the conspirators.

Decimus is no mere detail; he is the key. Brutus and Casssius fought for

Pompey and the Republic but Decimus had been loyal to Caesar for more than ten years. Why change now? Although Decimus said later that he acted to save the Republic, he was a hard-nosed man, the sort to be moved by fear, honor, and self-interest. And Decimus wasn't alone—other friends of Caesar also joined the conspiracy. That took more than a public relations misstep on Caesar's part—it took a crisis of trust. Caesar abused their friendship by breaking the unwritten rule of Roman life, that loyalty would be rewarded. Indeed, he convinced important friends that they were better off without him.

It was predictable that the Roman nobility would never accept a perpetual dictator. Ever jealous of their own privilege, they would sooner conspire to kill him than submit, as long as they thought they had a chance of getting away with murder. In winter 44 B.C. signs of the people's discontent gave them confidence. They might have hesitated but Caesar's imminent departure for the Parthian front forced their hand.

In 49 B.C., Caesar seemed to some like a second Hannibal—the great commander who rode in from the West and invaded Italy. In 44 B.C., Caesar seemed like a second Alexander the Great—like Pompey but more dangerous—on the cusp of a great war in the East that would bring him back in triumph as a king. Those who rode out with him, like Octavian, would reap glory and power. Those who stayed at home feared eclipse, even if they were loyalists. Caesar left several of his experienced generals at home. We do not know why, but he had a history of ditching supporters when they were no longer useful or if they threatened to outdo him.

All hope was gone that he would restore the Republic. Caesar was already Perpetual Dictator, already declared a god, already dismissive of both Senate and people, and already guilty of protesting too much that he didn't want to be rex. Now, it seemed as if he would be Lord of Asia like Alexander. Julius Rex was a far cry from the proconsul of Gaul. Many Romans feared the man who had installed the queen of Egypt and perhaps the son she claimed was his in his villa across the Tiber, the man who planned a massive expedition to conquer the same ancient Iran that Alexander had conquered—they feared that he would replace the Republic with a monarchy. Who doubted that a man who loved blood, grandeur, and power as much as Caesar was capable of it?

SOURCES OF EVIDENCE

Before turning to the conspirators and crime, a word is needed about our sources of evidence. If there ever was a full contemporary investigation report, it has long since disappeared. Cicero's correspondence includes a few dozen precious letters between him and a half dozen of the conspirators. They are fascinating but provide only limited evidence about the motives or the deed itself. Several of the conspirators issued coins that provide great clues. Archaeological remains in the city of Rome also add important information about the events of the Ides of March.

Several contemporaries wrote accounts of the assassination. Asinius Pollio (76 B.C.–A.D. 4) wrote what was probably the best history of the years from 60 B.C. to 44 B.C. This excellent historian was a friend of Caesar but was aware of his defects. Unfortunately, Pollio was not in Rome on the Ides of March. Livy (59 B.C.–A.D. 17) was born in Patavium (modern Padua) but came to Rome to complete his education. If he wasn't in Rome for the Ides, he was there a few years afterward, when the tale was still fresh. He included the death of Caesar in his monumental history of Rome. Strabo (ca. 62 B.C.–ca. A.D. 23), the famous geographer and historian, was born in Anatolia (Turkey) and came to live in Augustus's Rome. He included the death of Caesar in his history of the years ca. 145–30 B.C. Caesar's associate Oppius wrote a memoir of Caesar, and Brutus's stepson Bibulus wrote a similar book about Brutus. Brutus's friend Empylus wrote a short book on the death of Caesar. It would be instructive to be able to read these books today but, unfortunately, none of them survives. What remains of Livy includes only a capsule summary of his chapters on Caesar. Fortunately, some of the later ancient writers on the subject did read these books. Even more fortunately, two contemporary accounts do survive.

Cicero wrote one of those accounts in 44 B.C., possibly only a few weeks after the Ides. Cicero was an eyewitness. Unfortunately his account is just a brief paragraph. It confirms certain details in later versions while also containing several exaggerations.

Far more important, although somewhat later, is another, more detailed account by a contemporary, found in the *Life of Caesar Augustus*—that is, the life of the Emperor Augustus, the former Octavian, written by Nicolaus of Damascus (born in 64 B.C. and died on an unknown date but well after 4 B.C.). It is one of five surviving detailed ancient accounts of the conspiracy, the Ides, and the aftermath—our most important sources of information today. Nicolaus's account is often perceptive but it is not without problems. Although he was an adult in 44 B.C., Nicolaus wasn't in Rome then or even a Roman—he was a Greek from Syria. He wrote several decades afterward; exactly when is uncertain. He was biased—he drew in part on Augustus's autobiography, and, in fact, he worked for Augustus so he had a motive to defame the conspirators. On top of that, we don't actually have Nicolaus's work but only a version by a later abridger. Still, what survives is fascinating. More than any other ancient source, Nicolaus promotes the idea that private grudges rather than public duty moved the conspirators, with Brutus as an exception.

Plutarch, the famous author, a native of central Greece (ca. A.D. 45–before A.D. 125) narrates the conspiracy and assassination in three of his Roman biographies, Caesar, Brutus, and Antony. Although he wrote more than a century later, Plutarch was a scholar and he consulted earlier works. But he was also a student of Greek philosophy like Brutus, whom he makes his hero. Brutus played a very large role in the conspiracy against Caesar but Plutarch probably exaggerates it. Since Plutarch looms so large in the sources, and since he was Shakespeare's main source, we need to keep that in mind. Nicolaus, who was not under Brutus's spell, offers a counterweight.

Suetonius (ca. A.D. 70–well after A.D. 128) wrote in Latin the famous *Lives of the Twelve Caesars*, including one of Julius Caesar. Alternately gossipy and astute, admiring and critical, it includes a detailed account of the conspiracy and assassination. Like Plutarch, Suetonius was widely versed in the earlier sources. He admires Caesar enormously as a general but criticizes him as a politician and a man. A brilliant writer, Suetonius is seductive but not always right.

Appian (ca. A.D. 90–A.D. 160), a Greek from Alexandria, Egypt, lived most of his life in Rome. Among his several works is a history of Rome's civil wars. Of the five sources, his offers the longest connected historical narrative of Caesar's assassination. Like Plutarch and Suetonius, he too probably consulted Asinius Pollio. Also a good writer, Appian sees Caesar as first and foremost a soldier.

Finally, there is the latest source, Cassius Dio (ca. A.D. 164–after A.D. 229), a Greek senator who wrote an eighty-book history of Rome. He read widely in earlier histories but displays independence and astute analysis of his own. Unfortunately, he also makes errors of fact. A strong supporter of monarchy, he has little sympathy for Caesar's assassins.

By the standards of ancient history it's not a bad lineup, but by modern measures it's thin gruel. The evidence is based almost entirely on second-hand accounts and most of it is late. None of it is impartial—each author has an ax to grind. Supporters of the Roman emperors had little use for the conspirators, while the emperors' opponents looked back to the conspirators as role models if not secular saints.

Still, the five accounts are in basic agreement about the conspiracy and the crime. They disagree about certain important details. Faced with such sources, the historian has to exercise imagination, ingenuity, and caution. Above all, he or she needs to weigh the evidence at every point. So armed, let us turn to the men who had strong motives to kill Caesar.

CASSIUS

In January 45 B.C., Cassius accepted Caesar as an "old easygoing master." A little over a year later, in February 44 B.C., Cassius resolved to kill him. Brutus underwent a similar conversion, perhaps independently, or perhaps Cassius was the spark that set Brutus on fire.

It's unlikely that the conspiracy was in place before February. One reason is incentive—Caesar did not depose the tribunes and turn down the diadem until February. Another reason is danger—the many conspirators could not have kept the secret for long.

Gaius Cassius Longinus was an impressive man. Slightly older than Brutus, Cassius (born on October 3, around 86 B.C.) boasted several consuls in his family's history, including his father, a man defeated in battle by the rebel gladiator Spartacus. The name of Cassius's mother is not known, but a politician once mentioned her advice in a public speech, suggesting that she was someone to be reckoned with.

During his teenage years, Cassius had a fistfight at school with the son of the late dictator Sulla, who boasted about his father's power. Later writers took the fight as a sign of Cassius's lifelong hostility to tyrants. What it also shows is that he had a temper. Cicero once described him when angry as looking like the war god Mars, eyes flashing with courage. Caesar called Cassius pale and lean, a phrase he applied to Brutus, too. Shakespeare took the description of Cassius further. His Caesar says:

Yon Cassius has a lean and hungry look,
He thinks too much; such men are dangerous.

There is nothing hungry about a Roman portrait bust that has plausibly been identified as Cassius, but it is lean, as well as vigorous and determined. The marble bust shows a commanding figure in midlife. He has close-cropped hair, a prominent nose, angular cheekbones, sunken temples, and a rounded chin. He looks straight ahead with a tight-lipped and unsmiling appearance.

As far as the schoolboy fight, Pompey patched up the quarrel, which points to the political friendship between him and Cassius. Besides Pompey, Cicero was another important influence on young Cassius, who sought the statesman's company. Cicero described him as talented, industrious, and very brave. Also like Cicero, Cassius studied philosophy. He was a student on Rhodes and became fluent in Greek.

But Cassius thrilled to the sound of the trumpet. War was his forte. In that sense, he was more like Caesar than Brutus. Nor did Cassius suffer from any lack of interest in his own dignitas. Cicero once wrote to Cassius and called him "the bravest of men, one who, ever since you first set foot in the Forum, have done nothing unless it was filled to the brim with the most abundant dignitas."

The man found his moment in 53 b.c. in the Roman East. Cassius served as lieutenant governor and deputy commander to Marcus Licinius Crassus, governor of Syria. Crassus was eager to fight Parthia and win glory but he blundered into disaster—a crushing defeat near Carrhae (today, Harran, Turkey). His force of around forty thousand men suffered massive casualties. The Parthians added insult to injury by capturing several legionary eagles. Crassus was murdered in a postbattle conference with the Parthians.

The only bright spot in Rome's tarnished honor belonged to Cassius. He vainly urged caution before the battle and played a key role afterward in marching the survivors to safety in Syria. An estimated ten thousand men owed their lives to the worthy lieutenant governor.

From 53 b.c. to 51 b.c., Cassius served as virtual governor of Roman Syria. In 51 b.c. he ambushed a Parthian army raiding the province and fought a battle in which the senior Parthian general received a fatal wound. As a result, the Parthians withdrew from Syria. Cassius was able to claim victory. He wrote home that the Parthian War was over, and his report was read in the Senate.

It was vindication because earlier the senators had scoffed at him. When Cassius first wrote to them about the Parthian invasion of Syria, the general opinion was that he was concocting a cover story for his own looting. It was all a phony war, the senators said, with Cassius merely letting some neighboring Arabs into the province and then claiming they were Parthian invaders. In Rome, they said that Cassius was greedy. But then came an independent report from a Roman ally, confirming the Parthian attack, and people took Cassius seriously.

But the senators were right about Cassius's greed. Like most Roman governors, Cassius fleeced the provincials. Roman aristocrats looked down on commerce, but Cassius bought and sold Syrian merchandise with abandon and, if we can trust a late and gossipy source, earned himself the nickname "the date," in a reference to the fruit of the local palm tree. It was not a compliment. In this same period, Cassius invaded Judea and is said to have enslaved about thirty thousand Jews—and slaving was a big and profitable business.

When civil war came, Cassius supported Pompey. In 48 B.C. Cassius received command of a fleet that he used against Caesar's forces in Sicily and southern Italy. Caesar describes the two campaigns in his *Civil War* and praises Cassius's speed, aggressiveness, ingenuity, flexibility, energy, and overall effectiveness. By writing so warmly, perhaps Caesar was trying to attract Cassius to his camp or perhaps Cassius had already joined it. In any case, about a year after Caesar's victory at Pharsalus, Cassius defected to him.

The reconciliation took place in southern Anatolia, eased by support from Cassius's brother-in-law, Brutus. Later Cassius claimed that he almost assassinated Caesar then and there, but that sounds like a tall tale.

Cassius's defection was a slap to the die-hard combatants and a mortal insult to Pompey's sons. Yet Cassius could say that he continued to serve the Republic faithfully by promoting peace. Caesar welcomed him and appointed him as one of his generals. We don't know what command Cassius held but it seems unlikely that Caesar entrusted an important one to so recent an enemy. The return of peace found Cassius underemployed. Caesar promoted Brutus to governor even though Cassius was more qualified after his experience in Syria. But Caesar would not entrust Italian Gaul to a man with Cassius's military flair.

Still, Cassius did not assist Pompey's sons when they revolted in Hispania in 46 B.C. Having defected from Pompey's cause, he feared vengeance should Pompey's sons take Rome. Cassius wrote to Cicero in January 45 B.C.:

> I will die of anxiety and I would rather have an old and lenient master than to try out a new and cruel one. You know what a fool Cnaeus [Pompey] is; you know how he thinks cruelty is virtue; you know how he always thinks

himself mocked by us. I'm afraid that he'd want to mock us *à son tour* ["in his turn"—Cicero uses Greek, which is rendered here in French] clumsily with his sword.

Then Caesar won and changed the equation. After he removed the danger represented by the sons of Pompey he also removed his opponents' restraint about keeping Caesar alive.

Like many other Romans, Cassius was appalled by Caesar's monarchical behavior. Cicero claimed that Cassius came from a family that fought not only despotism but also even merely the concentration of power. Indeed, Cassius was one of only a very few senators who voted in February 44 B.C. against awarding a long list of special honors to Caesar. The act shows courage and respect for the ideals of the Republic. If any Roman took seriously a citizen's fundamental responsibility to defend the Republic by killing a man who wanted to be *rex*, it was Cassius.

But private grounds moved Cassius as well. He had his eyes set on high office, first the praetorship, then the consulship. In particular, he wanted to be urban praetor, the judge who heard cases between citizens. His main rival for this position was Brutus. In December 45 B.C., Brutus got the job. Cassius was appointed to one of the other praetorships, possibly the one who heard disputes between noncitizens.

Caesar supposedly told his friends that Cassius had a stronger case but he chose Brutus anyhow. Neither point is clear. True, Cassius excelled in the aftermath of Carrhae and the defense of Syria, but Brutus shone as governor of Italian Gaul, so why did Cassius have the stronger case? And if he did, why didn't he get the job? Perhaps the answer, as some said at the time, was that Caesar wanted to drive a wedge between Brutus and Cassius. This is plausible since Caesar also promised Brutus the consulship for 41 B.C. He passed over Cassius at first, although possibly later he gave Cassius too the nod as the other consul of 41 B.C.

If domestic politics injured Cassius's *dignitas*, perhaps foreign affairs did so, too. Cassius was Rome's most experienced and successful general against the Parthians. It is easy to imagine him disappointed when Caesar did not give him a command in the new war. Cassius would have to settle for the governorship of Syria, which Caesar promised him for 43 B.C. It wasn't much of a consolation, though, since Cassius had already been governor of Syria in all but name.

There was also a rumor that Caesar had an affair with Cassius's wife. Tertia was the daughter of Servilia and half sister of Brutus. Supposedly Servilia let Caesar have her, a story that Cicero made fun of. If the liaison happened, presumably it predated Tertia's marriage, but we have no idea of the truth of the tale or whether Cassius chafed at this gossip.

Finally, there were the lions of Megara. This small Greek city held some caged lions that Cassius was transporting to Rome to show in the games—and thereby to win political capital. When Caesar's general took Megara in 48 B.C. he confiscated the lions. Plutarch says that this added to Cassius's grievances against Caesar, but some think that he has confused Caius Cassius with his brother Lucius Cassius, who supported Caesar. So the story is inconclusive, although it sheds light on motives in Roman politics. (The lions got loose in a botched attempt to stop Caesar's troops and mauled innocent civilians.)

Cassius was a Roman's Roman. He had principles but he balanced them with pragmatism. He studied Greek philosophy but never made it his guiding star. There was a theory once that his hostility to Caesar was motivated by Epicurean philosophy—that is, by a Roman version of Epicureanism that emphasized freedom. But it's not clear that Cassius paid anything more than lip service to Epicureanism. His ambitions ran on a time-tested track. He wanted to rise in public service and become a consul like his ancestors. He was a first-rate military tactician. One ancient writer says that he had the single-mindedness of a gladiator.

Cassius was an educated man. He peppered his letters with Greek words. He knew philosophy and how to turn an elegant phrase. He could be witty or cutting and he had an edge. He was intense. As the philosopher Seneca later said, all his life Cassius drank only water, meaning he was abstemious. True, he enjoyed a good laugh but he was too prone to jesting or scoffing.

Cassius could manage the conspiracy but he lacked the authority to lead it. In asking men to assassinate Caesar, Cassius was asking them to commit murder. They had sworn oaths to hold Caesar sacrosanct and to defend him with their lives. Cassius was asking them to break those oaths. But it didn't matter how cogent an assassination plan Cassius put forward. Men refused to join the conspiracy unless the indispensable man joined first.

BRUTUS TURNS

Brutus was essential to the plot against Julius Caesar. No Brutus, no assassination. The conspirators insisted on him. Their principle was that to kill a king it takes a king—or at least a prince, and Brutus was practically a republican prince. He had the authority and the connections that Romans admired. Son of a Populist, nephew of one of the leading Best Men, enemy and then supporter of Pompey and Caesar in turn, son of Caesar's mistress and object of gossip about being Caesar's son, Brutus was all things to all people. He supposedly came from the oldest family in the Republic, the one that drove out the kings, and he also had a prominent tyrant slayer in his family tree. He had a public record going back a decade of standing for liberty and against dictatorship. Sometime during the 50s B.C. Brutus issued coins celebrating both Libertas, the goddess of liberty, and his ancestors who opposed kings and tyrants. In 54 B.C. he spoke against a proposed dictatorship for Pompey. Two years later he argued that a man who committed murder for the good of the Republic was innocent.

He was admired as a thinker and speaker. Nicolaus of Damascus puts it concisely if skeptically, "Marcus Brutus . . . was respected his whole life for his soundness of mind, for the fame of his ancestors and for his supposedly reasonable character."

Brutus's love for Greek philosophy calls for a balanced approach. Philosophy added depth and garnered respect. It allowed him to tap into time-honored ideals and to strike stirring poses. Brutus learned to recognize tyranny, to despise it and to rise against it. But Roman interest in Greek culture was rarely very substantial. Caesar's killers were practical men. Their demand for Brutus had little to do with his ability to quote Plato.

The conspirators said they were fighting for the Republic, by which they meant not only the idea, but also the power that came with it. For the Romans, as for most people, principle and profit were inseparable. Politics in Rome was a way to honor, money, and power. Caesar threatened to take too much. Brutus pointed the way to regaining what Caesar took away while also rekindling the Republic's ideals.

Above all, the conspirators wanted a leader who could keep them alive. Brutus would give them credibility in the storm sure to follow the murder. If a man of his pedigree and principles called Caesar a tyrant, then the public would believe him. Conversely, if Brutus stayed loyal to Caesar, he would cut the legs out from under the conspirators.

It also mattered that Brutus enjoyed Caesar's favor. Caesar had made Brutus governor, urban praetor, and consul. By risking everything to kill Caesar, Brutus would demonstrate his courage and his principles. True, he would also demonstrate ingratitude, but that paled in importance when compared to the survival of the Republic. Brutus was, in short, the best endorsement of the conspiracy and the best safety net for the conspirators.

The question is: what was in it for him? As recently as August 45 B.C., the answer seemed to be: nothing. Back then, Brutus wrote to a skeptical Cicero that he believed Caesar was ready to go over to the Best Men. Seven months later, Brutus entered the Senate House with a dagger at the ready. What changed?

Few characters in ancient history appear so fully in the round as Marcus Brutus. We can almost reconstruct his thoughts at this crucial turning point. His personality, his principles, his foibles, and his key relationships (with his wife, his mother, and his brother-in-law) all leave a mark in the evidence. In the end, though, the facts are tantalizingly incomplete, and so we have to resort, as usual, to informed speculation.

Brutus is also one of history's most misunderstood characters. For that, we can thank Shakespeare. The ancient sources make Brutus courageous, public-spirited, calculating, and ungrateful. Shakespeare makes Brutus instead into the model of ethics. In *The Tragedy of Julius Caesar*, Brutus agonizes over killing a friend he loves. The ancients say nothing about this. Plutarch's Brutus worries about the risks of killing Caesar but not the morality.

What makes Brutus a worthy adversary is that, like Caesar, he was multifaceted and iconic. Brutus stirred people by his philosophical mind, his lineage, his courage, his principles, and his love of freedom but he was also an opportunist and an extortionist. In Caesar, egotism, ambition, talent, ruthlessness, vision, populism, and revolution came together in a way that is still today best summed up in his name—Caesar. Caesar waded through rivers of blood in Gaul while Brutus carried the bloodiest dagger of Roman history, and yet each radiated personal charm.

Four things changed between August 45 B.C. and mid-February 44— Caesar, public opinion, Cassius, and Brutus's wife. During those critical seven months, Caesar frightened a large part of Roman public opinion into believing that he wanted to replace the Republic with a perpetual dictatorship, and possibly a kingship, in which both Senate and people would be subordinate to him. Not even the prize of the consulship could allow Brutus to continue believing that Caesar wanted to join the Best Men.

What did Caesar's perpetual dictatorship mean for Brutus? Plutarch interpreted a remark of Caesar to mean that Caesar considered Brutus his most suitable successor. "What then? Don't you think Brutus will wait for this bit of flesh?" Caesar said, touching his body. He was responding to people who accused Brutus of plotting against him. But this one-liner does not reveal Caesar's expectations. Caesar did not adopt Brutus posthumously as he did Octavian, nor did Caesar mention Brutus in his will as he mentioned others. Caesar promoted Brutus to the Republic's highest offices. Yet under Caesar power flowed away from those offices and toward Caesar and his friends. Plutarch added that Brutus could count on being the first man in Rome after Caesar's death, but that was not a reasonable expectation, not given the competition.

Either spontaneously or by concerted effort, a public relations campaign emerged to persuade Brutus to act. Graffiti appeared both on the tribunal where he sat as urban praetor and on the famous statue on the Capitoline

Hill of his supposed ancestor, Lucius Junius Brutus, who overthrew the kings. Tags like "If only now you were Brutus," "If only Brutus were alive," "Brutus, wake up!" and "You aren't really Brutus!" appeared. Some thought that these words, more than anything else, moved Brutus. He had already staked his reputation on his family's famous love of liberty, and now he had to uphold it.

Cicero may have alluded to those famous ancestors when he wrote, in his *Brutus* of 46 B.C., that he wished for Brutus "that Republic in which you could not only renew the fame of your two very distinguished families but also add to it." These were stirring words but surely not a call to Brutus to take up a dagger. In 46 B.C., Cicero still hoped that Caesar would restore the Republic.

As for Cassius, he turned his considerable strategic skills to convincing Brutus to join him against Caesar. On his visit to Brutus's house with which this chapter began, Cassius not only ended his feud over the urban praetor-ship, but he also asked Brutus pointedly what he would do at the upcoming Senate meeting. Cassius cited a rumor that Caesar's friends would propose that he be made king. Brutus said he would stay home but Cassius insisted: what if they were summoned as public officials? In that case, Brutus suppos-edly said, he would fulfill his duty by defending his country and die on be-half of liberty if necessary. Cassius is said to have cited the graffiti in reply, assuring Brutus that the authors were members of the Roman elite and not mere artisans or merchants—a snobbery that suits documented Roman prejudices only too well. These men didn't want Brutus to die, said Cassius, but to lead! Then came an embrace and a kiss and a conspiracy was born. Or so the story goes.

There was no polling in ancient Rome and no scientific measuring of public opinion. Brutus had no way of knowing whether the graffiti repre-sented public opinion. He couldn't be sure that the authors were people of quality and influence, as Cassius said. But the graffiti let him hope for the popular support that a conspiracy needed to succeed.

And then there was Porcia, Brutus's new wife. She was a strong woman. It is hard not to suspect that she nudged Brutus in a new direction. It was one thing for Brutus to turn his back on Cato's legacy when he was far from Cato's household, but quite another thing when he came home to Cato's daughter every night. No wonder that Porcia was said to be the only woman who shared in the secret of the plot. Finally, there was Servilia. There is no evidence that she knew of the plot, let alone that she opposed Caesar. Her hostility to Porcia suggests the opposite. Besides, there was no credit to be gained by Servilia for plotting the death of her former lover. In later years, Antony treated her with courtesy, which he surely would not have done if he thought that Servilia was part of the conspiracy. Still, the sources ask what anyone might wonder—whether simmering resentment over her affair with Caesar helped push Brutus to join the plot. He did not believe the rumor about Caesar being his father, because no Roman would contemplate the crime of killing his father. Believing and hearing are two different things, though, and perhaps Brutus nursed a grudge that now came out.

Self-interest moved Brutus away from Caesar. Philosophical conviction would not tolerate a tyrant. No Roman noble would ignore his family's honor and reputation, least of all Brutus, who wrote on the theme of duties within the family. He had to live up to the reputation of a Junius Brutus and a Servilia Ahala. He had the legacy of his late uncle, Cato, who was now not only his mentor but also his posthumous father-in-law. He had his wife, Porcia. He had his brother-in-law, Cassius. And perhaps he also had a score of shame to settle in regard to his mother, Servilia, and the insult of illegitimacy via her lover, Caesar. Brutus believed in ideals that were bigger than himself—in philosophy, in the Republic, and in his family. And so, once again, Brutus betrayed an older man who trusted him, just as he had earlier betrayed first Pompey and then Cato.

DECIMUS

In Plutarch's version, Brutus and Cassius now recruited Decimus to the conspiracy. It would not be surprising if the truth was the other way around and Decimus urged them. One thing is certain—Decimus played a central role. If Brutus was the heart of the conspiracy and Cassius the head, Decimus was the eyes and the ears. He was an insider. Of all the conspirators, only Decimus could be described as "a close friend of Caesar." If anyone in the conspiracy might have agonized about betraying a friend, it was Decimus. But there's not a scrap of remorse in any of the dozen surviving letters that Decimus wrote after the assassination.

Readers of Shakespeare might wonder why they have never heard of Decimus. He is misnamed in *Julius Caesar* as "Decius." Except for a scene in Caesar's house on the morning of the Ides of March, "Decius" plays very little role in the drama. That is not surprising when we consider that Shakespeare based his account on English translations of Plutarch and Appian. Decimus has some importance in Appian but Plutarch scorns him as insignificant. The ancient author who emphasizes Decimus's role in the plot against Caesar is Nicolaus of Damascus, and Shakespeare did not read him. Nor did he read Cassius Dio or Cicero's letters, other sources of Decimus's importance.

It was Decimus whom Caesar chose to accompany him to dinner on March 14. He was the conspirators' ace. Decimus was the best source of information about the dictator's thoughts and plans and the best hope of moving Caesar in whatever direction was needed. Who better to confirm that Caesar suspected nothing?

Decimus is widely recognized in the ancient sources as a major player in the conspiracy. Both Nicolaus of Damascus and Suetonius place him on an equal footing with Brutus and Cassius among the conspiracy's leaders. Nicolaus actually names Decimus first. Appian makes him next after Brutus and Cassius. Velleius Paterculus, a Roman soldier-statesman who wrote a history around 30 A.D., speaks of Decimus leading the conspirators along with Brutus and Cassius. Other sources name Decimus as one of the four most important conspirators. Plutarch is not very impressed with Decimus, whom he unfairly calls "neither active nor daring," but he recognizes Decimus's importance to the plot.

At only thirty-seven, Decimus had a brilliant record. A noble of impeccable pedigree and one of Caesar's confidants, Decimus stood near the pinnacle of power. Having excelled as a commander in Gaul both in the

Gallic War and the Civil War, Decimus governed the province for Caesar in 48–45 B.C. and added another military victory to his record, over the fierce Bellovaci. He was probably praetor in Rome in 45 B.C., certainly governor-designate of Italian Gaul for 44 B.C., and consul-designate for 42 B.C. Whether Decimus knew it or not, Caesar named him in his will as heir in the second degree, in the (unlikely) event that one of the three heirs in the first degree—Octavian and his cousins Quintus Pedius and Lucius Pinarius—was unavailable. He also named Decimus as one of the guardians of his adopted son, Octavian. Caesar unwittingly named other conspirators as guardians as well, although their names are not known to us.

Decimus brought two essential things to the conspiracy. He had Caesar's confidence and he had a band of gladiators. Without his trust in Decimus, Caesar would never have gone to the Senate on the Ides. Without the gladiators, the conspirators might not have survived the day themselves. Looking ahead, there was a third point. Decimus was about to start a term, given to him by Caesar, as governor of Italian Gaul. It was a strategic position, close to Rome and with two legions. Such a man could be enormously useful after the Ides.

Decimus owed even more to Caesar than Brutus did. Caesar had made Decimus's career and, until the Ides, Decimus seemingly repaid him with faithful support. In later years, no one earned more scorn for ingratitude from Caesar's loyalists than Decimus. The sources don't reveal his motives, so we can only engage in informed speculation.

Like Brutus and Cassius, Decimus might have felt that his first loyalty was to the Republic. When writing to Decimus in 43 B.C., Cicero portrayed him as part of a cause. For all his support of Caesar, for all his mother's flirtation with revolution, Decimus came from a family of Best Men and claimed descent from the founder of the Republic. Both Decimus's father and his grandfather had slaughtered Populists in the city of Rome in what they considered the defense of the Republic. Now it was Decimus's turn.

Yet, unlike Brutus or Cassius, Decimus was no philosopher, nor do his republican sentiments run very deep. In his eleven surviving single-authored letters—all from 44 or 43 B.C., ten of them to Cicero—Decimus refers only once to "liberating the Republic"; he is much more interested in military and political affairs. Although he was admirably brief as a writer, and although he was running a military campaign, his silence about why he fought is striking. By contrast, thirteen letters by Cicero to Decimus survive from the same period and five of them refer to liberty, tyranny, the assassination of Caesar, or the Republic.

When it comes to killing Caesar, self-interest suggests itself as Decimus's motive. Decimus was ambitious, competitive, proud, and violent. He cared very much about his dignitas, a subject that comes up frequently in his correspondence with Cicero. If Cicero was a good judge of character—and he often was—then Decimus wanted fame and greatness. Caesar being Caesar, it is easy to imagine him telling Decimus that there was no limit to his ambitions. Yet Caesar was too shrewd to believe it. He could see Decimus's limitations.

Decimus was the right man to conquer or govern Gaul but not to rule Rome. Decimus was a tactician, not a strategist. He took things personally, which made it difficult for him to postpone revenge, as a good leader needs to be able to do. Decimus was shrewd and capable of deceit but, like the Gauls whom he spent so much time with, he was passionate. For all his youth, Octavian's acumen and judgment made him much better suited to succeed Caesar. Decimus was a soldier while Octavian was a politician to the core.

Decimus was not the sort of person to shrug off the rise of a rival. He rose to the top by serving Caesar in the field in Gaul and the Civil War. Now others would have the chance to do the same in Parthia while Decimus stayed behind. In particular, the new man who would serve in Parthia was Octavian. After a long ride with him from Gaul to Italy in 45 B.C., Decimus had at least an inkling of Octavian's ruthless determination. If Decimus ever dreamed of being Caesar's heir, he had to worry about Octavian. The more Decimus valued the signs of affection bestowed on him by Caesar—the place in his second chariot, the companionship of the dining couch at Lepidus's—the more he might have resented the rise of Octavian.

Being governor of Italian Gaul and then consul was well and good, but Decimus knew where the real power lay in Caesar's world—with the army. And the army was closest to Decimus's heart. The army could win him the cherished goals of being hailed imperator, celebrating a triumph, and becoming one of the first men in Rome. By the end of 45 B.C. Octavian had joined the force that would fight Parthia while Decimus was still in Rome. Decimus might have reckoned that, once Caesar, Octavian, and a troupe of new heroes rode back home in triumph, he would be swept aside. Better to get rid of Caesar now and seize power while he still could.

Style perhaps played a role as well—Decimus was a very brave man and a hard man, and he might have bristled at the courtly affectations that were accruing to Caesar. Snobbery may have played a role. Like Antony, Decimus could sneer at Octavian as the heir of a freedman and a moneychanger. As a member of the old Roman elite, Decimus might not like rubbing shoulders with Caesar's new senators, men he thought were beneath him. With perhaps a few exceptions, they were not barbarians or ex-legionaries but, rather, wealthy citizens of northern Italy and southern Gaul, descendants of Roman immigrant families in Spain, and centurions from the urban elite of all Italy and not just Rome. Yet that might have been enough to disgust senators who traced their ancestry back to early Rome. We know the name of only one centurion whom Caesar elevated to the Senate but it is worth noting—Gaius Fuficius Fango. His was no doubt a proud name in his hometown of Acerrae, a small city near Naples, but to a Roman elitist it sounded like it came from the gutter.

Then there is Paula Valeria, Decimus's wife. She was a member of the Roman elite and was in touch with Cicero. Her brother is plausibly identified as Valerius Triarius, a man who fought with Pompey at Pharsalus and died either in that battle or before the end of the Civil War; Cicero became his children's guardian. Perhaps Paula, like Porcia, felt that she had family blood to avenge and so encouraged her husband to break with Caesar. Paula, remember, had divorced her first husband on the very day of his return to Rome from military service so she could marry Decimus. Such a woman would not hesitate to advise a change of allegiance.

The sources offer no trace of any personal grudge against Caesar but they give abundant evidence of other personal grudges on Decimus's part. Decimus's cold-blooded betrayal of his chief becomes easier to understand if emotions like fear, loathing, and resentment came into play. And so he turned on Caesar.

6

WANTED: ASSASSINS

Brutus, Cassius, and Decimus now mobilized followers. They had to decide how to kill Caesar and where and when, but first they needed to assemble a team. They had to move quickly but cautiously. Although Caesar had appointed many if not most of the 800–900 senators, quite a few senators had lost faith in the man who seemed to want to be king. Still, few were willing to commit murder, even on behalf of the Republic, and few were willing to risk their own lives. Fewer still could be trusted. Secrets did not last long in Rome. Besides, Caesar was planning to leave for the Parthian War on March 18. That left a window of about a month.

The leaders of the conspiracy wanted just the right number of followers. They needed enough men to surround Caesar and fight off his supporters but not so many men as to risk being discovered. They preferred trusted friends to new acquaintances. They wanted neither rash youths nor infirm elders. They sought men in the prime of life, like themselves. In the end, they focused on men around the age of forty, as were Brutus, Cassius, and

Decimus. They screened potential recruits with well-crafted and innocent-sounding questions.

UNKINDEST CUTTERS: CAESAR'S FRIENDS

It was one thing for Caesar to lose the support of Brutus and Cassius. They owed a lot to him, but they were not really his men and had fought for Pompey. It was another thing for Caesar to lose others like Decimus, the very men who followed him for years, from Gaul to the Civil War and beyond. But that is just what happened. Writing about eighty years later, the thinker-statesman Seneca claimed that the plot had more of Caesar's friends than his enemies in it. It's tempting to believe that Seneca was right.

According to Nicolaus of Damascus, the conspirator-friends included Caesar's civilian associates, his officers, and his soldiers. Nicolaus admits that some joined the plot because they were disturbed to see power go from the Republic into the hands of one man. They were also impressed by the quality of the men who led the plot, especially the Brutus family. But Nicolaus emphasizes their low, self-interested motives. They felt that Caesar hadn't rewarded them enough or that he had given away too much to the former supporters of Pompey. Nicolaus singles out some of Caesar's soldiers, both officers and ordinary men, for feeling this way. As for the politicians, some wanted to replace Caesar as the leading man (or men) in Rome. And then there was Caesar's famous policy of pardon or forgiveness toward his opponents in the Civil War. The policy earned gratitude and stirred anger.

Nicolaus makes Caesar's policy of clemency a central grievance of the conspirators. On the one hand, Caesar's clemency angered some of his longtime supporters, who wanted to see their former enemies humbled, not raised to equality. On the other hand, it annoyed the former Pompey supporters, Nicolaus says, to have to accept as a favor what they might have won on their own. Cato protested Caesar's arrogance in claiming the right to "pardon" his enemies. Writing in the same vein, another ancient writer sums up the case against Caesar. "His very power of granting favors," he says, "weighed heavily on free people."

For Nicolaus, the conspiracy was more a matter of court intrigue and petty jealousy than of liberty and the Republic. This may reflect his life experience. Before coming to the court of Augustus, the first Roman emperor, Nicolaus served at the court of the infamous King Herod in Judaea, a place that had no shortage of plots. He also served as tutor to the children of Antony and Cleopatra, also not a job to foster political innocence. Nicolaus's outlook on the conspiracy surely also reflects the situation of his later years, when he supported Augustus's regime, a monarchy that looked down on the conspirators as villains.

Jealousy is a primitive emotion, easily discernible in children and animals. Yet even sophisticated Romans might have felt resentful of Caesar. So much talent, so much good fortune, so much power in one man! Jealousy was surely not enough on its own to give birth to a conspiracy, but it might have emboldened the conspirators.

Nicolaus leaves out one selfish motive on the part of the conspirators—fear of Octavian's rising star. But since Nicolaus worked for Octavian Augustus he could hardly include that motive. Many people underestimated Octavian at the time because he was young and charming, but at least some of them surely felt threatened by the young favorite, especially when he joined the army for the Parthian War.

If Caesar's friends turned on him now, it was not the first time. In 49 B.C., at the outbreak of the Civil War, Caesar had lost his right-hand man in Gaul, Titus Labienus. The two had been political allies even earlier, and in 50 B.C. Caesar offered to support Labienus for consul. Yet Labienus chose Pompey in the Civil War. Why?

After seeing Caesar close-up in Gaul for eight years, Labienus knew how his commander operated. He knew that the real power in Caesar's Rome would go to military men and private advisors, not to senators and public officials. To be sure, the consulship that Caesar offered him was important, but a consulship in Caesar's Rome was not what it once was. Caesar's success in Gaul owed much more to Labienus than Caesar was willing to admit. If Caesar became first man in Rome, how long would he want Labienus around as a reminder? No wonder Labienus chose Pompey, especially if there is anything to the report that Labienus began to insist that Caesar treat him as an equal, which Caesar wouldn't do. Labienus fought against Caesar until the last, dying on the battlefield at Munda in March 45 B.C.

The conspirators might have considered Labienus's fate and concluded that bad things happened to men who were once close to Caesar.

We don't know the order in which the other conspirators were recruited. It is likely though that Gaius Trebonius, who was Caesar's longtime lieutenant, was an early convert. Not only was he immensely important, but he had already thought of killing Caesar. He was the only ex-consul in the conspiracy.

Trebonius was born around 90 B.C., making him about forty-six in 44 B.C. A key commander in Gaul and the Civil War, Trebonius had also done yeoman labor for Caesar as urban praetor in Rome in 48 B.C. and governor of Nearer Hispania in 46 B.C. Caesar rewarded Trebonius by naming him suffect (substitute) consul in 45 B.C. and choosing him as governor of the province of Asia (western Turkey) for 43 B.C. Yet perhaps Caesar insulted Trebonius when he appointed a one-day replacement for Trebonius's consular colleague, who died in office on December 31, 45 B.C. It suggested how little Caesar thought of the so-called high honor bestowed on Trebonius.

A great soldier under Caesar, Trebonius had a political career of his own before Gaul when he was quaestor in 60 B.C. and People's Tribune in 55 B.C. In the latter capacity, he proposed the law that gave Pompey and Crassus five-year special commands. Trebonius was also close to Cicero. The two exchanged letters and Trebonius helped the orator on his return from exile to Italy in 57 B.C. Cicero called Trebonius's father "an ardent patriot," which suggests that the father supported the Best Men. Trebonius was literate, charming, and very ambitious. He once wrote a poem based on a statement of Cicero, for example, and sent it to the orator as "a little gift." So Trebonius kept in touch with the Republic's greatest defender.

In short, Trebonius was no mere Caesarian loyalist—he knew how to think for himself. After the Ides, Cicero said that the Republic owed Trebonius a debt of thanks for preferring the liberty of the Roman People to the friendship of one man, and for choosing to drive away despotism rather than to share in it. Indeed, no one who had the friendship of Caesar would throw it away lightly.

It seems that Trebonius already decided to kill the dictator before Caesar returned from Hispania in 45 B.C. At least that is what Cicero claimed in a speech after the Ides of March. Trebonius was the man who, said Cicero, approached Mark Antony in Narbo (modern Narbonne, France) in summer 45 B.C. to recruit him for a plot against Caesar. Nothing came of it at the time but when the plot began gelling in February and March 44 B.C., Trebonius joined it. Afterward he expressed pride in his role in the events of the Ides and the hope that Rome would, at last, enjoy liberty in peace and quiet.

The two Servilius Casca brothers, Publius and Gaius, also joined the conspiracy. Both were senators but nothing is known of Gaius's career. Publius was elected People's Tribune for 43 B.C., which means that he had Caesar's support. There is a hint in one source that Publius was short of funds, while Cicero called him a true lover of the Republic. We can't be sure of either brother's motives.

Two of Caesar's less successful Gallic commanders joined the conspiracy as well: Servius Sulpicius Galba and Minucius Basilus. Both had reason for grudges. Galba's poor generalship nearly cost his legion their lives in eastern Gaul (today's Switzerland) in winter 57–56 B.C., as Caesar claims in his *Commentaries*. Galba no doubt saw things differently. Caesar supported his former officer for the consulship for 49 B.C., but Galba lost. This was enough, according to one ancient theory, to drive Galba into the conspiracy. Then too, Galba quarreled with Caesar because the latter insisted that Galba make good on an old debt. When Pompey was consul in 52 B.C., Galba guaranteed a loan that Pompey made, and Caesar wanted Galba to pay even after Caesar had confiscated Pompey's property. Galba objected in public and Caesar backed down, but Galba still owed money as late as January 45 B.C.

Judging from his one surviving letter, Galba was a man of action. His writing is efficient and to the point. He puts himself in the center of things and comes off as energetic, courageous, and important. He cared, in short, about his reputation. Caesar failed him in the polls, pinched his purse, and embarrassed him in the *Commentaries.*

Minucius Basilus had his moment in the Ardennes Forest in northern France in 53 B.C. when he happened on the rebel Ambiorix. He stopped a dangerous foe but then let Ambiorix escape. A frustrated Caesar attributed the whole thing to fortune and nothing else. In the Civil War, one Basilus commanded a legion for Caesar in the Illyrian campaign and was defeated—perhaps he was the same man. Caesar made Minucius Basilus one of the praetors for 45 B.C., but he didn't give him what every praetor wanted for the year following his office—a province to govern. Instead, he made him settle for a sum of money. This was a disappointment because in Roman government the real money was made by exploiting the provincials. The monetary gift was also close to an insult. The Romans called public office an honor, a term they would not have applied to a sum of money. Minucius Basilus, who came from a senatorial family, expected more. It was this, we are told, that made him join the conspirators. In effect, Caesar gave Minucius Basilus a golden handshake—and Minucius Basilus came back with a dagger.

Last but not least was Lucius Tillius Cimber. He had a close connection to Caesar, although the nature of it does not survive. No surprise, there, because recording all of Caesar's connections would take all the papyrus in Rome. A later source calls Cimber one of Caesar's "fellow soldiers," so perhaps he served in Gaul or the Civil War or both. He was praetor in 45 B.C. so he should have been at least forty then (the minimum age requirement for the job, although Caesar did not always observe the rules). Caesar assigned him the rich and important provinces of Bithynia and Pontus (in today's Turkey) for 44 B.C., which speaks to Cimber's favor in the dictator's eyes. Cicero said afterward that Cimber was deeply grateful to Caesar for his personal kindnesses but, to his credit, Cimber preferred his fatherland. Actually, Cimber seems to have been thinking more of his family, specifically his brother, who fought for Pompey. He took it hard that Caesar would not let his brother come back from exile.

Cimber had a reputation as a brawler and a heavy drinker. To the philosopher Seneca, Cimber's role in the conspiracy proves that even drunkards can be trusted with a secret. Cimber even supposedly make a joke about it. "Would I, who cannot tolerate my wine, tolerate anyone as a master?" he said.

POMPEY'S REVENGE

The names of twenty conspirators survive. They are not found on some comprehensive ancient list—none exists. Rather, the twenty names can be pieced together from various sources. We would not expect them to include all the conspirators. Indeed, the sources report a total of more than sixty or even more than eighty conspirators, although the latter number may be a scribal error. As we shall see, far fewer than sixty men actually attacked Caesar on the Ides of March. Nonetheless, as events showed, sixty is a plausible number for the total number of conspirators.

Sixty was not a small number and it raised the danger of a security risk. Still, an entourage usually accompanied Caesar, and so a considerable attack force might have been needed. No less important, the more men who joined the plot, the more backers there would be afterward to rally public opinion to their side.

Pompey supporters shared with the supporters of Caesar a common opposition to the drift toward monarchy. But they had additional motives. On the one hand, Caesar had pardoned them but, on the other hand, it was humiliating to be pardoned. The result, said Nicolaus of Damascus, was that "many people were angry at him because they had been saved by him."

Although some of Pompey's supporters, like Brutus and Cassius, did splendidly under Caesar, others suffered. They were men like Quintus Ligarius, forced to live in exile in North Africa until Cicero successfully pleaded his case before Caesar in 46 B.C. His brothers endured the indignity of going before the dictator on bended knees. Although Caesar personally disliked Ligarius and despite warnings to be careful who he pardoned, he decided to let Ligarius come home. Now Ligarius was so eager for revenge that he joined the conspiracy from a sickbed.

Another supporter of Pompey to join the plot was Pontius Aquila, the People's Tribune who refused to stand during Caesar's Spanish triumph in 45 B.C. He suffered humiliation at the dictator's hands and possibly property confiscation. It's likely that some of the Pompey allies in the conspiracy lost property under Caesar or knew friends or family who had, which provided another reason to want to kill him.

It's hard to say just how much property Caesar confiscated. In principle he pardoned his enemies and spared their property but in practice he engaged in some confiscation. Since Caesar's enemies were often rich or superrich, this potentially represented a huge transfer of wealth. But it wasn't only Caesar's enemies who lost their holdings, as Brutus later complained bitterly—neutrals were targeted as well. Caesar promised to pay compensation but it's doubtful that it was adequate, if it was paid at all. Besides, for many farmers, nothing could ever make up for the loss of their land.

The other Pompey supporters among the conspirators are little more than names to us. The other names of conspirators that have survived cannot be assigned to either group in the Civil War. Perhaps they remained neutral, as some Romans did, or perhaps we just don't know which side they had been on. They included Gaius Cassius of Parma and Decimus Turullius, both later admirals; and Pacuvius Antistius Labeo. Cassius of Parma was also a poet who did not hesitate to put his pen to political use.

Labeo was a friend of Brutus. He was present when Brutus cautiously sounded out two other prospective conspirators, both politicians with an interest in philosophy. Without revealing his intentions, Brutus probed them about political theory. One of them, Marcus Favonius, was an admirer of Brutus's late uncle Cato. A virulent enemy of Caesar, Favonius fought for Pompey but had few good words to say about him. Favonius received a pardon from Caesar after Pompey's death. Now he told Brutus that he thought civil war was even worse than a law-flouting monarchy.

In the same conversation, Brutus engaged one Statilius, another supporter of Cato, but, unlike him, an Epicurean and hence averse to politics. Statilius said that it was not proper for a wise and intelligent person to take on risks and worries because of bad and foolish people. Labeo disagreed. Brutus diplomatically said it was hard to decide. Afterward, he brought Labeo into the conspiracy but left Favonius and Statilius out.

CICERO AND ANTONY

The conspirators turned down two of the leading men of the day, Cicero and Antony.

It's been suggested that Cicero was really the guiding spirit of the conspiracy. He denied the charge. Cicero flattered Caesar, served as his host, and did business with him. His written record is mixed but one wonders what he said in private. Inasmuch as Cicero mourned the death of the Republic, idealized its lost liberty, and privately called Caesar a king, he certainly stirred men's souls. Cicero once said that Caesar had no fear of him, although Caesar knew that Cicero called him a rex, because Caesar knew that Cicero had no courage. By implication, a man with courage who believed as Cicero did would be a threat.

It's also true that Cicero was highly regarded for trust and goodwill by both Brutus and Cassius, yet they left him out. In their judgment, Cicero lacked daring. He was too old and too likely to put safety before the speed that was needed. Compared to the leading conspirators, Cicero was indeed old. He was over sixty, while Brutus, Cassius, Decimus, and Trebonius were all around forty. As things turned out, Cicero applauded the Ides assassination, but he considered it a botched job. The old man insisted that *he* would have done better.

Antony, another man aged about forty, is a more interesting case. Ultimately, Antony proved to be the mortal enemy of the conspirators. And yet, his name came up among them, and for good reason. For all his support of Caesar, Antony had no intention of burying the Republic. He was not willing to turn over to the dictator the choice of Rome's top public officials.

Antony's behavior in regard to Dolabella proves that. Dolabella was an ambitious demagogue who had caught Caesar's eye. Caesar was determined to promote him to consul, even though, at thirty-six, Dolabella was under the required age and had not held the praetorship. Antony was determined to stop it. He hated Dolabella for having committed adultery with his wife, whom Antony promptly divorced. He violently opposed Dolabella's radical politics and sent troops into the Roman Forum when he was Caesar's deputy in 47 B.C. to have eight hundred of Dolabella's supporters killed. Caesar had since reconciled with Dolabella and wanted him appointed Antony's co-consul when Caesar left for the Parthian War on March 18. Antony was adamant. He was a member of the priesthood of the augurs, men who interpreted the gods' will by observing the flights of birds. As an augur, Antony had the right to block the appointment of Dolabella.

Promising material for a conspirator, and Plutarch says that everyone wanted to approach Antony until Trebonius spoke up. He reported his failed attempt to recruit Antony to a plot against Caesar in Narbo the summer before. At this point, according to Plutarch, the conspirators did a 180-degree turn—now they wanted to kill Antony along with Caesar. Antony, they said, was a supporter of monarchy, an arrogant man, strong because of his easy familiarity with the soldiers, and powerful because he held the office of consul.

Like Decimus, Antony perhaps feared being eclipsed by Octavian, but there the similarities end. Antony might have reasoned that if Caesar were killed, the door would be open for the return to Rome of Pompey's surviving son, Sextus. As the man who auctioned off Pompey's property, Antony could not look forward to that. There was kinship, too, as Antony and Caesar were distant cousins. In addition, Antony's wife, the powerful Fulvia, whom he married in 47 B.C., was a staunch Populist. Perhaps she encouraged her husband's continued support of Caesar. Finally, there was Antony's sheer talent. Of all the Roman nobles, only he had a degree of Caesar's versatility—the combination of political cunning, oratorical fire, and battle command. Antony might simply have felt less threatened by Caesar than his peers, and more confident that he would replace him one day. So, Antony stayed loyal.

But what should the conspirators do about him?

THE PLAN

The conspirators had to work under the constraints of time, numbers, and politics. They needed to attack Caesar before he left Rome for the army on March 18, after which military security would protect him. The plotters were a loose coalition, not a tight revolutionary cell. As a mix of Best Men and Populists, they had to limit themselves to goals that everyone could agree on. They couldn't afford to drive anyone out of the group and risk betrayal.

Security was a concern. The plotters never gathered in the open but met secretly in small groups and in each other's houses. They never swore an oath or took pledges over sacrificial animals, as in some conspiracies, but they kept the secret. Perhaps it was the military experience of men like Cassius, Decimus, and Trebonius that allowed them to proceed so sure-footedly. Perhaps it was a kind of reverse "honor among thieves." According to Nicolaus, every conspirator revealed his own grudge against Caesar when he joined the plot, and the fear of being exposed in turn kept each one from talking. And perhaps it was a proud hostility to oaths that kept their lips sealed. Only tyrants make men swear oaths—the old Romans never did. So Brutus is reported to have said later. By ostentatiously not swearing an oath, the conspirators were almost swearing an oath, as if to say, "I declare that I support this conspiracy against a tyrant but I won't swear to it, not the way tyrants make men do!"

The Best Men wanted to go back to the way things were before Caesar. Doing that required killing not just Caesar but all the men around him, starting with Antony. Caesar's supporters among the conspirators would probably not agree to a purge. They supported Caesar's reforms and they had no intention of returning property confiscated from Pompey's supporters. Even they, however, agreed to kill Antony, who they considered too strong and too dangerous. Perhaps Decimus remembered how, on the return to Italy that summer, Antony shared Caesar's chariot while he was relegated to the second chariot.

Brutus disagreed. He objected that the conspirators were acting on behalf of law and justice and it would be clearly unjust to kill Antony. Killing Caesar would win them glory as tyrannicides—tyrant slayers. If they killed Antony or other friends of Caesar, people would consider the deed a private grudge and the work of the old faction of Pompey. Besides, Brutus hoped for a change of heart on Antony's part. He had a high opinion of Antony, who, like him, came from an old and noble family. Brutus saw Antony as clever, an ambitious man and passionate for glory. He believed that once Caesar was out of the way, Antony would follow their example and fight for the liberation of the fatherland.

Brutus believed that people opposed Caesar the rex, not Caesar the reformer. For him, therefore, the best strategy was to remove Caesar but leave his program intact. Brutus believed that once Caesar's faction was decapitated, it would fall apart. Ambitious men like Antony would accept the new reality and move on. Besides, it was absurd to think of restoring the Republic by killing a consul like Antony. A Dictator in Perpetuity was a monstrosity and had to go, but a consul was a sacred Roman office.

But what about the urban plebs? What about Caesar's soldiers? Brutus considered it possible to keep their support by maintaining all of Caesar's actions intact. Brutus refused to give the Best Men what they wanted. There would be no restoration of Pompey's supporters' property, no overturning of Caesar's acts, and no purge. Those whose property had been confiscated would receive public funds in compensation but the new owners would keep their land. Brutus was an assassin whose goal was not revolution but peace. So he alone of the conspirators opposed killing Antony, and he got his way. Brutus was indispensable to the plan.

Roman history, alas, did not provide support for this plan. It showed, rather, that in order to stop a domestic political movement by violence, you had to kill or at least drive out a man's followers as well as the leader. Even the founder of the Roman Republic, Marcus Brutus's supposed ancestor, Lucius Junius Brutus, did more than drive out the king. He also got rid of the king's wife and children, including his adult sons. Lucius Brutus also made sure that he had armed followers and that they secured the support of the Roman army.

What then, was Brutus thinking in 44 B.C.? Why did he imagine that the murder of one man would be enough to save the Roman Republic? As a Roman, he knew perfectly well that Caesar's followers would want to avenge his death. Most Romans admired what Sulla said: "No friend ever served me and no enemy ever wronged me whom I have not repaid in full."

Brutus knew that but he expected to win even so. He believed that both Senate and people would thank the conspirators for killing a tyrant. Anticipating that armed men would threaten vengeance, the conspirators prepared a stronghold in the heart of Rome with their own force of armed men to defend it. They did not think they would need it for long, though. They did not believe that any of Caesar's lieutenants could rally the men as Caesar had. Without a strong leader, the army would dissolve, especially because Brutus would meet the soldiers' demands.

The conspirators also thought that the matter of how and where they struck Caesar would make a difference. It was one thing to ambush him with hired thugs on the Appian Way, as the demagogue Clodius was killed in 52 B.C. It was another thing to kill Caesar by themselves in a public place in the heart of Rome. The very act could inform and change public opinion.

They considered other venues for the assassination. One possibility was an attack while Caesar was walking near his home on the Via Sacra, or Sacred Way, which was the oldest and most important street in the vicinity of the Forum. Another plan was to attack him during the elections for new consuls while he was crossing the bridge that voters crossed in Rome's formal (and primitive) voting procedure. Others wanted to attack at the time of a gladiatorial game, when no one would be suspicious of armed men. Instead, they decided on a different course. In its own way the plan was very like Caesar. It depended on speed and shock. It was risky. It was spectacular. With luck, it would swing public opinion in their direction, with Brutus's prestige and moderation taking care of the rest. If, however, that wasn't enough, they had an ace up their sleeve. Or so we might imagine.

The conspirators might have thought that this time would be different, and for the same reason that Caesar had cited: that no one wanted a return to civil war. They might have believed that public opinion, stoked by Brutus's oratory, would insist on a compromise between Caesar's supporters and the men who killed him. They knew Caesar's supporters and they were confident that they could do business with most of them.

It was a risk, but Brutus gambled that the Republic could still be saved. Like Caesar, he was willing to let the dice fly high.

DISMISSING THE BODYGUARD

Of course, security considerations came into play as well. It was best to strike when the dictator was vulnerable. It might have seemed as if he was always vulnerable because Caesar had no bodyguard, but Caesar was not without protection.

Sometime after returning to Rome in October 45 b.c., Caesar formally dismissed his Spanish bodyguard who protected him in the field. In principle, he relied solely on the informal protection of the senators and the knights. On the face of it, this was remarkable. If Roman history taught anything, it was that you could kill anyone. Assassination was not the rule in Rome but it wasn't rare, either.

True, other plots against Caesar had not amounted to much. Cassius supposedly conspired against him in 47 b.c. In 46 b.c., Cicero worried publicly about assassination plots against Caesar. In 45 b.c., Trebonius had tried to enlist Antony in a conspiracy. The fate of Caesar's former foe Marcus Claudius Marcellus that year—stabbed to death by a disgruntled friend—served as a warning. Meanwhile, Caesar's slave Philemon, his secretary, promised Caesar's enemies that he would poison his master. When the plot was discovered, Caesar showed mercy by sparing Philemon from torture; he was merely executed. Only the last plot was certainly real. The rest might have been just talk. But then, consider the case of Deiotarus.

In November 45, Deiotarus, king of the central Anatolian kingdom of Galatia, was the subject of a hearing in Rome. A former supporter of Pompey, for whom he fought in person at Pharsalus, Deiotarus was accused of plotting to murder Caesar when the dictator visited him during Caesar's Anatolian campaign in 47 B.C. Cicero, who defended Deiotarus, gave the whole thing a comic opera air, which was not hard to do, since the accuser was none other than Deiotarus's grandson, Castor, and the main witness for the prosecution was Deiotarus's doctor. Less funny was the venue of the hearing—Caesar's house, the Public Mansion, the official residence of the Chief Priest. Long ago the kings of Rome enjoyed the right of hearing cases in their palace and Caesar now insisted on no less.

The other thing that was not funny was the possibility that the charge was true. Brutus was one of Deiotarus's friends in Rome and we can only wonder if the two communicated about the subject of killing Caesar. In any case, Caesar did not render a verdict on the matter. He certainly did not take it as a reason to increase security.

More than assassination plots, it was bad press that got to Caesar, like the scathing verses of one Pitholaus. Caesar did not suppress them but he showed his displeasure. Another case: during the Civil War, Aulus Caecina published a pamphlet that so laid into Caesar that now he refused to grant the writer a pardon, in spite of Cicero's pleas.

Caesar's sources in Rome denounced conspiracies and nighttime meetings. Caesar did nothing but announce that he knew what was going on. Cassius Dio makes the striking statement that Caesar refused to hear information about the conspiracy and that he severely punished those who brought any such news. All the talk of plots had not amounted to much, and that could breed complacency on Caesar's part. "Let them talk about assassination," he might say, thinking that talk would blow off steam. Besides, he trusted his own judgment above all. In the field he sometimes acted in the absence of reliable intelligence. He made snap judgments and dealt with stereotypes and probabilities. He took risks that most commanders would shrink from.

Military intelligence was well and good, Caesar's career seemed to say, but it was no match for his own genius. All the more true in the case of the gossip and rumor that was the stuff of domestic political intelligence. Caesar's problem was probably not too little information but too much. One imagines a steady stream of rumors and tips of alleged threats. The difficulty was separating fact from fiction.

Caesar heard accusations that Brutus, Mark Antony, and Dolabella were each plotting revolution. He suspected Brutus and Cassius. He made a memorable quip about the supposed plotters: "I am not much in fear of these fat, long-haired fellows"—Antony and Dolabella—"but rather of those pale, thin ones," meaning Brutus and Cassius. He meant that Antony and Dolabella were slow, lusty, and affected, while Brutus and Cassius were intellectuals, and so they were dangerous.

Yet Caesar refused to take the risk seriously. He had too much faith in Brutus's character, and without Brutus, Cassius could do little. Caesar complained to his friends about Cassius but did nothing. He brushed off Brutus's accusers with a joke.

Why then did Caesar dismiss his bodyguard? Wasn't he inviting an attack? Ancient authors asked the same questions. One school of thought says that the dictator was arrogant. He knew about the danger but he convinced himself that it couldn't happen to him. He reasoned that the senators had all sworn oaths to guard him with their own lives. He put too much trust in the oath, some said, while others said that his enemies concocted the oath precisely in order to lure Caesar into giving up his bodyguard. As mentioned, Caesar had dismissed his Spanish bodyguard when he first arrived back in Rome.

There are those who argue that Caesar knew that killing him would only push Rome back into civil war and all its horrors. He was quoted as saying that his safety wasn't so much in his interest as in the Republic's. Caesar thought that no one would dare to assassinate him. As often happens, the victim engaged in what one scholar calls "the pleasure of deception." He deceived himself by overestimating how much he and his adversaries had in common.

One ancient theory says that Caesar was so depressed that he didn't care whether he lived or died, but why then did he prepare a major military campaign abroad? Three other matters better explain Caesar's willingness to court death: Sulla, soldiering, and sobriety.

Caesar was always looking over his shoulder at Sulla, the dictator who preceded him. Where Sulla was brutal, Caesar was mild. For example, Caesar replaced Sulla's executions with pardons. To the Roman mind, a bodyguard in the city of Rome smacked of *regnum*—monarchy. Far from having a bodyguard, a Roman senator was supposed to be easy to approach—accessibility was the mark of a free society. Even Sulla honored this code. When he stepped down as dictator, he dismissed his bodyguard and walked through the streets of Rome untouched, supposedly guarded only by his reputation. This, although he still had plenty of enemies, and although once, years earlier, he was attacked in Rome by men with hidden daggers. Caesar, we might conclude, wanted to do Sulla one better and give up his bodyguard even while he was still dictator.

Caesar was a soldier. He prided himself on his personal courage and he thrived on risk. He had earned a civic crown by scaling the walls of a rebel Greek city at age twenty and survived a near disaster on the River Sabis in Gaul at age forty-three, and he was not about to cringe in the streets of Rome at age fifty-five. For a man as proud as Caesar the danger of going without a bodyguard was not an argument against doing so but an argument in favor of it.

Courage served well in the field but politics and Rome required cunning. Caesar had shown cunning, but perhaps he had grown rusty. Nicolaus says that the conspirators easily tricked Caesar because he was "straightforward by nature and unused to political wiles because of his military campaigns abroad." An exaggeration, especially "straightforward," and yet it contains some truth. The political magician of the 60s B.C. was out of practice. What's more, he no longer seemed to enjoy Roman politics. He was used to giving orders, not unraveling plots. He made it clear that he couldn't wait to get back into the field.

If Caesar was in denial about politics, he assessed the value of a bodyguard with cold sobriety. He knew that no bodyguard could offer complete protection. In fact it was precisely bodyguards who had assassinated some of the great men of the past, like King Philip II of Macedon, a founder of empire like Caesar, or Viriathus the Lusitanian, a native rebel against Rome in the very part of Spain where Caesar had fought. Finally, there was Sertorius, a supporter of Marius like Caesar himself.

Besides, something very important must be kept in mind: not having a bodyguard did not mean lacking protection completely. As dictator, Caesar was accompanied in public by twenty-four *lictors*. These were strong men, each carrying a bound bundle of wooden rods with an executioner's axe on the outside. They served as guards, opened the way through crowds, and carried out arrests and whippings. They would not be useless in case of attack.

In addition, a crowd of friends and followers usually surrounded Caesar. This was truer than ever after the affair of the tribunes in January–February 44 B.C., when Caesar worried that he had behaved too high-handedly. He asked his friends to protect him in public. But when they in turn asked him to reestablish his bodyguard, Caesar refused.

We might suspect that some of the friends who accompanied him in public were chosen carefully. Imposing, dangerous-looking men, as well as, say, veterans, gladiators, and the odd cutthroat or two were likely recruits. The evidence comes from one ancient writer who says that the conspirators stood in awe of Caesar. They were afraid that, "even though he had no bodyguard, one of the men who were constantly around him would kill them" if they attacked Caesar. Finally, as we'll see, the gathering of soldiers for Caesar's impending departure for the front gave him one additional advantage when it came to deterring an attack.

The conspirators were well aware of all this. Cassius, Trebonius, and Decimus were among the best military minds in Rome. They understood the sober truth that the Senate House was the safest place to attack Caesar. Since only senators were allowed in the room during a meeting, the dictator would not have a throng of "friends" to protect him there. True, some of the senators, especially Caesar's new senators, were probably tough customers and although no weapons were allowed in the Senate, they might have smuggled some in. Help might come to Caesar from outside. So Cassius, Trebonius, and Decimus planned accordingly. After having pulled off an ambush against the Parthians in Syria in 51 B.C., for example, it was child's play for Cassius to trap Caesar in the Senate. Escaping his vengeful soldiers afterward posed more of a challenge.

DINNER AT LEPIDUS'S

On March 14, 44 B.C., the day before the Ides of March, the dictator went to dinner with his Master of the Horse. Marcus Aemilius Lepidus was a loyal friend to Caesar, which separated Lepidus from his two brothers-in-law, Brutus and Cassius. Like Cassius, Lepidus was married to one of Brutus's sisters. Like Brutus, Lepidus came from a prominent noble family. Like Decimus, Lepidus rose under Caesar but he was a diplomat and errand boy rather than a great general. Caesar let Lepidus celebrate a triumph in 46 B.C. for negotiating a settlement after trouble in Hispania, even though his military achievements were meager. Caesar made Lepidus his co-consul in 46 B.C. and his Master of the Horse in 45 and early 44 B.C. Such a man would never break with his patron and the conspirators surely never approached Lepidus.

Besides Caesar and Lepidus, Decimus was also present at dinner, brought by Caesar, according to Appian. Decimus might have used the occasion to brood on the honors that Lepidus had but which he, Decimus, really deserved—surely Decimus was more worthy of a triumph.

A formal Roman dining room had space for nine diners on three couches. Considering Caesar's status, Lepidus surely had a full complement of guests. The couches were typically arranged in a U shape around a table. The guests ate reclining, three per couch. As guest of honor, Caesar lay on one end of the middle couch. Beside him, at the end of the so-called lowest couch, reclined Lepidus, the host.

While reclining, Caesar added personal greetings at the bottom of documents written by a secretary. This was his habit at dinners and at the games as well. It offended some, but Caesar was a busy man.

A Roman banquet had at least three courses and as many as seven, and Lepidus might have served a long meal. A Roman banquet began in the afternoon, followed by a drinking session, which often stretched well into the evening. The sources agree that the topic of discussion that night was the best sort of death. Appian says that Caesar brought up the subject himself. And what was the best sort of death? Caesar's answer, according to Plutarch, was an unexpected death; a sudden one, says Appian; sudden and unexpected, says Suetonius. We could put Caesar on the psychiatrist's couch and say that, subconsciously, he welcomed assassination. But he was about to leave for battle, which is a much simpler explanation for his comments. It's understandable that he thought of sudden death as a warrior's death.

Suetonius adds that Caesar had discussed the subject on another occasion. The literate dictator read, in Xenophon's classic book, *The Education of Cyrus*, how King Cyrus of Persia gave orders for his funeral as his health declined. It is striking that Caesar compared himself to a king, and not just any king but a warrior king, one of history's great conquerors. Cyrus was also an absolute monarch and the king of the country that Caesar now stood poised to invade. In any case, Caesar said that Cyrus's plan was not for him—he wanted to die quickly and suddenly.

At least one of the other guests that evening knew that the dictator might soon have his wish.

7

CAESAR LEAVES HOME

Not long after five in the morning of March 15, 44 B.C., the first light was visible in the eastern sky above Rome. Romans were early risers, so Calpurnia, wife of Julius Caesar, was probably already awake after a night of uneasy sleep. She was in bed by Caesar's side that night when, suddenly, all the doors and windows of the bedroom opened and woke them both.

The noise roused Calpurnia from a bad dream. According to one version, she dreamt she was holding a murdered Caesar in her arms and mourning him. Other versions have Calpurnia dream that the front pediment of their house collapsed, with Caesar's corpse either present or just suggested. In one version, his body was streaming with blood. The Senate had given Caesar the right to put up this pediment to make the house look like a temple—he was a god, after all.

Calpurnia had plenty of reason to toss and turn. Daughter of a prominent noble family, she was Caesar's third wife (the first had died, while the second was divorced after adultery). Her father, Piso, was a former consul and a leading patron of philosophy. He and Caesar negotiated the marriage in 59 B.C. when Calpurnia was in her late teens. Now, fifteen years later, she was a mature woman. The marriage was childless. Although Caesar was absent from Rome for almost their entire marriage, she had plenty of time, living in the center of the city, to deepen her knowledge of Roman politics and its treacherous ways.

Rumors of plots to kill Caesar were widespread. Unfavorable omens were piling up, from menacing behavior by birds and weird lights in the sky to the discovery of a buried inscription with a threatening-sounding message, strangely crashing weapons, and men who seemed to catch on fire. Even the horses that Caesar had used to cross the Rubicon, now dedicated to the gods, supposedly stopped eating and started shedding tears. But if Calpurnia went in for prophecy, the most troubling item was Spurinna's prediction. A month before, Spurinna said that Caesar faced great danger for the next thirty days. The morning would bring the last day. It was the Ides of March, roughly, the midpoint of the month.

SPURINNA

Spurinna came from Etruria (roughly, modern Tuscany), possibly from the city of Tarquinia, where the name was prominent. In Roman eyes, it was a city of dead kings and live soothsayers. Rome's last kings had come from Tarquinia. Spurinna was a soothsayer—that is, he predicted the future by examining the internal organs of sacrificial animals or by interpreting lightning bolts or other omens. As an Etruscan, Spurinna was a Roman citizen, but he was also descended from a proud and separate culture. The Romans held Etruscan soothsayers in high regard and some leading politicians had personal soothsayers.

Spurinna served as Caesar's soothsayer at the infamous Lupercalia on February 15. Caesar sacrificed a bull that day. Spurinna made the chilling announcement that the beast had no heart—perhaps it had withered or been displaced in the chest cavity or perhaps its absence was a sorcerer's trick. Caesar was unmoved—he was famously unimpressed by omens.

Spurinna, though, said he was afraid. The ancients believed that the heart was the seat of thought as well as of life, and so, Spurinna said, he feared that not only Caesar's plans but also his life might come to a bad end. Then came another ominous sign when, at another sacrifice the next day, the victim's liver was lacking the lobe.

The evidence is suggestive rather than conclusive, but a reasonable modern interpretation of these events is as follows: Spurinna was trying to warn Caesar not to go too far and not to become a king. Spurinna was a friend of Caesar. Caesar put at least one soothsayer in the Senate. We don't know who but Spurinna is the leading candidate. Yet, like others rewarded by Caesar, Spurinna had principles. It seems that Spurinna came from an Etruscan aristocratic family that was as opposed to kings as Brutus, Cassius, and Decimus were.

February 15 was probably also the occasion when Spurinna warned Caesar that his life would be in danger for the next thirty days, a period ending with the Ides of March. This is subtly different from the famous warning in Shakespeare to "beware the Ides of March." Spurinna's notice referred to a month rather than a specific day. He could not have known that the conspirators would strike on March 15. He was not a conspirator and besides, they hadn't settled on that date yet. What Spurinna did know was that Caesar was planning to leave Rome in mid-March for the Parthian War. He also knew the rumors of plots to kill Caesar—any well-informed Roman did. "Thirty days" was a conventional time period for a prophetic warning. The result was a warning period that expired on the Ides of March.

Calpurnia no doubt knew about Spurinna's warning, which makes it easier to understand her troubled sleep on the night of March 14. The next morning at daybreak, around 5 A.M. or not much later, she begged Caesar not to go to the Senate meeting, or at least to carry out new sacrifices and check the omens first.

As for Caesar, one source says that he too had a bad dream—that he was flying above the clouds and shook the hand of Jupiter, king of the gods. But a bad dream might have been the least of Caesar's problems. When Caesar returned home from dinner at Lepidus's on the night of March 14, the meal did not sit well with him and his body felt sluggish. The next morning, he felt poorly. In particular, he is said to have suffered from vertigo. Could these have been the symptoms of an undetected epileptic seizure?

Even today, dizziness is often the mistaken description of the aftereffects of an undetected seizure (or even possibly a small seizure itself, although that seems less likely). One source says that Caesar experienced fainting and night terrors toward the close of his life, which might be seen in retrospect as signs of a seizure. If Caesar did suffer a seizure during the night of March 14–15, it might have left him with impaired judgment the next morning, even though he appeared normal. He might not even have been aware of the seizure.

Caution is needed, though, and not only because diagnosis is difficult on the basis of fragmentary details analyzed two thousand years after the fact. We can't even be certain that Caesar really had the symptoms in question. Some in the ancient world said that Caesar was merely pretending to be ill on the Ides as a cover for the real reason he wanted to postpone the Senate meeting—the omens disturbed him. We might also imagine that after the assassination Caesar's people invented the detail of his illness on the Ides as a way of explaining the great man's blindness to danger on the fateful day.

So, whether he was suffering from poor judgment after a seizure or he was too proud to admit weakness or he was, in fact, perfectly healthy, Caesar went on an early errand that morning. It was a protocol visit, a routine sacrifice to the god Jupiter, and only about three hundred yards away from the Public Mansion. The location was the residence of Cnaeus Domitius Calvinus. One of Caesar's generals, Calvinus was the dictator's choice for Master of the Horse in 43 B.C.

As it happened, Spurinna was also at Calvinus's house. There now took place the famous exchange between the dictator and the soothsayer. "The Ides of March have come," said Caesar. "Aye, they have come but not gone," replied the soothsayer in one of history's memorable comebacks.

Despite his bravado, Caesar took Spurinna's words to heart once back at the Public Mansion. According to some sources he ordered new sacrifices just as Calpurnia asked, and the omens were bad. Caesar hesitated for a long time and finally decided to stay home. He was not a superstitious man, but he knew that Spurrina and Calpurnia each had a finger to the political winds. Perhaps, he decided, it was better to be cautious in the face of all the conspiracy talk after all. Maybe Caesar respected Calpurnia's nose for trouble or maybe he just wanted peace in the household. Perhaps he felt dizzier than ever after the exertion of his visit to Calvinus's house.

Caesar decided to send the consul, Antony, to dismiss the Senate because Caesar would not be attending. It's not clear whether Antony was with Caesar in the Public Mansion at the time or whether Antony was elsewhere and reached by messenger.

Caesar would have missed the scheduled Senate meeting if not for the intervention of Decimus, who arrived at the Public Mansion later that morning. By that time, a lot was already going on in the city.

A GATHERING OF TOGAS

Rome was full of anticipation. It always was in March. It was less than a week until the first day of spring, the famous Roman spring. It was the season of Venus—Caesar's patron goddess was also the Roman goddess of spring. Caesar's contemporary the poet Lucretius (ca. 99 B.C. to ca. 55 B.C.), beautifully expresses the Roman attitude toward spring in a hymn to Venus in his great poem, *On the Nature of Things*:

> *Mother of Aeneas and his descendants, the Romans,*
> *The joy of men and gods, bountiful Venus,*
> *. . . .*
> *For as soon as you bring the sight of a spring day*
> *And the fruitful breeze blows freely from the west,*
> *The birds of the air, their hearts stirred,*
> *Give the first sign, goddess, of your arrival,*
> *And wild cattle range about their happy fields*
> *And cross rapid rivers: thus seized with delight*
> *Everyone eagerly follows you wherever you lead.*

The Ides of every month was sacred to Jupiter but the Ides of March was special because it was also the annual festival of Anna Perenna. She was a minor, obscure, but cherished goddess. On the day of her festival, people sacrificed for a good year. It was not a somber day, but, on the contrary, a time for drinking and carousing by both sexes in tents and grass huts. The festivities focused on a sacred spring in a grove north of the city at the first milestone of the Via Flaminia, about three miles north of the Roman Forum. With many people heading to the festival, some of Caesar's natural supporters, the working people of Rome, would be far from the center of town when the assassins struck.

They conspirators too began the day in a festive mood. While it was still dark out some them gathered at Cassius's house. Others, as we shall see, met elsewhere. They then accompanied Cassius and his son on a daybreak procession to the Roman Forum. It was the boy's coming-of-age ceremony, when he put on the Toga of Manhood, or *toga virilis*, a key moment for a Roman family. The men were all wearing togas as well. Brutus, who was the boy's uncle, was surely present.

The toga was the ceremonial public garment of a male Roman citizen. It was a large woolen cloth, off-white in color, dignified but heavy and unwieldy. The toga was worn over the left shoulder, draped under the right arm and back over the left arm and shoulder. It had to be folded, rolled, and draped over the body in an elaborate manner and without pins. This was difficult, if not impossible, to do alone, and those who could turned to a slave for help. Highest-ranking public officials had a reddish purple border on their toga.

Underneath his toga, a man wore a tunic, a simple garment held in place by a belt and covering the knees. In Rome today, average mid-March temperatures range from 43° to 61° Fahrenheit (6° to 16° Celsius), so men probably wore a heavy, woolen, winter tunic rather than a light, linen, summer tunic. Knights and senators were entitled to two reddish purple vertical stripes on their tunics, with narrow stripes for knights and broad stripes for senators.

Before leaving home, Brutus hitched a dagger on to his belt beneath his toga. Most if not all of the other conspirators probably did so as well, but Brutus was the only one who shared the secret with his wife. Calpurnia only feared what the day would bring, but Porcia knew.

As part of the Toga of Manhood ritual, a Roman boy could hardly escape at least one moral lecture about using his new freedom wisely. Now, many years after their own ceremonies, the conspirators stood poised on the most dramatic use of their freedom in their lives. Wisdom was another matter.

IN POMPEY'S SHADOW

After the ceremony in the Forum, the conspirators who were present, all dressed in togas, made their way to a meeting of the Senate. It was here that they planned to kill Caesar. After rejecting the possibility of doing the deed elsewhere, they decided to strike during a Senate meeting when Caesar would be unguarded, unsuspecting, and when many of the conspirators—who were senators—would be present, and they could carry weapons under their togas. It was here, at the site of the Senate meeting, that the rest of the conspirators, those who weren't at Cassius's house, gathered at dawn on the Ides.

A rumor may have given the conspirators an added reason to strike at this session. Caesar had called the Senate meeting. It was said that his cousin, Lucius Cotta, was going to make an important announcement as one of the priests in charge of the sacred Sybilline Books. Since, those books stated, only a king could defeat the Parthians, the priests were supposedly going to propose that Caesar be declared king. To soften the blow, it's possible that the title was meant to apply only outside of Rome—in Rome he would remain as dictator. But no less an authority than Cicero, who knew Cotta, stated that the rumor was false. In fact, the purpose of the Senate meeting was for Caesar to get Antony to give up his opposition to naming Dolabella as consul in Caesar's absence. The question is: did the conspirators believe the rumor, and if so, did it give them a nudge?

In any case, they decided to strike in the Senate. Shakespeare writes that Caesar was murdered in the Senate House on the Capitol—that is, on the

Capitoline Hill. The dramatic setting on high mirrors Caesar's pride and its undoing. But it is not true. The Roman Senate met from time to time on the Capitoline Hill, although in the Temple of Jupiter and not the Senate House, which was located elsewhere. But the Senate did not meet on the Capitoline on the Ides of March.

Unlike most modern senates, the Roman Senate had several different venues for meetings. They were all formally temples, including the Senate House itself, because legally the Senate could render a formal opinion only in consecrated space. Usually, though, the Senate met in the Roman Forum, where the Curia or Senate House was located. Originally called Curia Hostilia, after Rome's legendary third king, Tullus Hostilius, the Senate House was destroyed and rebuilt more than once. In 44 B.C., it was in the process of being rebuilt again by Caesar himself to be given his family name—it would be called the Julian Senate House (Curia Julia). And so, with construction still in progress, the Senate met in various other locations. The typical meeting place in this period was the Temple of Concord in the far west of the Forum.

But on March 15, the Senate met in the Portico of Pompey. To be precise, it met in the Senate House of Pompey (Curia Pompei or Curia Pompeia), a structure at the eastern end of that large complex opening onto the Portico and built to house Senate meetings. There were gladiatorial games in the Theater of Pompey that day, and Senate meetings were held in the Senate House of Pompey on days when there were games or shows in the theater.

The irony of attacking Caesar in a building dedicated to his enemy Pompey was clear. "It seemed as if some god was leading the man to the justice of Pompey," writes Plutarch. But the Portico of Pompey was a monument to Pompey's vain ambition, not to his loyalty to the Republic. "Murder for Pompey" was the slogan of a faction, not of men who put country above party. Worse still, the Senate House of Pompey was consecrated space, which made the conspirators not only murderers but also temple violators. Still, the conspirators planned to seize the public relations high ground.

They planned not just an assassination but an event. The conspirators believed that a murder in full view of the Senate would seize the public's imagination. "They thought that the act," wrote Appian, "precisely because it took place in the Senate, would appear to have been done not as a plot but on behalf of the country. . . . And the honor would remain their own because people would be well aware that they had begun it."

Then too, there was great symbolism in the Senate murder. It was believed that the senators assassinated the legendary Romulus after he changed from king to a tyrant. Plutarch cites a story that Romulus was killed in a Senate meeting in a temple, of all places, but the killers hid the body and kept the deed quiet. According to Appian, the conspirators of 44 B.C. believed that the Romulus story would resonate if they killed Caesar in a Senate meeting. Perhaps they also took note of an alternate version of Romulus's death in which the Roman nobility murdered Romulus at a meeting not of the Senate but of the assembly, when people were distracted by a violent rainstorm. The assembly supposedly took place, like the Senate meeting of the Ides of March, in the Field of Mars, where the Portico of Pompey was located.

To turn from politics to security, the Portico of Pompey was a godsend. The plotters faced threats both inside the Senate House and out, but the layout of the Portico favored them. The entrance to the Senate House of Pompey was in the Portico. If necessary, the conspirators could close off access to the complex. They had the manpower to do so on that day.

GLADIATORS AND SOLDIERS

A large group of gladiators gathered in the Portico of Pompey on the morning of the Ides. They were a team—a "family," as the Romans called groups of gladiators, no doubt named, as was usual, after their owner. They were probably known as the FAMILIA GLADIATORIA D BRUTI ALBINI, the gladiatorial "family" of Decimus Brutus Albinus.

The huge complex of the Portico, one of Rome's architectural wonders, held a theater at one end and a Senate House at the other, with a four-sided colonnade and park in between. Laid out as a rectangle, the Portico stretched eastward from the theater nearly 600 feet and was nearly 450 feet wide. The gladiators were positioned somewhere in the colonnade or the park. (At this hour of the day, there were probably none of the park's famous whores there to distract them.) The men were armed and preparing for a fight, but not an ordinary one.

Gladiatorial games were, in fact, underway in the theater—a venue for such events—but Decimus's men weren't part of them. Instead their job was to kidnap one of the gladiators who had violated his contract with Decimus by selling his services to the organizer of those games. Perhaps the organizer was an ambitious young official eager to catch Caesar's eye by his expenditure on public entertainment. The gladiator was clearly a good fighter—not one of those posers who fell over if you blew on him—and Decimus, his owner, said that he wanted him for his own upcoming games. This, at least, is the story told only by Nicolaus of Damascus. Others say that the gladiators were there to take part in the games, but Nicolaus's version is more plausible because it leaves the gladiators free to move at a moment's notice, which they couldn't do if they were competing. In any case, it speaks volumes about the level of violence in ancient Rome that Nicolaus's tale seemed perfectly normal.

The Romans took gladiatorial contests as seriously as we take football games today. By investing in a gladiatorial "family," a politician like Decimus hoped to win popular acclaim and political capital. The Romans called the games "gifts"—gifts to the people, that is. But Decimus was also investing in protection because gladiators doubled as private security forces. Many elite Romans, their names a roll call of republican glory—Cato, Sulla, Scipio—and their professions ranging from jurors and generals to art collectors, all employed gladiators as armed guards.

Take Birria and Eudamus, surely the most notorious gladiatorial guards of the era. In 52 B.C., they provoked a brawl on the Appian Way near Rome that led to the murder of the politician Clodius. Clodius was a Populist and demagogue, while Birria and Eudamus worked for his conservative archenemy, Milo. It was the evening of January 18 and they were bringing up the rear of the guard protecting Milo and his wife, Fausta, who were traveling in a litter. Then they came upon Clodius and his men. Eudamus and Birria started an argument and they noticed Clodius looking at them menacingly. So Birria ran Clodius through in the shoulder with his weapon, a *rhomphaia*.

This was no mean feat. The rhomphaia was a big, double-edged iron sword featuring a long wooden handle. It has been compared to a polearm or to the halberd used by Swiss armies in the Renaissance. The rhomphaia was a Thracian weapon, which suggests that Birria was Thracian. It required strength and skill to wield the rhomphaia properly. Considering that Clodius had the advantage of being on horseback while Birria was on foot, his achievement in wounding Clodius was all the greater. As an example of just what a gladiator could do in a fight, it helps explain why even veteran Roman soldiers were reluctant to attack gladiators.

Clodius's men carried him to the nearest tavern to recover, but Milo was hot on their heels. Milo ordered his men to drag him out and kill him, which they did. But the people loved Clodius and they mourned him mightily. There was a riot at his funeral in Rome that burned down the Senate House and upended the Republic. When Milo was put on trial, he got the best defense attorney money could buy: Cicero. The authorities surrounded the courthouse with soldiers in order to intimidate the jurors. The authorities wanted a guilty verdict to calm the people, and they got it. Milo was condemned to exile.

We don't know how many gladiators Decimus had, but the sources say there were a lot of them. Given their later role protecting the conspirators, it's hard to imagine fewer than 50 gladiators, but 100 or more is not out of the question. Too large a number of gladiators might have aroused suspicion, but Decimus was very close to Caesar, so few men would have dared challenge him. And Decimus was a very good liar indeed. No doubt he told Caesar about his plan to recover his wayward gladiator, and maybe the dictator smiled wryly at the thought of the fights he had once instigated in the streets of Rome. Maybe Decimus even reassured Caesar that the gladiators would double as security for him.

Caesar himself might have given these gladiators to Decimus as a token of friendship. Caesar had a fondness for gladiators. "He squandered all the power of his supreme talent," complained Cicero, "on *levitas popularis*," meaning "popular shallowness." He was Rome's greatest gladiatorial entrepreneur. Not only did he give Rome's most lavish gladiatorial games ever, but he also took a personal interest in the sport. The day before he crossed the Rubicon in January 49 B.C., he devoted several hours to watching gladiators training. In that same year he is recorded owning a very large number of gladiators in Capua, Italy's great training center for gladiators.

Decimus's gladiators could be useful in several ways. If a fight broke out to protect Caesar, the gladiators could intervene. If the assassins killed Caesar but then came under attack, the gladiators could protect them. If necessary, the gladiators could block the entrances to the Portico, and the Senate House had no direct access to the street—one had to go through the Portico. But the biggest threat that the gladiators faced lay not in the Portico but about half a mile away.

There, on the Tiber Island, a Roman legion had pitched its leather tents. If Cassius Dio is right, they were out on maneuvers in the suburbs of Rome that morning. In any case, by the afternoon they were back in camp and ready to be sent out on assignment.

Readers of Shakespeare's *Julius Caesar* will have the impression that Rome on the Ides of March was a civilian city. Nothing could be further from the truth. Outside the Sacred Boundary or *pomerium*, the ancient heart of Rome, the city was bristling with soldiers, both active-duty and demobilized. Armed soldiers were not allowed within the Sacred Boundary, a rule that was not always honored, but Caesar seems to have followed it.

The Tiber Island troops were under the command of Lepidus, a loyalist of Caesar who was about to finish his term as Master of the Horse, and so, the dictator's deputy. In four days, Lepidus was scheduled to leave Rome to take up a new job as governor of two important provinces, Narbonese Gaul (southern France) and Nearer Hispania (northeastern Spain), no doubt escorted by his legion. He was with the legion on the morning of the Ides.

Their camp on the Tiber Island made them an intimidating presence in Rome, even if they were less than full strength. In principle, a legion was made up of five thousand men, but legions were often understrength and Lepidus's force almost certainly was because you could not fit five thousand men on the island. It is no bigger than an average city block today. In antiquity, temples, shrines, and their grounds covered the island, leaving little open space.

We don't know much about the men but we can be sure that they were not new recruits. Perhaps some of them had served with Lepidus in Hispania during his earlier mission there. The cool professionalism that they would soon display shows that they were experienced troops. Perhaps Caesar thought of Lepidus's men as a deterrent to any would-be assassins, an insurance policy of sorts. If so, the policy had an additional protection clause—a second group of soldiers in Rome.

They were Caesar's discharged veterans. Between 47 B.C. and 44 B.C., up to fifteen thousand were settled on land in Italy but Caesar was still in the process of settling many more there. Some of those who already had land came to Rome to escort their old chief on his way to the Parthian front on March 18.

The veterans were stationed in temples and sacred precincts in various places outside the city walls of Rome. Like the men on the Tiber Island, they were armed. They were planning to march out to their new lands in the old-fashioned Roman style, following a banner, in military formation, led by a colonial commission. Presumably, they too would leave on March 18 for their new homes in Italy. Cicero called these veterans "country folk but very brave men and excellent citizens." They were certainly loyal to Caesar, but their commitment to the Senate was another matter.

No group of gladiators could protect the conspirators from thousands of Caesar's angry veterans for long, but they might give the conspirators enough time to persuade Caesar's angry soldiers that Rome's new leaders were offering even better terms for resettlement. And so there would be handshakes instead of civil war.

CRIES AND WHISPERS

Senate meetings began in the early morning. In times of emergency, meetings began at daybreak or even earlier, although legally a vote could not be taken before sunrise. On this day, though, the Senate probably met at what the Romans called the third hour, that is, around 8 or 9 A.M., when courts usually began the day. Yet the scheduled hour came and went, and Caesar was nowhere to be seen.

While they were waiting for the dictator to arrive, the praetors went about their business, which they carried out in the Portico of Pompey. Plutarch marvels at the calm and composure with which Brutus and Cassius listened to petitions, resolved disputes, or judged cases. He even mentions a litigant who promised to appeal to Caesar against Brutus's unfavorable verdict. Brutus replied, with a philosopher's precision, that Caesar neither did nor would prevent Brutus from behaving according to the laws.

But as the time passed and Caesar failed to appear, tension rose. Like Caesar, Brutus too endured sleepless nights leading up to the Ides of March. Various anecdotes claim to describe the nervous scene at the Portico of Pompey. A man approached the older Casca brother and scolded him for keeping a secret that, he announced, Brutus had revealed to him. Casca was unnecessarily frightened, as the man was just gossiping about Casca's run for office.

Then an augur and senator named Popilius Laenas took Brutus and Cassius aside to say that he joined in their prayers for success and urged them to hurry. The obvious question was, "prayers for success in what?" but Brutus and Cassius were too terrified to say anything. Finally, Brutus got awful news from home that Porcia was dead. It turned out to be a false rumor—she had just fainted from anxiety. But Brutus didn't know that yet, claim the sources, and he soldiered on.

The report came of the bad omens at Caesar's house, along with a rumor: the Senate might be dismissed. Thinking that Caesar wasn't coming, an attendant carried his golden chair—the special one, voted to him by the Senate—out of the hall. Later, in retrospect, that seemed like a bad omen.

But the conspirators had to worry about action and not omens. Dio claims that they decided to send Decimus to Caesar's house to try to talk him into coming because he was such a close friend of Caesar.

Decimus was about to enter a man's home to lure him to his death. That man was someone Decimus had served for more than a decade and who had honored and promoted Decimus in turn. True, he probably had left Decimus feeling unappreciated and overlooked, and true, he threatened to destroy the Republic and the values in which Decimus believed. Yet many people would label Decimus's behavior disgraceful, even while acknowledging that it took guts.

How could Decimus do it? Those in the know might have said afterward, "Like mother, like son." Sempronia had a reputation for brains, beauty, adultery, and revolutionary politics. She was accused of "masculine audacity." In 63 B.C. she broke with the conservative politics of her husband and her father and supported Catiline. He was a failed politician who advocated armed rebellion to obtain debt relief for both poor people and overextended aristocrats like Sempronia. While her husband was out of town, she opened their home to Catiline's Gallic allies—Allobroges, a tribe famous for its spear-wielding horsemen. Catiline's rebellion failed but Sempronia might have taught Decimus a thing or two about betrayal.

Whether he went to Caesar's on his own or at the call of others, Decimus was the linchpin of the plot. Unless he talked Caesar into coming to the Senate meeting, there would have been no attack that morning and probably no attack at all. Yes, Caesar would likely reschedule the Senate meeting for the next day or the day after, before he left for war. But with each day the risk increased that the plot would be discovered. It all came down to Decimus.

And so, he came to Caesar's home. The two men conversed among the mosaics and the marbles of the Public Mansion. We will never know the details of that conversation. One of the participants told the story to his advantage and the other was silent. Historians in ancient times did not hesitate to invent dialogue, reporting what the speakers "should" have said. Yet, most of what they state about Decimus and Caesar has the ring of truth.

Decimus, they say, argued that Caesar should not risk disappointing the Senate or, worse, seeming to insult or mock it. Caesar himself had called the meeting, and for business that required a quorum, so the house was full and it was already waiting for some time. If Caesar simply sent someone to dismiss the meeting because of Calpurnia's dreams, the senators would consider him a tyrant or a weakling. Some sources add that Decimus ridiculed the soothsayers. One writer even says that Decimus promised a vote in the Senate to declare Caesar king outside of Italy.

As the son of a noble family, Decimus had his finger on the pulse of the Senate, and Caesar knew it. But the key thing, one suspects, is that Decimus spoke as one soldier to another. They were comrades of the battlefield and Caesar was about to leave for another war, perhaps the greatest campaign of his career—this time without Decimus.

"What do you say, Caesar?" Decimus is supposed to have said. "Will someone of your stature pay attention to the dreams of a woman and the omens of foolish men?" Decimus told Caesar, in effect, to man up. Between two soldiers like Decimus and Caesar, an argument from masculinity is a trump card.

Caesar decided to go. He would postpone the meeting to another day but he would do it in person in the Senate House, thus showing the senators respect. Perhaps he was thinking that he would show something else, too—contempt for fear. What warrior could resist that?

In a seeming gesture of friendship, Decimus led Caesar out by the hand. To trick Julius Caesar was no mean feat, even if Caesar was in fact suffering from impaired judgment after a seizure. Decimus was a liar, a flimflam man, a brazen and audacious snake. In short he was much like Caesar.

Julius Caesar, the ultimate captain of his own fate, put his life in the hands of another. No writer could resist the drama of Caesar's decision. The sources give us a Caesar who is gullible, taken in by a schemer like Decimus—so says Nicolaus of Damascus. They give us a Caesar who is passive because he is led rather than a leader—so says Plutarch. They give us a Caesar who cares about appearances—so says Appian. They give us a Caesar who is arrogant because he ignores the warnings of the gods—so says Suetonius or Dio. Yet, there was another Caesar, a man who was a risk taker—indeed, a risk addict—and a gambler who couldn't resist one last roll of the dice. Appian, who sketches a Caesar who wanted a sudden death, comes closest to this side of the great commander's personality. The man who scaled walls as a young soldier in the East, fought his way through an ambush on the Sabis River in Gaul, and stole a march on more than one fierce enemy, could not resist the call of a fellow soldier to undertake a final mission.

Caesar decided to go to the Senate meeting not because he thought it was safe, one suspects, but because he thought it was dangerous. It was almost at the end of the fifth hour—that is, shortly before eleven o'clock—when Caesar went forth.

CAESAR ARRIVES

A litter carried by slaves brought Caesar through the streets of Rome. Festival of Anna Perenna or not, Caesar was thronged along the way by his twenty-four lictors, by most of Rome's public officials, and by a large and diverse crowd of citizens, foreigners, freedmen, and slaves. No doubt the multitude included favor seekers, well-wishers, rubberneckers, and maybe even a few bold catcallers. Many handed him small rolls of papyrus containing petitions or letters. Caesar immediately turned the rolls over to his attendants. It might have taken as long as forty-five minutes to reach the Portico of Pompey, so perhaps it was around 11:30 A.M. when he arrived. Meanwhile, word was sent to the senators that the dictator was on his way.

There was still time for Caesar to discover the plot, according to the sources. Barely had he left his door when another person's slave tried to reach him, but the press of people around the dictator was too great. The slave asked Calpurnia to let him stay until Caesar returned, presumably because he knew that something was afoot but not that it was set for that very day.

Then, a man named Artemidorus of Cnidus made his way through the crowd to hand Caesar a small roll and told him to read it himself and to do so quickly. Artemidorus knew the truth about the conspiracy. Caesar tried to read the roll more than once but the mob of people kept preventing him. He was still holding it in his hand, unopened, when he entered the Senate. Or so one version goes. On another account, Artemidorus couldn't break through the crowd to Caesar and someone else gave Caesar the roll he held as he went into the meeting. Suetonius merely says that Caesar got the roll from someone, but he claims that Caesar held it with other rolls in his left hand—the ill-omened hand for the Romans, as we can tell from the Latin word for left: *sinister*.

Who was Artemidorus to capture Caesar's attention? His hometown, Cnidus, was an important port city in southwestern Anatolia (Turkey). His father, Theopompus, was called "a friend of the deified Caesar, a man of great influence with him." Since 54 B.C. if not earlier, Theopompus had served Caesar as a diplomat. The dictator returned the favor by granting Cnidus "freedom"—that is, a certain amount of autonomy within Rome's empire—and immunity from direct taxation. Like his father, Artemidorus was a local bigwig. Plutarch calls him a teacher of Greek philosophy, which underestimates his importance but might explain how Artemidorus knew Brutus—through a common interest in philosophy. That is the only clue we have as to how Artemidorus was aware of the conspiracy.

Caesar finally arrived at the Portico of Pompey. No sooner did he get out of his litter than Popilius Laenas hurried up to speak to him. The same man had scared Brutus and Cassius before. Now, as he spoke at length to Caesar, the conspirators exchanged mutual looks of concern. Cassius and others supposedly reached for their weapons under their togas when Brutus smiled at them. He couldn't hear Popilius's words but he could see his face. He observed with relief that he was asking Caesar for some favor and not denouncing the plot. So Brutus signaled that all was well. Popilius is said to have kissed Caesar's hand as he said goodbye. Once again, we have only questionable sources for this melodramatic story.

Before Caesar went into the room, he had to wait for the magistrates to conduct the customary sacrifices and the soothsayers to take the auspices. Once again, they were unfavorable. The sources agree that the priests sacrificed several victims. The soothsayers examined the entrails but they did not like what they saw. The sources now offer two very different versions of what happened next. Nicolaus paints a dark picture. The soothsayers saw an avenging spirit in the omens; Caesar got angry and turned to face west, which was an even worse omen since the west symbolized sunset and death. Then Caesar's friends talked him into putting off the meeting—at a guess, without entering the Senate House at all.

What changed Caesar's mind? Nicolaus lays the blame squarely on the shoulders of Decimus, in whose mouth is put the memorable phrase, "make your own manly excellence an auspicious omen." He says Decimus scorned the soothsayers and so changed Caesar's mind. In the end, Decimus took Caesar by the hand and led him into the Senate House with Caesar following in silence. If this story is true, then Decimus becomes an even more pivotal player: even more cold-blooded and two-faced. Caesar is almost passive.

But no other source tells the tale, so perhaps it was a piece of venom invented after the fact. Nicolaus's patron, Augustus, loathed Decimus. The other sources leave out Decimus and emphasize Caesar's hubris instead. They have him insistent in the face of the bad omens. This sounds like the Caesar of old and, in fact, Appian says that Caesar reminded the soothsayers of a similar bad omen back on the campaign when he crushed Pompey's armies in Hispania.

The *capsarii* had long since entered the Senate House. They were slaves and it was their job to carry the *capsae*, containers holding scrolls that served as books in Rome. Each capsa was made of beechwood and stood about a foot high. Each could carry six scrolls. But today, some of the capsae held something additional and unexpected. If the slaves noticed that they were carrying extra weight, they said nothing. Slaves knew better than to challenge their masters.

The other senators had already entered the chamber. There was nothing left except for Caesar to go in. It was around noon.

8

MURDER

BEFORE CAESAR ENTERED THE SENATE HOUSE AROUND NOON ON
the Ides of March, he laughed. He thereby dismissed the soothsayers and
their bad omens. So Appian says. It's a gesture worthy of a poet, and as good
historians we must be highly skeptical and yet, Caesar wrote his own rules.
It might even be true.

THE ROOM

When it comes to the details of Pompey's Senate House, educated guesses
are the best we can do. All that survives is part of two or possibly three
foundation walls and perhaps some of the marble decorations. It's clear that
the Senate House was the biggest building in the Portico. A person entered
the Senate House from the Portico by walking up from the garden. The
interior was no doubt lined with marble and might conceivably have been
decorated with large columns, perhaps representing two different decorative
styles.

As Caesar entered the Senate House, he could have seen hanging inside it a famous painting by a Greek master of a warrior holding a round shield. But was the warrior in the process of going up or going down? That, said the Roman scholar Pliny the Elder, was open to question.

If Caesar turned around before going in the door, he would have seen beyond the double row of plane trees—their branches still bare on the cusp of spring—Pompey's Temple of Venus the Victorious perched atop the Theater of Pompey at the far side of the complex.

As he stepped inside, Caesar would have entered a place that was large but not imposing. We imagine that Caesar was killed in a grand space. The impression comes from the great neoclassical paintings, above all from Jean-Léon Gérôme's iconic work *The Death of Caesar* (1867). In fact, the Senate House of Pompey was relatively small. It was somewhat smaller than Caesar's Senate House, whose interior covered about 5,000 square feet. It was probably not as tall as Caesar's Senate House either, whose roof rose to a height of almost 105 feet.

Senatorial rules of procedure dictated the layout of the space inside Pompey's Senate House. Senators voted by division—that is, they crossed the center aisle to walk over to the side of the room where the senator proposing a motion was sitting. For that reason, the seats in a Roman Senate House were arranged along two sides of the building, with a broad central aisle. Perhaps the seats in Pompey's Senate House were arranged on three broad steps as in Caesar's Senate House.

At the far end of the room stood a tribunal—a low, raised platform for the presiding officer, who sat on his chair of office. Usually the consul presided, but, in Caesar's case, it was the dictator. In Pompey's Senate House, Pompey's statue probably stood on the tribunal, perhaps in the middle near the rear wall of the building like the famous Statue of Victory in Caesar's Senate House. No details of Pompey's statue survive. We don't know if it was marble or terra cotta or whether Pompey was garbed traditionally in a toga or depicted in the nude like some Greek potentate, which was the latest fashion for Roman generals and politicians.

There was probably room for about three hundred senators in Pompey's Senate House. They would have needed the space for the meeting of March 15, 44 B.C. Attendance was often sparse at Senate meetings, but a quorum was required for certain items of business, such as consultation with priests, which was on the agenda that day. Hence, a quorum was needed, and the sources state that it was achieved. Caesar had raised the number of senators from about 600 to 900. The quorum, however, probably remained at 200, as it had been before, given the difficulties from time to time in making the quorum.

So there were at least 200 senators present on March 15, 44 B.C. Add the ten People's Tribunes and, say, a dozen secretaries, slaves, and other assistants, and the result is a minimum of about 225 men and perhaps 300 in the Curia of Pompey on the Ides of March.

But at least two senators at the Portico of Pompey that day were not in the room. The conspirators were worried about Antony. Thanks to Brutus they wouldn't kill him but they insisted on neutralizing him. They worried that Antony might lead friends in the Senate House to come to Caesar's defense. If enough of them joined in, they could have overwhelmed the conspirators through force of numbers, especially if any of them carried hidden daggers. Antony was physically strong and a splendid leader. He could have played a key role, maybe even turned the tide. It was essential to keep him out.

So the plotters assigned Trebonius the role of chatting up Antony and keeping him outside the Senate. Not only was Trebonius a seasoned officer himself, but he went back a long way with Antony. The two of them had commanded adjoining sectors at the siege of Alesia in 52 B.C. in Gaul. And in 45 B.C., Trebonius had tried to recruit Antony against Caesar. By the time they met under the Portico outside Pompey's Senate House that morning, the two old comrades had years' worth of war stories to chew over.

As Caesar entered the room, the senators rose. The dictator looked splendid. Caesar was wearing the special toga of a triumphant general, dyed a reddish purple and embroidered with gold. The Senate had given him the right to wear it and he put it on for formal occasions.

Among the senators there that day who were not in on the plot were

Favonius, the friend of Cato whom Brutus rejected for the conspiracy; Dolabella, the consul-to-be if Caesar had his way; Cinna, the praetor; and Cicero. The great orator planned to attack Antony for trying to deny Dolabella his consulship.

Caesar took his seat on the tribunal—on his golden chair, which was now back in place. The conspirators were armed and ready.

THE WEAPONS

In Gérôme's *Death of Caesar,* the assassins walk out of the Senate House, waving their triumphant swords. It's a dramatic image and the swords look great, but the assassins—with one possible exception—used daggers, not swords. The sources are clear about this. Some if not all of the conspirators wore a dagger under their toga. Daggers had been hidden in the capsae, the storage baskets the slaves carried. Besides, swords were the wrong weapon for the occasion. They were too big for close-quarters action and they were too big to hide.

But the Romans never tired of thinking of their soldiers and their heroes in the arena as swordsmen—literally, gladiators, from the Latin *gladius* for "sword." Daggers get much less attention in Roman literature and art, yet Roman soldiers made extensive use of daggers. To be precise, they used the military dagger or *pugio* (plural, *pugiones*). *Pugio* is related to the Latin words *pugnus,* "fist" and *pugil,* "boxer"; the English word *pugilist* comes from the latter. The pugio or military dagger was a standard part of a legionary's equipment by the first century A.D. and probably already so by the second half of the first century B.C. But the Romans' reticence about daggers is not surprising. Swords offer distance from the target but knifework is close range. It is a bloody, gruesome business. Few feel comfortable talking about it, and fewer still doing it.

In its construction, a Roman military dagger exemplifies efficiency. The blade was iron and, in the Late Republic, about six to eight inches long and about two inches wide. Double-edged, the blade was leaf-shaped, with a slight spine running down the middle, and ending in a sharp tip. Such a weapon was perfectly designed to stab through the human chest, which is, on average, about six to eight inches thick.

The blade was held by a strong bronze or wooden handle ending in a pommel. A cross guard, secured through the top of the blade, protected the user's hand. The military dagger sat in a metal frame scabbard mounted to a soldier's belt by rings or a buckle.

A martial artist who works with replicas of Roman weapons today describes the Roman military dagger as smooth, streamlined, and remarkably light. It rides well against the hip, behind the back, or on the stomach, and can be grasped quickly. It was the right weapon to hide under a toga.

Remarkably, we know what two of the assassins' daggers looked like. A coin issued by Brutus—of which more later—shows two military daggers used on the Ides of March. The two daggers are not identical. Rather, each has a different hilt. The right dagger's hilt is decorated with two flat disks. The left dagger has a cross-shaped hilt. These might seem minor points to us but the details are not likely to have escaped a contemporary's eye, especially not a soldier's eye.

Since the coin was meant to be read from left to right (the direction of the inscription), it is tempting to believe that the first dagger, the dagger on the left—the one with the cross-shaped hilt—belonged to Brutus, whose name is on the other side of the coin. In that case, the dagger on the right— the one with a two-disk hilt—was Cassius's. Archaeologists have found both kinds of daggers in use in the first century B.C. In the current state of the evidence, cross-shaped daggers are rare, so perhaps Brutus's dagger looked really distinctive to people at the time.

The primary purpose of the Roman military dagger was to kill at close range. It was well suited for use in brawls, fracases, and security duty but it played an important role on the battlefield as well. Combat would leave many of the enemy wounded but still dangerous. The Roman military dagger was an efficient way to dispatch them, with its double edge (for slashing throats) and sharp point for stabbing (throats, eyes, groins, and chests) to make sure the enemy was truly dead and no further threat. Roman soldiers probably sometimes preferred to use their military daggers rather than their

swords in order to limit wear and tear on the latter, which were more expensive and so harder to replace. For instance, it made sense to use a dagger,
and not a sword, to cut off a dead man's finger for his ring or an ear for an
earring.

A dagger was also large enough for use off the battlefield, to trim
branches for firewood, defensive walling, or palisades, and yet small enough
to cut meat for meals (and dressing game). But many soldiers also carried
a small sheath knife, for eating, shaving, and general small tasks. Thus a
Roman soldier had a sword—the main tool, expensive and well cared for,
subject to frequent inspection for condition; a dagger—the workaday sharp
implement also used in combat as a backup and "mercy" tool; and a sheath/
utility knife—kept as sharp as can be for finer domestic work and eating
utensil. On the Ides of March, the military dagger would prove its worth.

THE DEED

Even before Caesar sat down, some of the conspirators stood behind his
chair while others gathered around him, as if they were going to pay their
respects or bring some matter to his attention. They were really forming a
perimeter. Sixty men could not have approached Caesar without arousing
suspicion. Besides, there wasn't room for sixty men on the tribunal. More
likely, about a dozen conspirators gathered around the seated dictator, with
others poised to join them later in a second wave. Cassius was there from
the start and supposedly glanced at the statue of Pompey as if to draw support from his old friend and enemy of Caesar.

The attack on Caesar, as we now know, was neither random nor improvised. The five main ancient sources are in general agreement, although they
differ in some details. The story that they tell points to careful, advance
planning. To succeed, the attack had to be sudden and swift before Caesar's
supporters had time to help. Centurions, for example, were among Caesar's
new senators. They were in the room and could have jumped to the dictator's assistance. But the conspiracy did not lack military minds who had
thought the operation through.

To return to the scene in the Senate House, after Caesar was seated, Tillius Cimber took the lead. The hard-drinking scrapper had Caesar's favor and so he was unlikely to arouse suspicion. He came up to the dictator and presented a petition on behalf of his exiled brother. The others joined him, clasping Caesar's hands and kissing his breast and his head.

These moves offer another sign of careful planning on the part of the conspirators because they mirror an earlier assassination attempt in 47 B.C. The intended victim then was the abusive governor of Further Hispania. The conspirators approached him in a public building in Corduba (modern Córdoba, Spain) as if they were going to present a petition. Then one of them grabbed him with his left hand and stabbed him with a military dagger twice. They killed one of his attendants but the governor survived. He was Quintus Cassius Longinus.

We can be sure that the conspirators of 44 B.C. knew about this event. For one thing, the next governor of Further Hispania was Trebonius. For another, Quintus Cassius Longinus was probably a brother of Cassius the conspirator. So, by drawing near Caesar with a petition on the Ides of March, the plotters were following an earlier scenario—no, they were improving it, because unlike the governor, Caesar had no attendants to protect him.

Cimber disrespected Caesar by coming up to him with his hands out instead of keeping them humbly beneath his toga. Then Cimber took hold of Caesar's toga and held it so tightly that he kept Caesar from getting up. Caesar was angry. Now Cimber pulled the toga from Caesar's shoulder. According to Suetonius Caesar exclaimed, "Why, this is violence!" This expression, found only in Suetonius, expresses Caesar's sudden realization. Whether he actually said this or not, it seems likely that the truth flashed before his eyes. The omens had been right after all and he had been wrong. But it was too late. As agreed on in advance, pulling down Caesar's toga was the signal to start the attack.

The honor of the first blow went to Publius Servilius Casca. He too was a friend of Caesar. Perhaps he was chosen because the Pompey supporters in the conspiracy insisted that a friend of Caesar go first, or perhaps because Casca was an experienced killer. We can only speculate about that. Since he was a senator, he was at least in his early thirties but probably not much older. Knife fighting has never been dainty. Very few soldiers, even good ones, have what it takes to stab a man to death. It takes sheer physical strength and a certain brutality to drive a dagger through a man's flesh, but the circumstances that day also demanded fearlessness. Casca had to strike in cold blood in front of several hundred witnesses and with the knowledge that retaliation was likely. One imagines that he was young and strong.

Nicolaus, Plutarch, and Appian say that Casca had a sword. Or do they? The Greek word they use, *ksiphos*, can also refer to a dagger, and it probably does so here. Elsewhere they generally refer precisely to a dagger (*ksiphidion* or *egkheiridion*). The use instead of a word that could mean "sword" adds a certain grandeur to the first blow. It didn't make the stroke accurate, though. Casca struck from above. He aimed for Caesar's neck and missed. A neck strike should have been fatal but Casca hit Caesar in the breast. Nicolaus says that Casca was nervous, but Caesar was a moving target.

Four of the five main ancient sources agree that Caesar tried to defend himself, while Dio says that there were too many attackers for Caesar to do or say anything in response. Nicolaus simply says that Caesar stood up to defend himself. Plutarch says Caesar turned around and grabbed Casca's dagger by the handle (here Plutarch indeed calls it a dagger). Appian adds that he hurled Casca away with great violence. Suetonius says that Caesar caught Casca's arm and stabbed him with his stylus—a pointed, iron instrument, about the size and shape of a pencil, used for writing on a wax tablet. He adds that Caesar tried to get up but was unable because of the next blow.

Of all the sources, Appian most emphasizes Caesar's military qualities. He has Caesar respond to the assassins with "anger and shouting." Plutarch says that Caesar cried out in Latin, "Impious Casca!"—or, in another version, "Accursed Casca! What are you doing?" Either version is understandable considering that Caesar considered Casca a friend. Suetonius claims that Caesar merely groaned without uttering a word in the attack, and Dio says that Caesar was unable to say anything, but a warrior like Caesar would probably have shouted something in defiance. Meanwhile, Casca cried out to his brother Gaius for help. Plutarch and Nicolaus say that Casca shouted in Greek to make sure he was heard above the din. If Casca was a thug, evidently he was an educated thug. According to Nicolaus, Gaius Casca obeyed his brother's call and delivered the second blow, which struck the dictator in the ribs.

Pause for a moment, as the other assassins draw their daggers, to contemplate the Roman nobility. They believed that they were carrying out their sworn duty to defend the Republic. By attacking Caesar, the assassins believed, they were covering themselves with glory. They did it out of conviction, they did it out of self-interest, they did it out of hatred, they did it out of jealousy, and they did it out of honor. They were the descendants of the senators who murdered the reforming Gracchi brothers in 133 B.C. and 121 B.C., and of the patricians who sat like statues dressed in togas when the Gauls sacked Rome in 387 B.C. and thus died fearlessly.

The conspirators surrounded Caesar in a circle—again, a sign of careful planning. The blows now came fast and furious. If Caesar was indeed standing, he could not have stayed on his feet for long, probably for less than a minute. Plutarch's description of Caesar being driven here and there like a wild beast sounds like poetic exaggeration. In short order, Caesar fell not far from his chair.

The attack almost sounds choreographed, even ritualistic. Two ancient sources use the language of a sacrifice to describe the attack, suggesting a common and perhaps a contemporary source.

None of the sources names all of the attackers. Nicolaus mentions three besides Casca—Cassius, who planted a slanting blow across the face; Decimus, who struck deep under the ribs; and Minucius Basilus, who missed and struck Rubrius on the thigh. Nicolaus also says that Cassius tried for a second blow but struck Brutus's hand instead. Appian agrees that Cassius struck Caesar in the face but says that Brutus stabbed him in the thigh and Bucolianus in the back. Plutarch says that Brutus struck Caesar in the groin—a site that sounds a little too good to be true for Caesar's alleged love child.

Ah, Brutus, the famous center of Shakespeare's description of the assassination! Caesar's cry of "Et tu, Brute?" or "You too, Brutus?" is not in the ancient sources. It was a Renaissance invention. Suetonius and Dio include a report that when Brutus rushed at Caesar or, even less credibly, after Brutus struck him powerfully, Caesar said, in Greek, "kai su, teknon" which means, "you too, child." Both authors express doubt about Caesar actually saying this. Regardless, a lively scholarly debate has long been going on as to what he meant if he did say it.

One possibility is that the dying Caesar was acknowledging Brutus as his son—and perhaps insulting him as a bastard and condemning him as a man who kills his own father. Another possibility is that Caesar was cursing Brutus. "The same to you!" is a familiar phrase on ancient curse tablets. A third possibility is that Caesar was interrupted in midsentence. Had he continued, he might have said something like, "You too, child, will one day taste power like mine." At least one of the later emperors said something similar to a young successor, and he might have been quoting Caesar.

A great man's last words make for an ever-fascinating theme. "You too, child" is a classic contribution to the corpus. In all likelihood though, Caesar said nothing of the kind. The story was probably invented later, when a debate raged over Brutus's role that day. It is easier to imagine Caesar's last words as an indignant cry against the villainy of Casca—a final war cry from an old soldier who had stumbled unknowingly onto his last battlefield.

But Caesar didn't only utter last words. He carried out a last gesture. All the five main sources except Nicolaus state that Caesar covered his face—Nicolaus makes no mention of this. Caesar's was a gesture of protection, of resignation and, perhaps, of modesty. Suetonius states, and Dio implies, that Caesar made his gesture as soon as he realized that he was being attacked from all sides. As Suetonius makes clear, what Caesar did was wrap his toga over his head. But when? According to Plutarch, it was only when he saw Brutus approach him with a dagger that Caesar did so. Less probable, Appian has Caesar do it after Brutus strikes him. Suetonius adds that Caesar also drew his toga over his legs for the sake of decency—an antidote, as it were, to the lifetime of peccadillos that Suetonius refers to in his biography. Valerius Maximus, a Roman writer of the first century A.D., makes it a gesture of immodesty as well. It showed that Caesar was less a man than a god returning home.

We'll never know just how Caesar responded to Brutus that day, if he responded at all. Caesar was closer to Decimus, who had lied to him that very day. We might expect that Decimus's betrayal hurt Caesar more than Brutus's betrayal. Yet there was a third party in the relationship between Brutus and Caesar—Servilia. Caesar's connection to Servilia was a matter of the heart, and the heart has its reasons. So perhaps Brutus's betrayal stung most sharply.

It probably took only a few minutes for Caesar to die. If they all lined up, if no one hesitated and if everything worked with complete efficiency, then twenty or more assassins could probably have each stabbed Caesar before he died. But few things work so smoothly. Besides, Caesar moved and fought back. The attackers were confused and overexcited, and in the turmoil some of them missed Caesar and stabbed each other. Brutus, for example, had a wound in his hand.

So, if they wanted to be able to say, "I stabbed Caesar," some of the attackers would have had to settle for stabbing the dead body. Caesar's heavy woolen tunic and toga surely soaked up most of his blood. The assassins had Caesar's blood on their daggers, but little of it stained their own clothing.

Caesar received twenty-three wounds. No fewer than eight ancient sources say that. Twenty conspirators are known by name, of whom one, Trebonius, presumably did not stab Caesar because he stood outside the room. That leaves four additional attackers, unless some struck more than once. What about the other thirty-six of the sixty conspirators? Maybe some were Roman knights and so ineligible to attend a Senate meeting. Maybe some were senators but stayed home that day, perhaps out of cowardice. But most were probably there on the Ides and yet did not stab Caesar.

Nicolaus explicitly says otherwise, that there was none of the conspirators still left who failed to strike Caesar's corpse on the ground, so that they all seemed to share in the deed. He also says, alone of the sources, that Caesar received thirty-five wounds. Perhaps, because he enjoyed the patronage of the emperor Augustus, Nicolaus maximized the crime against Caesar—he also says there were more than eighty conspirators in total. It's also possible that Nicolaus simply got his numbers from a different source than the others and that the sources disagreed. Nicolaus's argument that every conspirator struck Caesar dead if not alive may be true, but it sounds like a poetic touch, echoing the mistreatment of Hector's corpse in the *Iliad*. The reality was probably less melodramatic.

Some conspirators were assigned to defense. Their job was surely to back the killers up by holding off rescuers and keep an exit path clear. The plotters had to be prepared for a response. Even without arms, a counterattack by dozens of senators could have overwhelmed the killers, especially if some of Caesar's friends had also smuggled in daggers to the room. Yet that turned out not to be the case, and the assassins moved so quickly that most observers responded with shocked inaction. But not Cicero, not if what he says later is true, not if he derived great joy from seeing with his own eyes the just death of a tyrant.

Still, Caesar had many friends in the room and even more outside, where his virtual bodyguards were waiting. The door to the Senate House was kept open during sessions, and the sons of senators were encouraged to stand outside and watch. Cassius's son, in his freshly minted manhood, might have been there to observe his father murder the dictator.

It's a little-known fact but there were two rescuers in the Senate House that day.

THEIR FINEST HOUR

Among the senators present were Lucius Marcius Censorinus and Gaius Calvisius Sabinus. Both supporters of Caesar, they were otherwise oil and water. Censorinus was the product of an old and prestigious Roman family but one that had taken its share of knocks. Calvisius was an Italian whose family name wasn't even Latin. Yet before the morning was over, the two men would be bound together by unbreakable ties.

Censorinus came from a noble house that claimed descent both from a king of Rome and the satyr Marsyas, a character out of myth and a symbol of liberty. The family went in for no-holds-barred fighting. In the Second Punic War (218–201 B.C.) they broke oaths to Carthaginians. During the wars between Marius and Sulla they beheaded a consul and displayed his head on the speaker's platform. All's fair in war. Censorinus was the son of a man who, like Caesar, was a staunch supporter of Marius and an opponent of Sulla. Censorinus's uncle, another strong Marian, was captured by Sulla and killed. The family was probably short of money in later years, which might explain why Censorinus took on the undesirable role of a seller of public property like Antony. Although nothing else of Censorinus's earlier career is known, two things are clear. He had held public office, as senators had to, and he knew how to fight—future events show that.

Calvisius offers a richer story. He was an Italian from Spoletium (Spoleto) who made his way in the world as a soldier. During the Civil War he served as one of Caesar's officers. In 48 B.C., after they crossed the Adriatic, Caesar sent Calvisius with five cohorts and a few horsemen—about 2,500 men—through the rugged Greek hill country of Aetolia to the fertile plain on the Corinthian Gulf. There he met up with friendly locals and expelled enemy garrisons from the cities. That won Caesar the territory and a rich source of grain for his troops. After Caesar's victory in the Civil War, Calvisius was rewarded with a term as governor of the Roman province of Africa (modern Tunisia). He was currently praetor.

Calvisius and Censorinus were about to have their finest hour together.

Of all of Caesar's friends in the Senate House that day, they were the only two to come to his defense. Everyone else was too shocked and horrified to react, according to Plutarch. Precisely how and when Calvisius and Censorinus responded is not known. Nicolaus tells us only that the conspirators bore down on them and that the two resisted for a little while before they fled because of the number of their opponents. This is another sign of careful planning by the conspirators, who were prepared to meet resistance. More men might have risen to Caesar's aid and in that case the reserve force of gladiators would have come in handy.

Calvisius and Censorinus are forgotten today. In practical terms, they accomplished nothing. But they went down on the honor roll of the party of Caesar's friends.

POMPEY'S REVENGE

A physician named Antistius examined Caesar's body afterward. Perhaps he was one of the doctors who advised Caesar on the morning of the Ides against going to the Senate. In any case, Antistius concluded that of the twenty-three wounds, only one was fatal—the second wound, which was in his breast. Assuming that this was Gaius Casca's wound to Caesar's ribs, then he was the man who actually carried out the murder. That only one wound was fatal would not be surprising, because it is not easy to inflict a fatal stab wound—not in the heat of a nervous moment, and not through a heavy woolen toga and tunic. We can't be certain that Antistius was right, however.

With his death, Caesar closed a circle. In 60 B.C. he had joined Pompey and Crassus to divide the Roman state behind the scenes like three potentates. Crassus was tortured and then killed by the Parthians to whom he had surrendered after Carrhae in 53 B.C. After turning on Caesar and losing at Pharsalus, Pompey was murdered on the beach in Alexandria in 48 B.C. Now Caesar was dead and a round of murder and betrayal was over.

The irony of the great Caesar being killed in Rome was lost on no one. The conqueror of the world was murdered within a mile or two of his birth. Florus, a first-century A.D. Roman writer, probably put it best, "Thus he who had filled the whole world with the blood of his fellow-citizens at last filled the Senate House with his own."

Caesar was a master commander, a deft politician, an elegant orator, and a lapidary literary stylist. His victories in the field, his championship of the common man and the provinces, his wit, his verve, his charm, and his vision of reform all continue to excite admiration. His cold-blooded career of killing in Gaul still horrifies. His egotism seemingly knew no bounds.

Conqueror, creator, and dictator, Caesar was great but at least in the last stages of his career, not wise. His job after civil war was to heal Rome. Instead, he took with one hand what he gave with the other. He pardoned his noble enemies without asking their pardon in return. He spared their lives but in some cases not their land. He gave them the titles they coveted while shrinking their power. The cruel truth is that he might have been better off killing his noble enemies from the outset.

He passed laws to help the masses but he curbed elections and so weakened self-government. After going to war in the name of the People's Tribunes, he threatened one People's Tribune with death and deposed two others.

Caesar showed off when he should have worked behind the scenes. He rebranded the center of Rome with his family's name, as if the city were his property. He made himself dictator for life and flaunted the trappings of monarchy. He took the queen of Egypt as his mistress and allegedly the mother of his son and installed her in his villa on the edge of town. He promoted his eighteen-year-old grandnephew over his forty-year-old lieutenants and hinted that he intended to build a dynasty. He began a new war that threatened to win him overwhelming power.

After offending both masses and elite, Caesar refused to take a proper bodyguard because it was beneath the dignity of a man of destiny such as himself. He dared his enemies to strike and so they did.

Caesar fell at the foot of the statue of Pompey, his former political partner, his former son-in-law, and his former archenemy. The blood flowed from his woolen garments to the statue base.

Writing within months if not weeks of the event, Cicero highlights the irony of it all,

> In that Senate, the greater part of which he had chosen, in Pompey's Senate House, in front of the statue of Pompey himself, with so many of his centurions watching—that he was to lie there, slaughtered by the most noble of the citizens (some of whom he furnished with everything they had) and not only would none of his friends approach his body but not even any of his slaves.

Julius Caesar lay dead, but the Republic he had left behind, still seethed in agony. Julius Caesar was dead but not buried.

9

A REPUBLIC IN THE BALANCE

I<small>T WAS A SCENE OUT OF THE ROMAN PAST. THE SENATORS,</small> wrapped in their togas and accompanied by their armed slaves, marched through the streets of Rome. They folded their togas around their left arms like shields as their ancestors did a century earlier when they killed the Gracchi and their revolutionary supporters. The senators this day had a bodyguard of gladiators, while their ancestors had Cretan archers, but otherwise, the groups were similar. One foot in the past, the men who killed Caesar marched to restore the Republic.

On the afternoon of the Ides of March, the conspirators executed the second part of their plan. The first part, assassinating the dictator in the Senate House of Pompey, had succeeded. Now came the next phase. The plan: While they rallied public support and protected themselves from the vengeance of Caesar's soldiers, the Senate would retake control of the Republic. Then they would look beyond Rome and take control of Caesar's thirty-five legions while preventing rebellion and securing the frontiers. But things didn't work out that way.

The conventional wisdom about the assassins is that they knew how to kill their man but they hadn't the slightest idea what to do next. Like all hindsight, that view is twenty-twenty. It goes back to Cicero, who confided in a letter in May 44 B.C. that he thought the assassination was done "with manly spirit but childish judgment." Cicero was too harsh. Caesar's killers achieved their goal of stopping one man from ruling Rome. Now they wanted to revitalize the Republic.

Who would represent the conspirators to the Senate and the people after the assassination? Not Decimus—he was a military man. He had spent most of his adult life in Gaul and had little experience of Roman politics. Besides, he quickly became the focus of public anger after the assassination. Decimus's job was to provide the assassins security with his gladiators. He probably wanted to settle things in Rome quickly and then head for his comfort zone—the governorship and the armies of Italian Gaul.

Cassius knew Roman politics better but he too was a soldier at heart. As an accomplished orator and a man admired for his character and his famous name, Brutus was the clear choice as the public face of the conspiracy. But could he outmanuever Antony and Caesar's other leading supporters?

The Ides of March was a cleanup, not a coup, as Brutus saw it. Once the tyrant was removed, the Republic would function constitutionally again. The wisdom of the Senate would then guide both the people and the elected officials who executed the laws. This was a moderate goal but revolutions are hard on moderates. Revolutions reward extremes. Brutus wanted to return power to the Senate and the people, but the Senate lacked leadership and the people were divided. That left the army. In the five years since Caesar crossed the Rubicon, no one had ruled Rome without an army. And for sixty years before that, the shadow of military dictatorship often loomed. Only a miracle could leave the army out of the equation now.

Did the assassins understand that? Apparently they did but not well enough. They might have reasoned that with Caesar gone, his men would be loyal not to his memory but to whoever seemed to be the new Caesar—to whoever seemed strong enough to get them land and money. Even Brutus knew that but he miscalculated. He underestimated the price it would take and the speed and the determination with which Caesar's veterans would come to Rome to demand it.

The conspirators failed to expect the unexpected. Brutus, Cassius, and Decimus thought they could light a political fire and neatly put it out, but you cannot manage a revolution. They worried about their peers like Antony and Lepidus. Instead, their fate rested in the hands of Caesar's veterans. The conspirators should have worried about them, just as they should have worried about a precocious teenager who was not even in Italy— Octavian.

MARCH 15: FROM THE PORTICO OF POMPEY TO THE CAPITOLINE HILL

Uproar followed the death of Caesar. The senators fled the room shouting. The crowd outside the Senate House cried out in response. Some said the whole Senate had joined in the murder, others that a great army had come for the deed. Meanwhile, spectators ran from the gladiatorial games in the Theater of Pompey about six hundred feet away at the other end of the Portico. Rumors flew of gladiators or soldiers on a rampage.

Antony quickly made his way home, afraid for his life. The story that he exchanged his consul's toga for slave's clothes in order to escape sounds like something an enemy made up later. Still, some Romans hid themselves in their homes; some put on disguises and fled to their country villas. Everyone expected a bloodbath as in past Roman revolutions.

Meanwhile, the assassins emerged from the Senate. Brutus spoke. Some say that earlier he tried to address the senators in the Senate House of Pompey but they ran for the door. Appian says the conspirators expected the other senators to join them enthusiastically once they saw the assassination. In fact, many senators supported them, but fear ruled the moment. And yet, this was only the first scene of the drama that was Rome after Caesar. There would be time for political calculation later.

Others say that Brutus spoke to the people outside the Senate chamber and that other assassins spoke there, too. Brutus tried to calm the crowd.

More important, he seized the rhetorical high ground. There was no reason to be upset, he said, because nothing bad had happened. This was not murder, said Brutus, but the killing of a tyrant.

First came the daggers, then the honeyed words, and then came more daggers. That was the conspirators' strategy. Killing Caesar did not give them the keys to the kingdom—it merely opened the door. To take control of Rome they had to negotiate with Caesar's advisors, win the support of the urban plebs, and neutralize Caesar's soldiers. That would take time, which required a defensive base as well as a publicity and diplomacy blitz.

The conspirators now made a show of force by marching from the Portico of Pompey to the Roman Forum and up the Capitoline Hill, a distance of a little more than one-half mile. They had planned this move in advance. They had no intention of going alone. Cassius, Brutus, and Decimus led them, along with Decimus's gladiators as well as a large number of slaves, no doubt all armed.

In the most arresting image of the afternoon, the conspirators walked in the streets of Rome with their daggers drawn—"naked," as the ancient expression says—and their hands still bloody. Nicolaus says they ran in flight; Plutarch says they were most definitely not in flight but were radiant and confident. They agree that the men cried out as they went that they had acted on behalf of the public's liberty. No doubt, but there was also a warrior's simple pride in having killed a rival. Their bloody parade was something like a gladiator's victory lap in the arena. Appian claims that one assassin carried a freedman's felt cap on the end of a spear as a symbol of liberty. Cicero claims that some of them called out his name as they marched.

There is more to trust in the report that some non-assassins now took out their weapons and joined the march to the Capitoline. Between them, Appian and Plutarch name some half-dozen men. There was Marcus Favonius, the friend of Cato whom Brutus rejected for the conspiracy. Publius Cornelius Lentulus Spinther was the son of the consul of 57 B.C. Later he wrote to Cicero and had the nerve to lie, saying that he shared in the deed and the danger with Brutus and Cassius. One Gaius Octavius was probably

Gaius Octavius Balbus, no doubt a senator. Marcus Aquinus and one Patiscus both later fought for Brutus and Cassius. Lucius Staius Murcus fought for Caesar in the Civil War but now changed sides. He would soon become governor of Syria. Finally, there was Dolabella, Caesar's handpicked consul-in-waiting, who jumped ship and joined the assassins.

People ran through the streets to the Forum, galvanized by the news of Caesar's murder. Yet the center of Rome was probably less crowded than usual because many had gone to celebrate the Anna Perenna festival. Still the sources report looting and frightened people barricading themselves into their homes—perhaps accurate descriptions of panic.

The Capitoline was the smallest of Rome's hills. At about twenty-three acres in size, it was not much bigger than today's St. Peter's Square, but it was a natural fortress lined by rocky cliffs. The Capitoline Hill's main landmark was the huge Temple of Jupiter in the south, Rome's most important religious site. The northern end of the hill was known as the Arx, or Citadel. It had no walls but it was a natural fortress. The Citadel held a temple of Juno, the Roman mint, and a place of augury, where you could see all the way to the Alban Mount nearly twenty miles to the south. The saddle between the two hills was called the Asylum. Legend has it that Romulus made the place a sanctuary for foreign refugees that he wanted to attract to Rome. Several steep staircases and stepped streets provided access to the top but they could be blocked. In short, the Capitoline was easily defensible.

As soon as they reached the Capitoline, the conspirators divided the terrain into sectors and formed a defensive perimeter. The high ground was a force multiplier so they had chosen well. Anyone who attacked them on the Capitoline faced a bloody battle.

The hill was a symbolic as well as physical plateau. Between the Citadel and the Temple of Jupiter, the Capitoline Hill stood for Rome's heart and sinew, as if it were a cross between the Vatican and the Tower of London. There the men who killed Caesar could both give thanks to the gods and look down on their enemies. One source put it plainly when he said that the assassins "occupied the Capitol."

MARCH 15: THE WILL OF THE PEOPLE

If they used their legion and their veterans against the assassins' gladiators, Caesar's loyalists would have had the upper hand militarily. But on the afternoon of March 15, the focus was on persuasion. The assassins tried to win the support of the Roman people, who were divided. Some thought the killing of Caesar was the fairest of deeds and some thought it the most foul. To those who favored the assassins, Caesar had misused his mighty power and so was "justly slain"—*iure caesus*, to use a term from the old Roman law code, the Twelve Tables. To Cassius, Caesar was "the wickedest man ever killed." To Cicero, the conspirators were liberators who rightly placed the liberty of their fatherland before the ties of friendship.

Other Romans still supported Caesar. To Caesar's dear friend Gaius Matius, Caesar was a great man who had tried to leave all Romans safe and sound only to be murdered by those close to him. As Caesar's friends saw things, the dictator showed mercy to his opponents, and they paid him back with treachery and ingratitude. Caesar's supporters could accuse the killers of being motivated by "jealousy of his fortune and power." The assassins also seemed impious. By killing Caesar in a hall where the Senate met, the assassins acted in consecrated space. They were guilty, in effect, of committing murder in a temple.

The Roman people could forgive the assassins or condemn them. But how did you win the support of the Roman people? There were no opinion polls and no plebiscites. What mattered most was how the people reacted to public speeches. Applause, cheers, boos, and even rioting would be the signs of the public will.

For five days after the assassination, the Public Meeting (*contio*, in Latin) served as the instrument for gauging public opinion. It was a formal gathering called by a magistrate, featuring a variety of speeches but no voting. Public Meetings typically took place in the Roman Forum adjacent to the Capitoline Hill on the southeast. At least five separate Public Meetings were held between March 15 and March 19.

The Capitoline provided easy access to the Forum. The Rostra or

Speaker's Platform lay practically at the foot of the hill. There, the conspirators could take part in the contest for popular support. They had a chance to win over the ordinary people of Rome—the urban plebs. The plebeians were longtime backers of Caesar, but in the last six months they had started to change their minds. The plebeians loved election campaigns because they brought attention and payoffs from men running for office. But Caesar cut back on elections because he appointed most public officials himself. The plebeians resented that and they also resented his attack on their champions, the People's Tribunes. That gave Brutus and Cassius an opening, and so did Antony's unpopularity.

People remembered how Antony sent troops into the Forum in 47 B.C. and killed eight hundred supporters of debt relief. The people's champion on that occasion was Dolabella, and now *he* had joined the liberators on the Capitoline. Dolabella was also now consul like Antony. In short, the liberators had a chance of swinging the urban plebs to their side. They planned to make the most of the opportunity.

As the afternoon of the Ides proceeded without further bloodshed, a group of people began trickling up to the Capitoline. They included both senators and ordinary Romans, probably most of them friends or clients of the conspirators. One of them was Cicero.

Cicero wrote a very short letter to Minucius Basilus, one of the assassins. "Congratulations!" said Cicero, who added that he was rejoicing, that he loved his correspondent and wanted to be kept up to date. But what was he offering congratulations about? That's unclear. Some see it as acknowledgment of the assassination. If his later comments are any indication, Cicero was ecstatic at the murder of Caesar. To Decimus he called it the greatest deed in history. "Has anything greater ever been done, by holy Jupiter," he asked in a speech in 43 B.C., "not only in this city but in the whole world, anything more glorious and more valued in the eternal memory of men?" When Brutus addressed his visitors, he got enough of a response in this vein to make him decide to call a Public Meeting and give a formal speech to the people.

Along with Cassius and other conspirators, Brutus now came down from the Capitoline to the Forum. Nicolaus of Damascus says that gladiators and slaves protected them, but Nicolaus scoffed at Brutus's "supposed reasonableness," and so maybe Nicolaus invented this detail to take Brutus down a peg. The people would not respond well to such a sight, and with the Capitoline easy to retreat to, the conspirators were probably willing to leave their security behind. Plutarch, who saw Brutus as a hero, says only that a group of eminent men flanked Brutus. In any case, Brutus reached the Speaker's Platform near the foot of the Capitoline Hill. Just a month earlier, Caesar had sat on the same platform when Antony climbed up and twice put a diadem on his head, only to have Caesar remove it.

Brutus did not look his best since his hand was still injured from the wound he received in Caesar's murder. Yet, as he prepared to speak, something beautiful happened—silence. On a tumultuous day before a mixed crowd of ordinary Romans who were ready to shout him down, Brutus inspired orderly behavior. As he came forward, the audience received his words with great calm.

Brutus was a very good speaker if not an exciting one. He was frank, simple, and generous, and he had what the Romans called *gravitas*, that is, seriousness or substance. Cicero, writing privately, found his speeches tedious and lax and other critics called them dull and cold. But those qualities might have proved reassuring on this occasion.

We cannot reconstruct Brutus's speech. Cassius and others spoke as well, and, as usual, the sources offer only the gist of what the speakers "should" have said. So, the speakers criticized Caesar and praised the rule of the people. They said that they had not killed Caesar for the sake of power but only to be free, independent, and governed rightly. They referred to their ancestors who had expelled the kings and said that Caesar was even worse than the kings because he took power by violence. Appian, who writes scathingly about the conspirators, accuses them of boastfulness and self-congratulation. He says they especially thanked Decimus for providing gladiators at a key moment. He also says they advocated the recall of the tribunes deposed by Caesar. And he says they asked for something incendiary—the recall from Spain of Sextus Pompey, the surviving son of

Pompey, who was still fighting Caesar's lieutenants. Nicolaus is probably referring to Cassius when he has a speaker say that lengthy planning went into the assassination because of the presence of Caesar's troops and great commanders. That speaker also warns that greater evils might erupt.

Why then did the people treat Brutus so kindly? The sources disagree markedly. Cicero wrote to his friend Atticus that the people were "burning with enthusiasm" for Brutus and Cassius in the days following the assassination. Nicolaus says that many people came to join the men on the Capitoline on March 15 and 16, when Caesar's friends were still terrified. Appian maintains just the opposite—the people hated the assassins but they were intimidated into silence. Appian claims that Brutus and Cassius had hired a claque of foreigners, freedmen, and slaves to infiltrate the assembly and silence the real Roman citizens. But the Romans commonly tossed around such charges and we don't have to take them seriously. Plutarch says that the crowd was silent out of respect for Brutus and pity for Caesar. They admired Brutus's words but disapproved of the assassination. Nicolaus says that the people were confused and anxious about what the next revolutionary deed might be. That, and their respect for Brutus and his famous family, explains their silence.

Consider another possibility. Perhaps the people recognized that Brutus was that rarest of all things—an honest man. Perhaps they reasoned thus: If Brutus wanted power, why didn't he have troops at the city's gates? If he cared only for himself, why didn't he stick with his benefactor, Caesar? Perhaps the Romans understood that Brutus really meant what he later said— that his goal was liberty and peace.

Then came a disturbing note for the conspirators. Another senator, the praetor Lucius Cornelius Cinna, rose to speak. He was the brother of the late Cornelia, Caesar's first wife, and uncle of the late and much-loved Julia, Caesar's daughter. Cinna's father was a famous Populist and supporter of Marius. Caesar had made Cinna praetor for 44 B.C., an act of kindness to a man who had suffered persecution because of Sulla. Cinna accepted the honor but now he theatrically took off his toga of office and scorned it as the gift of a tyrant. Although not a conspirator, he condemned Caesar and praised his killers as tyrant slayers who deserved public honors. The crowd reacted with so much anger that the conspirators had to return to the Capitoline. Plutarch says this showed how much the people objected to the assassination, but their real objection was to Cinna's disgraceful behavior. Caesar was not only Cinna's benefactor but also his late sister's husband, which created a kinship relationship by marriage—violating that relationship as Cinna had done was not something the Romans took lightly. In short, Cinna was the wrong salesman for the assassination.

It was probably that same afternoon that Dolabella got a more favorable reaction to the conspiracy when he too called a Public Meeting and delivered a formal speech. Although Antony had not yet given up his objections to the appointment, Dolabella put on his toga of office as consul and addressed the Roman people in the Forum. He turned on his former champion, Caesar, and praised the assassins. Some sources say that Dolabella even proposed making the Ides of March the birthday of the state. The supporters of the conspirators took heart at the sight of a consul on their side.

The bottom line is that the Roman people had not yet made up their mind. They watched and waited and gathered information about the various players in the great drama. Public opinion was still up for grabs.

In addition to speaking to the Roman people, the conspirators decided to open negotiations with Antony. He was the highest-ranking person in Rome and he might want to make peace, especially because they had spared his life. They sent a delegation of ex-consuls to talk to him. Just what the terms were, we do not know. Cicero, who reports the news, says that they wanted him to tell Antony to defend the Republic, which sounds like an invitation to dump Caesar's friends and join them. Cicero wasn't having any of it. Reporting that he didn't trust Antony, he refused to join the other ex-consuls who went on the mission.

On the contrary, Cicero wanted the liberators, as he called them, to do an end run around Antony. On that "first day on the Capitoline," as he wrote later, he declared that Brutus and Cassius should call the Senate to a meeting on the Capitoline Hill. As praetors, they had the right to do so, and the Capitoline did indeed house Senate meetings from time to time in the Temple of Jupiter. "By the immortal gods," he wrote, what couldn't have been accomplished then, when "all the good men, even those who were only moderately good, were joyful, while the criminals were powerless?"

A supporter of Antony later wrote that after Caesar's assassination, the Republic seemed to be in the hands of "the two Brutuses [that is, Brutus and Decimus] and Cassius" and "the whole state moved towards them." That was an exaggeration, but perhaps it captures the excited mood of the assassins. If Appian is right, most of the senators sympathized with the assassins. In that case, what of the great number of senators appointed by Caesar? Appian says that even some of them found his actions repugnant or they were cynical turncoats like Cinna. Some senators gave the assassins the honorable name of tyrant slayer or tyrannicide. Others wanted to vote them public honors. Alive, Caesar had injured the conspirators' dignitas. Now that they had killed him many of their peers approved of their deed.

But that was probably not clear yet on the afternoon of March 15. Earlier that day the conspirators saw how few senators stood by them. Why expect more to show up now? No one would be impressed by the rulings of a rump Senate. Or so they might have thought. Besides, it might have been getting late and Senate meetings were illegal after dark. Better to keep the pressure on Antony by rallying public support to their cause.

MARCH 15: CAESAR GOES HOME

Meanwhile, back at the Senate House of Pompey, Caesar's corpse lay unattended. Caesar's friends left it there. His supporters fled from the Portico of Pompey but not before some of them made other arrangements. The story goes that one repentant Caesar supporter even paused before leaving the Senate House to spit out angry words over the body, "Enough service to a tyrant."

Only three slaves remained behind to tend to Caesar's body, which they put into a litter. These three ordinary slaves carried Caesar's litter home, a sad contrast to the grand escort that had brought him to the Portico of Pompey that morning. Since it took four slaves to carry a litter, the three bearers walked haltingly and with many stops. The curtains of the litter were raised and people could see Caesar's hands hanging down and his wounded face. According to Nicolaus, they cried at the sight.

The slaves' route took them past the foot of the Capitoline and through the Forum. Mourning, groans, and lamentation followed them on both sides from the streets, doorways, and rooftops. When they finally neared Caesar's house, an even greater shrieking greeted them. A crowd of women and slaves emerged accompanying Calpurnia. Remembering her warning that morning, she called Caesar's name and said that destiny had treated him even worse than she had expected.

Suetonius says that the conspirators planned to drag Caesar's body to the Tiber after killing him as well as confiscate his property and revoke his decrees, but that they held back out of fear of Antony and Lepidus. That's not credible. Maybe that is what Cicero had in mind for the Senate meeting he wanted to hold on the Capitoline Hill that day. Neither a moderate like Brutus nor the most hard-bitten cynic would have stood for it. The assassins needed Caesar's corpse as a bargaining chip.

Sometime before the day ended, a storm hit Rome. There was tremendous thunder with violent and heavy rain. To some, it seemed like the heavens were proclaiming Pompey's revenge over his rival.

As the sun set on the Ides of March—around 6:15 P.M. on March 15 in Rome—nothing was clear. Antony and Lepidus promised a response the next day to the embassy of ex-consuls. Everyone wondered what would happen next. Both sides had weapons and the outcome was uncertain. It was hard to think about the public interest when people feared for their own safety.

MARCH 16:
A GATHERING AT ANTONY'S HOUSE

The fate of Rome was decided in hundreds of gatherings during the days after Caesar's murder. They ranged from nighttime consultations in private homes to sessions of the Senate that began at dawn, from huddled councils in the occupied buildings of the Capitoline to a formal reading of the dictator's will in a posh town house, and from groups of armed men surging through the streets with shouted threats to public assemblies in the Roman Forum.

The story of the days following the Ides of March is a paradox. On the one hand, they are part of probably the best-documented year in Roman history thanks to Cicero's many surviving letters. On the other hand, Cicero says little about the March days and the other sources often disagree. The overall picture is clear but the details require a certain amount of guesswork.

The men who seized and defended the Capitoline Hill feared an attack from Caesar's soldiers. The first step came in the afternoon of March 15. Lepidus moved his soldiers from the Tiber Island to the Field of Mars, the site of the assassination. Then, in the night, he moved them again to the Roman Forum, on the east side of the Capitoline Hill. They probably marched along the road that led eastward to the city walls then they passed through the Carmental Gate and skirted the Capitoline Hill along the street known as the Vicus Iugarius, which led to the Forum. You could not legally bring an army within the walls of Rome, but the Civil War had seen many laws broken and the war had ended only months before. Pompey and even Cicero, that great republican, had each in his day summoned soldiers into Rome to put down unrest.

The next day, March 16, was a day of speeches, saber rattling, and plotting. At dawn in the Roman Forum, Lepidus called a Public Meeting and delivered a speech against the assassins. Antony was in attendance. He wore armor, as was his right as consul. Lepidus probably wore military garb as well. The audience is likely to have included Caesar's veterans and ordinary Romans as well as the troops that Lepidus commanded. Lepidus was ready to take his troops and assault the Capitoline Hill in order to avenge Caesar. The attack would surely succeed and kill at least some of the conspirators, perhaps including his two brothers-in-law, Brutus and Cassius. But Lepidus waited for a meeting later that day.

It was a gathering of Caesar's close supporters in Mark Antony's house. This was a grand structure, complete with two colonnaded courts and a bath. It covered about 24,000 square feet, about the size of a modern mansion and much larger than the average luxury house in Rome in its era. Formerly the town house of Pompey the Great, it was acquired by Antony when he disposed of Pompey's properties for Caesar. It was located in an elegant and fashionable residential district called *Carinae,* or the Keels, because certain buildings there looked like ships' keels.

The meeting lasted until evening. Lepidus and Caesar's faithful lieutenant Aulus Hirtius were key players but other Caesar supporters were there, too. Lepidus argued for a military attack on the assassins in the name of avenging Caesar. Someone else agreed, calling it both unholy and unsafe to leave Caesar's death unavenged—unholy presumably because these men had sworn to defend Caesar with their lives and unsafe because once the assassins gained power, they would exchange their present inactivity for something dangerous. Hirtius disagreed; he argued for negotiations and friendship. Killing the assassins would start a vendetta by their powerful friends and relatives and call down certain condemnation by the Senate. Then, too, if they started a war, they would have to face Decimus, who was about to become governor of Italian Gaul, a position to which Caesar had appointed him. This strategic province housed two legions capable of reaching Rome in less than two weeks. If they looked like winners, more troops would follow.

Other provinces were also matters of concern. Gaius Matius feared an uprising in Belgian Gaul at the news of Caesar's death; not until mid-April did the good news come to Rome that the tribes there had promised obedience. Supporters of Pompey controlled Syria and much of Hispania. Sextus Pompey had warships and, he would soon claim, seven legions. No match for the thirty-five legions that Caesar had gathered for war with Parthia, but to whom would those legions be loyal?

Antony's was the most important voice both because he was consul and because he was a man with a record of getting things done. He favored negotiation. Antony had no troops of his own and probably was not eager to see Lepidus get the credit for any military success. Besides, Antony perhaps learned his lesson from the backlash after he unleashed the army in the Forum in 47 B.C. He may have concluded that it was better to hold the soldiers in the background as an intimidating presence than to use them for bloodshed and recriminations.

In the short term, therefore, Brutus was right and Cassius was wrong—letting Antony live on March 15 was the smart move. In the long term, however, Antony would prove to be a deadly enemy to the liberators, a far shrewder operator than they had expected. Even then, however, he was not their biggest problem.

The conferees at Antony's house decided to negotiate. They would merely postpone vengeance, hoping to be able to wean Decimus's army away from him. To the ex-consuls sent from the Capitoline Hill, the conferees replied with stern words about having to drive out the few guilty parties who had killed Caesar or else suffer a divine curse. But they proposed a Senate meeting in which the two sides could work out a common course. The men on the Capitoline Hill were happy to agree on a session for the next day, March 17.

What followed was a long night in Rome, lit with fires as a sign of activity. Antony stationed guards around the city for safety's sake. The assassins sent men to one senator's house after another, trying to drum up support. At the same time, leaders of Caesar's veterans prowled the streets, trying to intimidate the friends of the assassins and issuing threats about the consequences if anyone interfered with their land grants. Meanwhile, people began to notice just how few assassins and their friends there were. Those who first cheered the death of the tyrant began to have second thoughts.

But the most important event of the night took place in the Public Mansion. Antony got control both of Caesar's private fortune and his state papers, either because Calpurnia thought they would be safer with him than in her house or because he ordered it as consul. According to Plutarch, Caesar's fortune amounted to 4,000 talents—that is, a huge sum, on the order of 250,000 pounds of silver. In politics, money and knowledge are both power, and Antony now had plenty of each.

MARCH 17: THE SENATE MEETS

Before first light on the morning of March 17, the senators began gathering for a session to start at daybreak. The Senate met in the Temple of Tellus, a Roman earth goddess. We know of no other Senate meeting in this location. The Temple of Jupiter on the Capitoline was under occupation. The Temple of Concord sat at the foot of the Capitoline, in reach of Decimus's gladiators. The Senate House of Pompey was a ghoulish thought. There were other temples in Rome, but the Temple of Tellus was on the Carinae, far from the Capitoline Hill and close to Antony's house, so it seemed safe. Still, Lepidus made a show of strength and brought troops to the temple, where they occupied the entrances—and a good thing, too. Cinna appeared for the meeting, this time wearing his praetorian robe. When some people, including Caesar's veterans, saw him, they promptly stoned him and chased him into a nearby house that they were about to set on fire when Lepidus and his soldiers arrived to stop them.

By now, March 17, more of Caesar's veterans were starting to arrive in Rome from the towns where he had settled them or from the confiscated lands they had acquired. Some came on their own initiative, others in response to calls from Antony, Lepidus, or other friends of Caesar. Honor and self-interest alike gave the soldiers grounds to strike. Caesar was their chief and their patron but now he was dead and they were afraid of losing everything. Nicolaus claims that most of the conspirators' supporters melted away at the sight of the veteran soldiers—an exaggeration, no doubt, but the direction of the wind was beginning to shift.

The Temple of Tellus offered reminders both of the Republic's defenders and its enemies. It was built on land confiscated long ago from a leader of the Early Republic who was accused of wanting to be a king, and who was convicted and executed. A statue of Ceres, goddess of agriculture, paid for from his property, stood in front of the temple. So did a statue of Cicero's brother Quintus, put up recently by Cicero. Quintus was a symbol of dangerous times—he served Caesar as a commander in Gaul and Britain before then supporting Pompey in the Civil War and finally receiving Caesar's pardon. So much for the exterior of the Temple of Tellus—as they deliberated inside the temple, the senators looked at a map of Italy painted on an interior wall, a vivid reminder of the heart of the empire at stake.

The Senate meeting was long and dramatic even though the assassins did not dare come down from the Capitoline. Supporters such as Cicero represented their side. What the senators decided in the end is well documented in reliable sources. The details of the debate come largely from Appian and Dio, making them plausible rather than factual. As consul, Antony set the tone of compromise from the outset. The speakers included Cicero and Caesar's father-in-law, Piso. Debate was vigorous. It turned out that many if not most senators had been uneasy with Caesar and his kinglike ways. Some said the murderers deserved a reward for killing a tyrant, others that they should merely be thanked as public benefactors.

Lucius Munatius Plancus made an impression as a voice of moderation. A trusted officer of Caesar in Gaul and the Civil War, Plancus was about to take up the governorship of Transalpine Gaul, but he was also close to Cicero.

One of those who favored rewarding the assassins for killing a tyrant was Tiberius Claudius Nero. He had served Caesar as a commander in the Civil War as well as an official in Gaul, but apparently he found Caesar's monarchical ways unbearable. (Ironically, he would later father a son who became Emperor Tiberius.)

Neither a reward nor thanks were acceptable to Caesar's friends, but even they were willing to give the killers amnesty on the grounds of their distinguished families. Caesar's enemies demanded a vote on the character of Caesar, but Antony intervened. If Caesar was declared a tyrant then his administrative arrangements around the empire would be null and void. Meanwhile, anyone who held high office thanks to Caesar would have to resign. Since Caesar had arranged Rome's public offices for the next five years, hundreds of men would have to resign, and they had no intention of doing so. Dolabella, whom Antony now recognized as co-consul, did an about-face from his support of the assassins the day before. Now that his own job was on the line, he spoke strongly against calling Caesar a tyrant or honoring the murderers.

Meanwhile, a crowd gathered outside, and Antony and Lepidus went out to address it. "Peace!" called some and "vengeance!" cried others. Antony said that as consul he couldn't support vengeance, tempted though he was. When one in the crowd threatened Antony, he loosened his tunic to show the armor beneath it. He used the occasion to remind people of Caesar's clemency and of the oaths that his murderers had abused.

The advocates of vengeance called on Lepidus to carry out their will. Before he could answer, they insisted that he come to the Roman Forum, where they could hear him better, so he did. Lepidus stood on the Speaker's Platform and made for a sad sight. He groaned and wept there for a long time. When he recovered, he spoke. He said he remembered standing there just yesterday, as it seemed, with Caesar, and now he was forced to ask what the people wanted him to do about Caesar's murder. Once again, cries both for peace and vengeance rang out. Like Antony, Lepidus admitted to wanting vengeance, but it was more important, he said, to spare Roman lives.

When they returned to the Senate, Antony spoke in favor of a compromise—extending protection to the assassins and ratifying Caesar's acts. If Appian is right, he was not subtle about the danger posed by the thousands of Caesar's veterans who were in Rome and armed. They wanted their land and they wanted Caesar's memory honored—or else. Antony proposed that the assassins be spared only as an act of clemency.

Cicero gave a long speech. He summarized Rome's current state: the Capitol was occupied, the Forum filled with arms and the whole city with fear. He agreed with Antony about the need to compromise, leaving the assassins unpunished and Caesar's acts in force. His preferences were different no doubt, since Cicero called Caesar a king in private. What Cicero did achieve was to substitute the notion of amnesty for clemency. The word *clemency* was too closely tied to Caesar. He gave the senators a history lesson, citing the case of Athens where, after a bloody civil war, the people wisely passed an amnesty, and then went on to prosperity at home and victory abroad. Cicero actually used the Greek word, *amnestia*. He advised the senators to act in a similar spirit for the sake of moving forward.

After the speeches, a decree passed guaranteeing the assassins immunity from prosecution while also ratifying all Caesar's acts and decrees, but only "since it is advantageous to the state." The friends of the assassins—surely including Cicero—insisted on this condition because anything more favorable to Caesar might sound like a condemnation of the murder. Ironically, men like Decimus, Brutus, and Cassius stood to gain from the ratification of Caesar's acts, because it confirmed them as public officials. Meanwhile, under pressure from Caesar's veterans, the Senate passed two more decrees confirming the new colonists who were about to take possession of their lands as well as those who already held theirs.

It was at this meeting or one shortly afterward that Antony moved to abolish the dictatorship. The Senate agreed. So Caesar was not only Rome's most powerful dictator ever but also its last.

Antony's reputation soared as people hailed him for his statesmanship. But Cicero never trusted Antony and considered this merely a tactical retreat. He believed that Antony wanted Caesar's power and that he would push for it as soon as possible. But Cicero himself had no taste for compromise. For him, restoring the Republic meant crushing Caesar's supporters.

At least one person was undoubtedly happy with the compromise of March 17—Brutus. True, the assassins failed to have Caesar branded a tyrant. True, they failed to get the honor they craved. But Brutus wanted peace and moderation, and he got it. As far as he was concerned, the tyrant was dead. The Senate and the People could regain their power; Rome could move on.

Cicero later said in private that he called for a compromise only because the liberators, as he called them, had already lost. He couldn't speak freely in that Senate meeting, he said. What choice did he have but to defend the veterans with all his power of argument, seeing that they were present and armed, and he had no bodyguard? In public though, he praised Antony for his speech in the Senate and for his goodwill.

MARCH 17: RECONCILIATION

That same day, March 17, the conspirators invited the Roman people to the Capitoline and a large number accepted. Brutus addressed them, speaking, it seems, either in or near the Temple of Jupiter, where the Senate often met. Appian reports what Brutus is supposed to have said. After delivering the speech, Brutus prepared it for publication. Appian's words might reflect the published version.

Before publication, Brutus sent a draft to Cicero for his comments. Cicero wrote privately that the speech was the height of elegance in both its sentiments and its words but that it lacked fire. Cicero wanted thunderbolts in the manner of Demosthenes, the great Greek orator who combined elegance with gravitas. Appian's version of the speech has no thunderbolts but it is a hard-hitting speech.

Brutus met head-on the charges against the conspirators, that by killing Caesar they violated their oaths and by occupying the Capitol they were making peace impossible. As for the latter charge, Brutus said they were forced to take refuge on the Capitoline Hill because of the sudden and unexpected attack on Cinna. That was false since the conspirators climbed the hill before that attack, but it made for a good story. Turning to the subject of Caesar, the oath to hold him sacrosanct was made under compulsion, said Brutus, so it had no force.

Brutus painted a scathing but accurate portrait of Caesar. The defrocked governor of Gaul invaded his own country, killing a large number of its best and noblest citizens, including the strongest supporters of the Republic. He denied Romans their liberty and insisted that he, Caesar, arrange all things according to his command. He attacked the People's Tribunes, officials whom all Romans were sworn to consider sacred and inviolable.

Then Brutus turned to a key constituency, Caesar's veterans. He understood their anxiety about getting or keeping the land that Caesar had promised them. Brutus protested what he called slander directed against him and the other conspirators. They would never take the veterans' new holdings away from them. The men deserved those lands because of their glorious service in Gaul and Britain. Brutus objected only to Caesar's practice of stealing property from his political enemies in Italy. The conspirators would now pay compensation to the former landowners from public funds but they would guarantee the veterans what they now had. They swore that by the god Jupiter himself.

Caesar, said Brutus, purposely drove a wedge between the veterans and the former landowners to stir up trouble. Sulla behaved similarly. Brutus cleverly lumped Caesar and Sulla together, which might have reminded some in the audience that Brutus's father was a Populist who had opposed Sulla. To sum up the speech in a phrase, Caesar was a tyrant.

Fine words but not enough. In retrospect, Brutus's speech was a lost opportunity. To succeed in Roman politics now, you couldn't just let the soldiers keep what they had—you had to give them more. Caesar's generosity was yesterday's news. Rather than waste precious resources on his rich, landowning friends, Brutus should have lavished those resources on the soldiers. If Brutus didn't have something new to offer the troops then somebody else would.

If Brutus could defend himself, he might say Caesar's veterans were a lost cause, especially in the emotional days following their fallen chief's murder. Better to focus now on the political game in Rome, for which Brutus needed the support of former Pompey allies and others whose land had been confiscated. If he failed politically, there would be time later to buy other soldiers, less wedded to Caesar than men who needed to keep Caesar's memory alive in order to protect their property.

Brutus might say one other thing, too. If the Ides of March proved anything, it proved that the military did not decide everything in Roman politics. For all his military power, Caesar had lost legitimacy among large parts of the Roman people and the Senate, including some of his closest supporters. That cost him his life. So, Brutus might reply, it was vitally important to win the debate.

But such arguments do not convince. It was worth trying to buy the loyalty of Caesar's soldiers, if only to force Caesar's supporters into bankruptcy if they wanted to compete to keep the soldiers loyal. And the soldiers, in the end, had a very loud voice.

At the time Brutus's speech appeared to be a hit. People called it fair and righteous. The conspirators seemed not only bold but also caring. The crowd promised support.

Next came the consuls' time to speak. They addressed the Roman people from the Speaker's Platform, below the Capitoline, and explained what the Senate had decided. In addition to Antony and Dolabella, Cicero spoke as well. Dio says that the conspirators sent a letter down the hill in which they promised not to confiscate anyone's property and said they considered all of Caesar's acts valid. In other words, they reassured Caesar's veterans that they could keep their lands. They called for harmony among all citizens and even, says Dio, swore the strongest oaths—ironic, if true, considering Brutus's critique of oaths.

The people now called for the conspirators to come down from the Capitoline. Brutus and Cassius agreed but only on condition that hostages were provided. And so Antony and Lepidus sent their sons up the hill. Antony's son was a mere toddler. Hostages were not unusual as a way of safeguarding a conference in times of civil war. Their use shows just how uneasy the peace was.

Brutus and Cassius came down. The delighted crowd broke into shouts and applause. They wouldn't let the consuls speak until they first shook hands with their enemies, as they did. Perhaps, as Appian says, Antony and Dolabella fretted that the political initiative had passed to the conspirators. To some, it looked like the majority of Romans were glad to be rid of Caesar's one-man rule.

Caesar's supporters now hosted their friends or relatives among the conspirators for dinner. Under a promise of safety, Brutus went to his brother-in-law Lepidus, while Cassius went to Antony. There followed surely the two most tense reconciliation dinners in Rome's long history. No details survive of Brutus's dinner at Lepidus's, but Lepidus might have felt Caesar's presence there, just as he felt it on the Speaker's Platform that morning.

After all, Caesar had dined at Lepidus's only the day before his assassination. At his dinner with Cassius, Antony is said to have engaged in black humor. He asked Cassius if he had a dagger under his armpit, possibly a reference to the famous assassination of a would-be tyrant by Brutus's ancestor, Servilius Ahala, who concealed a military dagger under his armpit. If so, it was a subtle dig at Cassius, who lacked such a family tree. Cassius supposedly responded harshly, saying that he certainly did have a dagger—and a big one—if Antony was eager to be a tyrant. But big daggers don't fit under armpits.

It was not difficult for educated nobles like Antony and Cassius to exchange barbs and break bread. Coming out on top of the political struggle would be harder. Restoring peace in Rome without another civil war would be the toughest task of all.

10

A FUNERAL TO REMEMBER

Caesar was dead but not buried. In a city that made political theater out of the matter of laying its noble dead to rest, this was no small point. The struggle for Rome's future now shifted from Caesar's acts and the assassins' status to Caesar's funeral and the process of mourning. The tense atmosphere was about to get even more stressful.

MARCH 18: A PUBLIC FUNERAL?

Cassius pressed the point the day after his dinner party at Antony's. The Senate was meeting again in a session pushed for by Piso, Caesar's father-in-law. Caesar had named Piso the guardian of his last will and testament. Now Piso demanded that Caesar's will be read in public and that Caesar get a state funeral, a rare honor that had been given only to Sulla and a few others. Antony strongly supported both measures but Cassius just as strongly opposed them. So, in private, did Cicero's friend Atticus. He predicted that a public funeral would destroy the conspirators' cause. Funerals for Roman

nobles were usually private but even they were often political; public funerals packed a stronger punch still. Perhaps Atticus thought of Sulla's splendid
and intimidating military rites thirty-five years earlier. Ironically, on that
occasion, Lepidus's father had strongly opposed the public ceremony but
he was outvoted. More recently, massive violence had broken out at the
private funeral of the demagogue Clodius in 52 B.C. But Brutus gave in on
both points. The Senate voted in favor of reading Caesar's will in public and
holding a state funeral. Antony secured the right to give the funeral oration.
The same meeting confirmed Caesar's status as a god.

In retrospect, allowing Caesar's funeral was a mistake, but Brutus might
have said there was no choice. Popular desire for compromise demanded it.
Besides, as Appian has Antony say, Caesar's soldiers would never tolerate it
if Caesar's body were dragged, abused, and cast out like a tyrant's corpse.
How could they feel secure about their property if the man who gave it
to them was treated so outrageously? Perhaps Brutus took comfort in the
behavior of Lepidus's soldiers at the Temple of Tellus the day before when
they saved Cinna from a mob that included Caesar's veterans. Perhaps he
reasoned that the same soldiers would keep things from getting out of hand
at Caesar's funeral. Perhaps Lepidus even promised that. We don't know.

A great deal depended on the soldiers, both the legionaries and the veterans. Brutus would probably never admit that the Senate was at their mercy
but, by the same token, he didn't oppose what they wanted.

MARCH 19: LAST WILL AND TESTAMENT

The next day, March 19, Antony presided over the reading of Caesar's
will in Antony's house. It was the document Caesar had signed the previous September 15 in his villa south of Rome and then given to the Vestal
Virgins for safekeeping. Neither Antony nor Decimus, Caesar's traveling
companions on the journey from Gaul back to Italy the previous summer,
got much. The big winner was Octavian. He inherited three-quarters of
Caesar's private fortune while the rest went to Octavian's cousins Pedius and
Pinarius, also descended from Caesar's sister. Caesar posthumously adopted

JULIUS
CAESAR.
This marble
bust shows
something
of the man's
force and
intelligence
as well as his
wrinkles and
sunken cheeks.
(Scala/Art Resource, NY)

COIN OF JULIUS CAESAR, 44 B.C. The dictator is shown in profile with wreathed head and identified as CAESAR IMPERATOR, that is, as conquering general. (© BnF, Dist. RMN-Grand Palais / Art Resource, NY)

POMPEY THE GREAT. Caesar's great rival. (Alinari/Art Resource, NY)

MARK ANTONY. This marble bust shows the soldier-statesman who supported Caesar in all his vigor. *(Alinari/Art Resource, NY)*

OCTAVIAN. The man who would later become the emperor Augustus is shown with a beard as a sign of mourning for Julius Caesar. *(Erich Lessing/Art Resource, NY)*

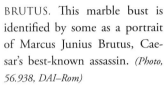

BRUTUS. This marble bust is identified by some as a portrait of Marcus Junius Brutus, Caesar's best-known assassin. *(Photo, 56.938, DAI–Rom)*

CICERO. Rome's greatest orator was a leading opponent of Caesar. *(Alinari/Art Resource, NY)*

ROMAN WOMAN OF THE UPPER CLASSES. Notice her elaborately folded clothing, carefully groomed hair, and calm expression. Gilded Bronze Statue of an unidentified person, late first century B.C., from the Cartoceto Group from Pergola. *(Scala/ Art Resource, NY)*

RELIEF OF CLEOPATRA AND CAESARION. Temple of Hathor, Dendera, Egypt. Elsewhere Cleopatra is depicted as a Greek, but here she and her son by Caesar are shown as Egyptians. *(HIP/ Art Resource, NY)*

FORUM OF JULIUS CAESAR. Temple of
Venus Genetrix (Venus the Mother) and
statue of Caesar on horseback, conception
of the artist Olindo Grossi (1909–2002).
(© American Academy in Rome 2014)

CASSIUS. A marble bust identified by
some as Gaius Cassius Longinus, one of
Caesar's leading assassins as well as Brutus's
brother-in-law. *(Montreal, Museum of Fine Arts)*

GARDENS AND PORTICO OF POMPEY. As conceived by the Italian artist Augusto Trabacchi (d. 1975). (© *American Academy in Rome 2014*)

EID MAR. The Ides of March on a silver denarius of Marcus Junius Brutus, who is depicted in profile on one side, with two daggers and a liberty cap on the other side. (© *The Trustees of the British Museum / Art Resource, NY*)

THE DEATH OF CAESAR. The legend as depicted in an oil painting from 1867 by the French artist Jean-Léon Gérôme. (*Walters Art Museum, Baltimore*)

Octavian into his family and gave him his name—Caesar. He named several of his assassins as guardians of his son should one be born to him. Their names are not known but Decimus was probably one of them because Caesar gave him an additional honor: he named Decimus as heir in the second degree, in case the first heirs were unable or unwilling to take up their inheritance. Antony received a similar honor.

Surely Decimus knew or guessed Caesar's choice of Octavian when he joined the conspiracy, but loyal Antony might have been surprised. Making Caesar's name all the more valuable, Caesar left a huge political contribution to the Roman people. He bequeathed every citizen a cash bonus of three hundred sesterces (equal to 75 denarii), just a little less than the amount he gave them at his triumphs in 46 B.C. In addition, Caesar converted his estate across the Tiber, Caesar's Gardens, now housing Cleopatra, into a public park. Even from beyond the grave, Caesar was the consummate politician, catering to his supporters among the urban plebs.

Caesar's will was probably read in public. At any rate, word of its provisions got out. Caesar's generosity turned the heat up on the men who killed him, especially Decimus, whose status as an alternate heir and assassin was scandalous.

Let us pause and consider what the scene looked like to Antony on March 19. It was the eve of Caesar's funeral. Antony's patron, Caesar, was dead. He had barely mentioned Antony in his will. Instead, Caesar had made Octavian his heir. Antony's enemy Dolabella had seized the consulship and Antony had to accept that. Antony's colleague Lepidus had an army and he did not. Neither the Senate nor the people had turned their righteous anger on the murderers. By confirming Caesar's acts, the Senate left Decimus about to take up the governorship of Italian Gaul and another assassin, Trebonius, about to become governor of Roman Asia (western Turkey). These were two important provinces because Italian Gaul was of great military value and Roman Asia could be milked for its wealth. However, things weren't all negative for Antony. By managing the compromise of March 17, he had scored points with moderate public opinion, and by arranging approval for a public funeral, he had pleased Caesar's supporters.

Still, Antony's future looked uncertain. His "friends" included rivals like Octavian and Lepidus. Then there were the assassins and their allies, many of them Pompey allies who wanted their property back. As the man who had auctioned off Pompey's property, Antony had to worry about their vengeance, especially with Sextus Pompey waiting in the wings.

In this tangle of troubles there appeared a red thread—Caesar's funeral. As consul, friend, and Caesar's distant relative, Antony had obtained the right to deliver the funeral oration. Suddenly he had the best soapbox in Rome—and he seized the occasion. Like Brutus, Antony was married to a woman who could steer him toward action. Fulvia, Antony's wife, was Clodius's widow. She had played an active role in the demagogue's funeral in 52 B.C. and she could show Antony how these things were done. In Rome, funerals and mourning were women's work, but a woman as able as Fulvia could leverage them to her advantage in a man's world.

But there was another important factor besides Antony's actions. Day by day, Caesar's veterans poured into Rome "in vast numbers." This influx was a game changer. It was not predictable. Yes, the call would go out—that was to be expected. Yes, Caesar's troops loved him when he was alive. But most men had only one way to get to Rome—on foot. Many had to walk a hundred miles or more. Yet they came. They loved Caesar, they hated his murder, and they feared for their newfound wealth. Their journey was informal and disorganized, and yet, in its own quiet way, it was a march on Rome every bit as effective as if the legions had come with standards raised and trumpets blowing.

Caesar was dead but Caesarism lived on. That was the secret of Roman politics that was revealed in the third week of March 44 B.C. The Senate still met and issued decrees. The people still commanded enough respect that the magistrates courted them in public speeches. Yet, in the final analysis, it was Caesar's veterans converging on Rome with their weapons who had the last say. They might have forgotten their loyalty to Caesar if the assassins had paid them a bonus or increased their land allotments, but the assassins offered too little to win their trust. Cassius saw it coming and, as a military man, perhaps Decimus did, too.

As consul, as a successful general, and as Caesar's close ally, Antony was now the natural leader of a large force. If he played his hand well at Caesar's funeral he could cement his position. On March 17, he had supported amnesty, but now, Antony went for the jugular. Without formally repealing the amnesty, he showed who really ran Rome. Antony was an opportunist but, given his vulnerability, who wouldn't be?

MARCH 20: THEY CAME TO BURY CAESAR

Shakespeare plays up the drama of Caesar's funeral. He should only have known! The real funeral was even more theatrical than the product of the Bard's pen.

The funerals of Roman nobles always were shows. The classic elements were: the body lying in state for seven days; a funeral procession carrying the body to the Roman Forum; a family member or professional actor dressed in beeswax mask and costume to represent the deceased while others in the procession wore beeswax masks of famous ancestors of the deceased; a funeral oration delivered from the Speaker's Platform; the burial; and a banquet. Caesar's spectacular funeral combined music, acting, a procession, a chorus, a eulogy, props, a funeral pyre to rival a Gallic chieftain's, and, finally, a riot. The assassination of Caesar could not compare to Caesar's funeral. A murder carried out indoors before several hundred members of the Roman elite followed by a parade to the Capitol of gladiators and dagger-wielding senators was no small thing, but it could not match an event that filled the Roman Forum with many thousands of people.

Caesar had left instructions for his funeral with his niece, Atia, Octavian's mother. But Caesar did not plan on being murdered and the funeral highlighted that crime. Someone must have adapted Caesar's plan, and that someone was probably Antony.

In recent decades Rome had seen several spectacular funerals. The greatest was the public funeral for Sulla the Dictator in 78 B.C. Sulla died in his villa on the Bay of Naples. His body was carried to Rome on a golden litter, preceded by trumpeters and horsemen, and followed by armed infantrymen with his military standards and fasces in the very front. Once in Rome, a procession made its way through the streets, allegedly carrying more than two thousand golden crowns, which were the gifts of his legions, his friends and various cities. The entire Senate, all the public officials, many knights, and all his legions marched, all in their proper uniforms, carrying gilded standards and silver-plated shields. No fewer than 210 carts carried the aromatic herbs and spices donated by Roman matrons, useful both to hide the smell of Sulla's worm-eaten corpse and to sweeten the odor of burning flesh on the pyre. After a funeral oration was delivered from the Speaker's Platform, a group of strong senators carried the bier to the Field of Mars, traditionally reserved for the burial of kings. As the perfumed pyre burned, the knights and the army marched past. The remains were buried in a tomb in the Field of Mars.

One element of Sulla's funeral should not be overlooked—fear, specifically fear of his armed soldiers. Fear brought out all the priests and priestesses of Rome, each in his proper robe to escort the body. Fear made the senators, knights, and urban plebs join in his supporters' cries of farewell, even those who hated Sulla.

In 69 B.C., Caesar organized a memorable funeral for his aunt Julia. She was the widow of Sulla's great enemy, Marius. Caesar delivered the funeral oration, praising his family as well as its descent from gods and kings. It was an announcement of sorts that the Populists were back and Sulla was gone—and that the sky was the limit when it came to Caesar's ambition.

Finally, there was Clodius's funeral in 52 B.C., a radically different event. Improvised on short notice after the demagogue's murder on the Appian Way, it was a case of populism run wild. Clodius's wounded body was shown to the public at his house, then a crowd brought it to the Forum the next day. There was neither the usual procession nor any masks of the deceased or his ancestors. The crowd cut off an attempt by the People's Tribunes to speak. The crowd then rioted and burned the Senate House, in whose ruins afterward they cremated Clodius. After further rioting around Rome, the crowd held a funeral banquet. Antony, who supported Clodius, was probably at the funeral, but even if not, he could learn anything he wanted to know from Fulvia. Fulvia had incited Clodius's supporters by displaying his corpse and its wounds the night it was brought back to Rome.

Like Sulla's funeral, Clodius's funeral no doubt engendered fear, but this time it was fear of the mob rather than of the soldiers. Caesar's funeral managed to combine both.

Before his funeral began, the organizers set up a gilded shrine on the Speaker's Platform and a funeral pyre on the Field of Mars beside Julia's tomb. The shrine, modeled to look like the Temple of Mother Venus, would hold the corpse. Heralds informed the public not to join the funeral procession, as the day wouldn't be long enough for the crowd expected. Instead, they told people to take any convenient route to the Field of Mars in order to bring their gifts for the pyre.

The procession no doubt began at the Public Mansion. Musicians and dancers took part as well as men carrying busts of Caesar. Actors, perhaps five—one for each of Caesar's triumphs—took part, too, each wearing a beeswax mask of Caesar and each dressed in a triumphal robe. As usual in a noble's funeral, the actors were trained to imitate the pace and bearing of the deceased.

Roman funeral masks were not death masks but life masks, cast while a person was still alive. Modern experiments with beeswax funeral masks show that they are uncannily lifelike. A wealthy man like Caesar would have used the most sensitive and expensive wax available, often imported from a far-off place, to make a vivid mask. Between their gait and their masks, the actor or actors who represented Caesar gave the eerie impression of a dead man come back to life.

Torchbearers and freedmen—those just freed by Caesar's will—probably walked before the corpse. Public officials, present and past, carried the body on an ivory couch covered with purple and gold. Normally the corpse was visible but this time it was covered and a wax image represented the dead man.

Piso, Caesar's father-in-law, led the body into the Forum. At this point, a very large number of armed men—Caesar's veterans, surely—ran to escort it as a kind of bodyguard. With loud cries coming from the procession,

they placed the corpse on its ivory couch in the shrine on the Speaker's Platform. At the head of the shrine stood a trophy, most likely a spear, holding
up the toga that Caesar wore on the Ides of March. There followed a long
period of more wailing and lament and armed men clashing their shields. If
Appian is right, the armed men began to regret the amnesty of March 17.

A large crowd was present. Presumably it was not a representative sample
of Roman public opinion but was stacked with Caesar's supporters, including many of his veterans. The conspirators stayed far away; in fact the prudent among them were probably barricaded at home.

Women attended Roman funerals. Calpurnia was surely there along with
Atia and the other women of Caesar's family. Cleopatra was surely not since
monarchs were banned from entering Rome's sacred boundary. She was
probably on the other side of the River Tiber in Caesar's villa.

It was finally time for Antony to speak. The consul had the honor of
delivering the eulogy. This is Shakespeare's "Friends, Romans, Country-
men" speech—a phrase that Antony did not use. But what did he say? The
sources differ starkly about that. Cicero, Appian, Plutarch, and Dio all have
Antony give an emotional speech, but Suetonius says that Antony did not
give a proper funeral oration at all. Rather, he says that Antony merely had
a herald read aloud the decrees in which the senators gave Caesar divine and
human honors, promising to defend his safety, and then Antony added a
few words of his own. Cicero, who says that Antony gave a rabble-rousing
speech, is more plausible than Suetonius. True, Cicero is biased, since he
was Antony's political opponent, and besides, Cicero didn't attend the
funeral. Still, when he addressed the Senate in October 44 and referred to
the speech, Cicero probably could not completely misrepresent a funeral
oration that Antony gave about six months earlier in the presence of many
in the room. Perhaps Suetonius was misled by the massive anti-Antony propaganda of later years. In any case, whatever Antony did or didn't say in his
formal address, he was the star performer in the melodrama that followed,
and his theatrics did more than his rhetoric to inflame the crowd.

Appian gives a generally plausible, if overly dramatic, account of Antony's speech. Antony read a list of the honors voted to Caesar by the Senate and the people. He emphasized Caesar's clemency and his status as the Father of His Country. He pointed out the bitter irony that a man who did no harm to anyone who sought refuge with him was then murdered in turn. He denied that Caesar was a tyrant. He recalled the senators' promise, on pain of a curse, to hold Caesar sacred and inviolable, and to avenge any harm to him. Antony turned to Jupiter, whose temple loomed above on the Capitoline Hill, saying that Antony himself was ready to take revenge but he had a duty to uphold the amnesty. At that, a hubbub arose from the senators present. Antony backpedaled and made a bland statement about letting bygones be bygones, with a warning about the danger of civil war.

Antony then performed a variation on the usual hymn and lament. He praised Caesar as a god and rapidly recited his achievements—the wars, battles, victories, peoples conquered, and spoils sent home. He bent down and rose again, lifted his hands to heaven, mourned, and wept. He ran arpeggios from high to low with his voice. Then he supposedly uncovered Caesar's body—an implausible detail—lifted his robe on a spear point, and raised it up, torn as it was by the assassin's blows and stained with the dictator's dried blood.

The most remarkable feature was that Antony now had the assembled people join in, as if he were the leader and they the chorus. The audience chanted to the sound of a flute while they took turns with Antony reciting Caesar's deeds and his suffering.

Now an actor impersonating Caesar spoke. He named names, listing the men for whom Caesar did favors, including the murderers. Then, in one of history's more inspired uses of sarcasm, he delivered a line from a Roman tragedy that seemed tailored for the occasion. "Did I save them just so that they could destroy me?" It was even bitterer than the phrase that Shakespeare puts into Antony's mouth when, in Shakespeare's funeral speech, Antony repeatedly calls the assassins "honorable men."

The actor impersonating Caesar moved the people to a near-riot pitch. The ingratitude of the murderers, especially Decimus, infuriated them.

Now, on the Speaker's Platform, a wax image of Caesar was raised above the body and rotated by a mechanical device so that it showed all the man's wounds, including those on his face.

The crowd took matters into its own hands. They took Caesar's bier and carried it on their shoulders. They ignored the plan to cremate him in the Field of Mars. Instead, they tried to bring the bier to the Temple of Jupiter on the Capitoline or to the Senate House of Pompey for cremation. Dio says that Lepidus's soldiers prevented them for fear that they would destroy those and the surrounding buildings. Some called for cremation in the Senate House of Pompey, but they didn't prevail. In the end, the people brought the bier into the Forum, threw together a pyre of dry branches and benches from the nearby law courts, and cremated it there, near the Royal Residence, where Caesar presided as Chief Priest. Later, the word went out that two "beings" bearing swords directed them—figures reminiscent of the twin gods Castor and Pollux. Was that just a tale told afterward or did someone actually dress up two actors to guide the crowd?

People now offered gifts to the dead man. Musicians and actors took off the robes from Caesar's triumphs, tore them into shreds, and threw them into the flames. Legionaries from the veteran units threw in the arms with which they had adorned themselves for the funeral. Women added their jewels or their children's robes and amulets.

Finally, there was a riot. Cicero says that rioters consisted of slaves and poor people or "ruffians, mostly slaves," but one wonders if some of them weren't Caesar's veterans. It's hard not to suspect that the riot was organized beforehand. Antony, who once belonged to Clodius's gang himself, and Fulvia, Clodius's widow and an able recruiter of armed men, are the obvious culprits. Caesar had abolished the gangs, but Caesar was dead. Either Antony or Fulvia or both could have worked in advance with their old friends from the gangs, perhaps with the veterans, too.

The crowd surged to the homes of Brutus and Cassius with torches and they were barely kept away—perhaps by Decimus's gladiators. The assassins had to be careful that day, and we happen to know that at least one of them—Publius Servilius Casca—was strongly guarded. The crowd succeeded in burning the house of one Lucius Bellienus, otherwise unknown but probably a supporter of the assassins. Cicero claims that the same torches that were used to burn Caesar's body were used on Bellienus's house. Then the rioters turned on an unfortunate victim, the People's Tribune and poet Helvius Cinna. He was a supporter of Caesar but the crowd mistook him for the hated praetor Cornelius Cinna. They killed and decapitated Helvius, parading his head through the streets. The soldiers did nothing that we know of to stop the riots or to protect the homes of the conspirators.

Cicero had no doubt that Antony was to blame. In a blistering speech to the Senate the next year, Cicero said of Antony, "The pretty funeral oration was yours, the emotional appeal was yours, the exhortation was yours—you, you, I say, you lit those torches!" By then, the compromise of March 17 had fallen apart and the lines were drawn. Cicero's words need to be taken with a grain of salt. And yet, Antony was the answer to that old Roman question, *cui bono?*—Who benefits?

For Antony, the funeral was a precious chance to claim the leadership of Caesar's party. To do so, he needed to lay it on thick and to curry favor with Caesar's veterans. He said that he stood by the amnesty but his performance suggested otherwise.

The assassins judged that the Roman people wanted peace and compromise. They were right. What the assassins misjudged was Antony's ruthlessness and Caesar's veterans. When the veterans flooded Rome they gave Antony an opportunity—or perhaps they forced his hand.

MARCH 20 AND AFTER: MOURNING AS DIPLOMACY

Eventually the funeral pyre burned out and Caesar's remains were brought to the family tomb in the Field of Mars. Mourning, however, continued. Foreigners as well as Romans lamented Caesar. Suetonius opens a window into Rome's ethnic politics with this statement: "At the height of public mourning a multitude of foreign peoples lamented around the pyre, each in its own way, and especially the Jews, who even on successive nights crowded the funeral site." The outsize Jewish presence among the mourners deserves comment.

A Roman general, victorious in various provinces, would have many foreign clients. Caesar had the greatest number of them all. Besides, he had made a name for himself as one who championed various foreign elites, especially in Italian Gaul but also in the so-called Province (the Provence region of France) and Hispania (Spain) as well as in various other communities around the empire. One of Caesar's most successful and long-lasting alliances was with various Jewish communities.

His relationship with the Jews was very different from that of Pompey—who conquered Judea, looted the Temple, deported Jewish slaves to Rome, and paved the way for the country to be diminished and divided. Caesar, by contrast, declared Judea an ally and friend of the Roman people, restored its territorial integrity, reduced taxes, and allowed the rebuilding of the walls of Jerusalem. He granted privileges to Roman and other diaspora Jewish communities.

Caesar's friendliness toward the Jews marks a refreshing change from the verbal hostility of many elite Romans such as Cicero, Horace, Tacitus, and Juvenal, not to mention Pompey's brutality. Yet the relationship between Caesar and the Jews was surely a marriage of convenience. In Egypt in 48 B.C., Jewish troops came to Caesar's rescue against his Egyptian enemies. Caesar remembered this and perhaps saw Judea as a base against Parthia. In the Land of Israel, chances are that many saw Caesar as an occupier—better than Pompey but still unwelcome. And Caesar favored Antipater, father of King Herod, who was hated both by the rabbis and by many in the Jewish masses.

The Jews who mourned Caesar night after night might have genuinely admired him. Even if they disliked Caesar, perhaps they wanted to be on good terms with Caesar's friends if they saw them as the likely winners in the power struggle.

AFTER MARCH 20: "ET TU, DECIME?"

Caesar's funeral was as good a show as Sulla's and nearly as violent in its aftermath as Clodius's. The amnesty was still in effect, but the funeral and riot compromised it. Afterward, the consuls ruled that no one but soldiers could bear arms, which defanged Decimus's gladiators. No wonder the conspirators felt that they had to lie low or even to run for their lives.

Decimus was the most hated man in Rome. Other friends of Caesar betrayed the dictator on the Ides, but only Decimus had dined with Caesar the night before and only Decimus had lured the dictator from his house to his death. Only Decimus protected the assassins with gladiators. To top it off, Caesar mentioned Decimus in his will. For the Roman public, it was all too much. Antony might have evoked nods of approval when, a few months later, he called Decimus a poisoner. No one is recorded saying "Et tu, Decime?" but that sums up how people felt.

A remarkable letter survives from Decimus to Brutus and Cassius. The date is uncertain but if may have been written soon after Caesar's funeral. In it, Decimus bemoans his position. He says that Caesar's close colleague Hirtius visited him at home the evening before and made clear that Antony's state of mind was very bad and very treacherous.

According to Decimus, Hirtius reported that Antony said that he couldn't give Decimus his province of Italian Gaul. Further, Antony said it was unsafe for any of the assassins to stay in Rome, not with the soldiers and the people aroused as they were.

All lies, said Decimus. He claimed that Hirtius made clear what Antony really thought—that with only "a moderate boost in the dignitas of the assassins," the assassins would be safe from popular agitators. What did Decimus have in mind by a "moderate boost in dignitas"?

Decimus said that he had lost hope. He asked for a senatorial commission to travel abroad on public business, and Hirtius agreed, but Decimus doubted that Hirtius could actually obtain it. Public opinion had turned on the assassins, and Decimus said he wouldn't be surprised if he and his friends were declared public enemies. Therefore, his advice was "we must give in to fortune." Exile was the solution. Sextus Pompey in Hispania or Caecilius Bassus, the rebel governor of Syria, represented their best hope.

The last paragraph of his letter was, it seems, a postscript. In it Decimus announced a new plan. He had taken heart, perhaps based on new information. He now told Hirtius that he wanted to stay in Rome after all and he demanded a public bodyguard. This, it appears, would suffice as the "moderate boost in dignitas" that Decimus referred to earlier.

It might seem strange that Decimus, of all people, the man who betrayed Caesar, would call a person treacherous, as he called Antony. But Decimus was not someone to see himself as others saw him. In several letters written over the next year he complained about those who vilified him and attacked his dignity. They were malicious, he said. He had no doubt but that he represented his country, while his enemies were "a most wicked conspiracy." Betray Caesar? As far as Decimus was concerned he had done nothing wrong, and that was that.

In the end, Decimus stayed in Rome without a bodyguard until early April, when he finally went to Italian Gaul. There he had two armies under his command as well as his infamous gladiators.

As for Brutus and Cassius, their status in Rome after the Ides was not as bad as Decimus's, but it wasn't good. They had drawn their daggers on the Ides of March. Within a week, an influx of Caesar's veterans into Rome gave Antony swords and shields. Finally, in mid-April, Brutus and Cassius left the city. By then a new factor had emerged on the political scene.

The men who killed Caesar were caught in a contradiction. What they needed to secure their status was a military coup. Instead, they committed murder and made speeches. Revolution, as Mao said, is not a dinner party.

Emerson said that when you strike at a king, you must kill him. The conspirators thought they had done just that by killing Caesar, but they were wrong. The king wasn't Caesar but Caesarism—the idea that a general and his armies could conquer the Republic. The only way to kill that idea was to defend the Republic by defeating its enemies once and for all. But doing that would take more than speeches. It would take an army and the determination to use it in a war.

The conspirators had lost Caesar's veterans in Rome. Now they needed to start raising an army, both in Italy and in the east, by attracting as many battle-hardened soldiers as possible. If they already understood that on the Ides of March, they may not have admitted it. To do so meant accepting the paradox that only the legions could save the Republic from being run by the legions.

Part Three

The

ROAD

BACK

11

THE STRUGGLE FOR ITALY

BY THE TIME THE MESSENGER GOT TO APOLLONIA (TODAY, POJANI in Albania), he was stressed and gloomy. A freedman, he had left Rome about ten days earlier on the afternoon of the Ides of March. He hurried across the Adriatic Sea even though it was a dangerous time of year for sailing. In his hands he held the fate of a man or maybe a country. Julius Caesar's niece, Atia, sent him to her son, Octavian, with a letter containing the news of Caesar's murder. With the future uncertain, Atia recommended that Octavian come home. So did the messenger. He emphasized both the danger to Caesar's family and the large number of assassins (or so he thought).

It was a shock and a comedown to Octavian. Four months earlier, he arrived in the strategic city of Apollonia. It was a thriving port and the naval link between northern Greece and the harbor of Brundisium (modern Brindisi) in southern Italy, where a highway led to Rome. Apollonia was also the gateway to the Via Egnatia, the great road that ran all the way east to Byzantium (modern Istanbul). No wonder Apollonia was the staging point for much of the army that Caesar gathered for his Parthian campaign. There were six legions, a large number of cavalry and light-armed troops, as well as abundant weapons and military machines. Octavian was there to learn the art of war and to prepare to march east with his uncle the dictator, who had appointed Octavian Master of the Horse. Now, everything had changed.

At eighteen, Octavian was preparing for a career at the top. During his stay in Apollonia he hobnobbed with the army's officers and drilled with the cavalry. He had an informal council of friends with him, of whom the most important was Marcus Vipsanius Agrippa. About the same age as Octavian and raised with him in Rome, Agrippa was drawn to a soldier's life. His advice now was for Octavian to approach the army and convince it to march on Rome and avenge Caesar. Meanwhile, some officers went to Octavian and offered to fight for him in order to avenge Caesar, but Octavian declined. He was too young and inexperienced, the attitude of the Roman people was too uncertain, and the number of enemies too great. About the soldiers, though, he had no doubts. While Caesar had lived they enjoyed his good fortune. Caesar gave them offices and wealth and gifts beyond their wildest dreams. They would avenge him.

There would be time later to circle back to the soldiers. For now, Octavian needed to see for himself the lay of the land in Rome. He also needed to consult the wise men of Caesar's inner circle and financiers who could bankroll his ambitions. So he took a relatively small entourage and braved the still-wintry Adriatic. Instead of landing at Brundisium they chose a point even farther south where the strait is narrower. After disembarking, Octavian went on foot not to the port city of Brundisium but to Lupiae (modern Lecce), a small, inland town. The cautious young man worried that his enemies held Brundisium and he wasn't taking any chances.

Messages arrived from Rome with up-to-date news about Caesar's funeral, the turn against the assassins, and Antony's success in gathering support from Caesar's veterans. Most important was the news of Caesar's last will, naming Octavian his son and heir, and giving him three-fourths of Caesar's huge estate. Octavian cried but he barely dried his tears before moving on. His mother wrote and warned about his enemies. His stepfather wrote and urged him to give up his inheritance and retire to the safety of private life. Octavian wasn't having any of that. He knew that Caesar owed everything to taking strategic risks and he planned to do likewise.

He now knew that Brundisium was safe, so he headed there. The troops there welcomed him and hailed him as Caesar. The road to Rome lay open. Rome itself was another matter because it was full of people who would not accept without a fight the man who would be Caesar.

For both the men who killed Caesar and those who wanted to avenge him, it was a time of struggle. For their women, it was a time of rallying support on the home front. For Cicero, the last lion of the Republic, it was a time of heroic resistance from the well of the Senate. And for Octavian and Antony, the two men who wanted to inherit Caesar's mantle, it was a time of rivalry.

Decimus and Cassius quickly came to the conclusion that the only thing that mattered was the soldiers and the resources to pay them. It took Brutus longer to reach the same end but he got there, too. So much for turning the state back over to the Senate and the people—that was premature while Antony and Octavian had armies at their disposal. To restore the Republic the assassins and their supporters would have to fight. If they won, then, after reestablishing peace, if they moved slowly and wisely and made necessary reforms, they could have the Republic back. For now it was a distant goal.

For three years after the assassination, the Roman commonwealth unraveled and came together again, but in a new and garish pattern. Armies marched, soldiers mutinied, tax collectors squeezed, secret messages flew, aristocratic ladies plotted, assassins' daggers flashed, orators thundered, the Senate debated and decreed, the people rallied, battle roared, and even the specter of Pompey rose again in the West—all in all, a story that could have filled a third book of *Commentaries* had Caesar been alive to write it.

The world without Caesar was still a world about Caesar. His wealth, his soldiers, his supporters in the urban plebs, his advisors, his contacts abroad, and even his mistress—all were in contention. Octavian claimed Caesar's heritage, but the young man's hold on that would be only as secure as his stomach for a fight and his ability to navigate in a storm.

Rome after Caesar resembled Macedon after Alexander. In each case, the great man's marshals fought over the empire that he had won. Both were warrior cultures that could not suddenly embrace the arts of peace. In each case, the army missed its fallen chief—while always keeping an eye out for a good deal with a new chief. "Vengeance" and "loyalty" became the watchwords of the day, often with grotesque results. Romans were hunted down and murdered merely for sympathizing with Caesar's assassins, but that was less gruesome than what had happened in Macedon—the murder of Alexander's mother, widow, and sons.

Even dead, Caesar set the tone in Rome for the years following the Ides of March. "Where were you on the Ides of March?" became the unspoken question of the day. For Antony and especially for Octavian, loyalty to Caesar—*pietas*, in Latin—was a key card to play. The assassins, meanwhile, brandished their daggers like primitive victory trophies. Love Caesar or hate him, conquest and power still made Roman hearts beat faster. Even Brutus rendered homage to Caesar by putting an image of himself on his coins while still alive, a practice that Caesar had begun, thereby overturning centuries of Roman tradition that frowned on something so immodest.

THE GATHERING STORM

Antony kept his options open in March and April 44 B.C. He arranged land allotments in Italy for Caesar's veterans while suppressing a radical movement in Rome. He showed respect to the Senate and Caesar's assassins, especially Brutus. Antony and Brutus always shared a certain mutual regard. As two members of the old Roman nobility, they were confident they could settle the world's fate with a handshake. Not Cicero. He had little sympathy for Antony and suspected him as an enemy of the Best Men. A new man who had risen from the Central Italian aristocracy, Cicero felt no class solidarity with Antony. He despised Antony for marrying Fulvia, the widow of Cicero's archenemy, Clodius. He was convinced that Antony was forging alleged decrees of Caesar—which had the force of law—and making off with Caesar's fortune. Cicero always believed the assassins made a mistake by letting Antony live on the Ides of March.

Left on his own Antony might have become a prince of the Republic like Pompey or like Caesar without the monarchical airs. A son of the Roman nobility, Antony had residual respect for the system, and he had skills as an orator and as a general to rise to the top of it. But no one was willing to leave him on his own. Brutus and Cassius challenged Antony first from various places in Italy and then from the East. Sextus Pompey represented a growing threat in Hispania and Massilia. Decimus honed his army in the foothills of northern Italy's Alps. The other provincial governors ran hot and cold on Antony. Beginning in summer of 44 B.C., Cicero rallied opposition to Antony in the Senate. Last but not least there was Caesar's heir, young Octavian. He challenged Antony for the leadership of Caesar's faction. Octavian raised a private army among Caesar's veterans, siphoned off some of the legions returned from Macedonia, and rallied support among the urban plebs of Rome.

Faced with these challenges, Antony decided to use his position as consul to amass a power base. His opponents did not leave that decision unchallenged. Ultimately, Antony became a revolutionary who wrecked what was left of Rome's traditional government, although he was forced into it.

During a brief trip to Rome in April, Octavian officially accepted his adoption by Caesar. Afterward, Octavian began to call himself Caesar. Most of the ancient sources refer to him by that name. To avoid confusion, even if not historically accurate, we will continue to call him Octavian, although to his contemporaries, he was Caesar.

One title that Octavian did not inherit was Chief Priest. Before Caesar's death, the Senate had decreed that Caesar's son or adopted son would replace him as Chief Priest. But Antony ignored that decree and now arranged for Lepidus to become Chief Priest. Antony did not want the office to go to Octavian and, besides, he saw the value of building bridges with Lepidus, who was about to take office as governor of the important provinces of Narbonese Gaul and Nearer Hispania. For good measure, Antony had his daughter engaged to Lepidus's son, probably the same son who had been a hostage on the Capitoline on March 17.

Around the same time that Octavian came to Rome, Cleopatra left. She did not depart quickly after the Ides of March. Cleopatra wasn't just a bereft mistress but a queen, and she needed to ensure the continued friendship for Egypt of Rome's new rulers—whoever they would be. She might even have been hoping to get official recognition for Caesarion, Caesar's alleged son. If so, she failed.

No sooner had the ashes cooled on Caesar's funeral pyre than men wanted to consecrate the spot. A column and altar were erected there at the behest of the man known as Herophilus or Amatius, the demagogue who claimed to be the son or grandson of Marius and who had once upstaged Caesar in his villa. Neither of the two consuls, Antony or Dolabella, favored such monuments. Dolabella supported the assassins (for now) while Antony had no use for anything with so radically populist a taint and so likely to shine glory on Caesar's adopted son, Octavian. Antony was able to have Amatius-Herophilus executed and Dolabella could order certain rabble-rousers thrown to death from the Tarpeian Rock—an archaic punishment for traitors. But neither of them dared stop the other pressure group behind the monument—Caesar's veterans.

The veterans now erected a new column, possibly with Octavian's support. Carved from a single block of ornamental marble, it stood twenty feet high and contained an inscription: TO THE FATHER OF THE FATHERLAND. It was a title voted for by the Senate. A statue of Caesar posssibly topped the column.

The column on the site of Caesar's cremation was a reminder and a challenge. It recalled the great honor of being cremated within the Sacred Boundary of the city. It defied the assassins and anyone who thought that Caesar had been justly killed. Finally, it brought up unfinished business—the cult of Caesar's divinity that the Senate had established before his death but which had been left by the wayside.

In September 44 B.C., Antony set up a competing statue of Caesar at the other end of the Roman Forum on the Speaker's Platform. This was a compromise. It honored Caesar without stirring up the emotions of the site of his funeral pyre. But it had something to offend everyone—Caesar's veterans, who wanted the maximum respect for their old chief, and republicans, who wanted no honors for Caesar at all. As Antony discovered, revolutionary times are hard on moderates.

Octavian had no such problems. With his stepfather's estate on the Bay of Naples as a base, he wooed prominent supporters of Caesar. He also met Cicero, whom he was determined to make an ally. Octavian courted the great orator. Cicero had mixed feelings about the high-powered youth. But as summer approached and a rift opened between Antony and Octavian, Cicero began to think of Octavian as the lesser of two evils and a useful tool. It was a gamble.

Octavian was ruthless, energetic, and determined to have not only Caesar's name but also his power. It was a tall order for an eighteen-year-old in a still fairly conservative society, but Octavian's age was also an advantage. Since he had little invested in the old system, he had little inhibition about overturning it. And the veterans' cry for blood vengeance for Caesar suited his purposes.

Antony and Octavian dueled over money—Antony blocked Octavian's access to Caesar's funds—and Caesar's legacy. To pay Caesar's promised bequest to the Roman people, Octavian raised the funds on his own, and so endeared himself to the ordinary folk of Rome. In late July, Octavian put on the funeral games in honor of his adoptive father. Antony had to tolerate this, although he refused to allow the display of a golden chair and wreath—honors that the Senate had granted Caesar when still alive. Octavian later claimed that the urban plebs and Caesar's veterans supported him against Antony.

When a comet appeared during the games, Octavian turned what was usually considered an ill omen in Rome into a symbol of Caesar's new place in heaven with the gods. This made splendid propaganda. Unusually bright, the comet was visible during the daylight hours, and so caught the public's attention. When a soothsayer saw it as a sign of the dawning of a new age, the notion resonated with the Roman people.

Antony, meanwhile, pivoted. In April, he conciliated the Senate. He made it possible for Brutus and Cassius to remain praetors although absent from Rome. Although Caesar himself had named Antony as High Priest for the worship of Caesar as a god, Antony did nothing to go forward with the new religion. But then the presence of Octavian forced Antony away from the Senate and toward Caesar's veterans and the urban plebs. In late April and early May, he visited the veterans in Campania and promised them more land.

Meanwhile, Antony prepared to deal with Decimus, who was now governor of Italian Gaul. The Senate had assigned Antony a different province after his consulship ended on December 31, Macedonia. It was an important position, especially since Macedonia included six legions that had been chosen for Caesar's Parthian Expedition. Italian Gaul was more important, however, because its location controlled Italy. So Antony made clear that he intended to switch provinces—trading Macedonia for Italian Gaul—while also keeping the six legions. It was a dark cloud on the horizon.

In the spring of 44 B.C., no one trusted anyone in Rome. Everyone talked peace but feared war. The few moderates, men like Hirtius, Caesar's friend and one of the consul-designates for 43 B.C., had little room for maneuver in such a climate. As spring became summer, each of the leading players began turning his attention away from talk and toward arms. For Antony and Octavian their base consisted of Caesar's veterans and the legions in Macedonia that had been allocated for Parthia. For Decimus, it was the legions of Italian Gaul as supplemented by his allies in the Senate. For Brutus and Cassius, it was the armies stationed in the East.

Each attracted supporters from the Roman political and military leadership class. Each side needed money—a lot of money, and money in a hurry, because the urban plebs had to be appeased and soldiers had to be armed, fed, and paid. The result was taxation, and, soon enough, looting and murder.

Caesar had predicted a new civil war if he died. He understood something about the Romans very well, that they liked to fight. Politics fascinated them, but it did not take much to make Romans resort to the sword.

Only a few of the older generations of leaders were left and they returned to the scene for one last act, doing what they had always done best, only more so. For Cicero that meant giving speeches, holding meetings, and writing letters to make deals, all for the cause of the Republic. He pushed hard against the man whom he considered the biggest threat—Antony. For Servilia, it meant behind-the-scenes maneuvering to advance her son and save her family.

It's a reasonable guess that even before they raised their daggers against Caesar, Brutus and Cassius considered the possibility that they might have to leave Rome. It was not news to Roman politicians that men who played for the highest stakes sometimes had to go into exile and regroup. There was plenty of precedent for going east to raise money and manpower. Sulla, Pompey, and Caesar had all done so and only Pompey failed—and even he won great success on his first expedition in the East. Both Brutus and Cassius had substantial connections in the East dating back ten years and they also had the support of Deiotarus, the king of Galatia, who had been accused of trying to assassinate Caesar. There was also the intriguing possibility of help from Parthia.

FLY ON THE WALL

Antium (Anzio, of World War II fame) was a seaside town south of Rome where Brutus and Cassius withdrew after leaving the capital in April 44 B.C. Lined with villas, the area was virtually Rome's Gold Coast. Cicero's villa was nearby at Astura, and he called it "a delightful place, right by the sea." But Brutus did not go to Antium for the waters. He held a virtual court in exile there.

Brutus tried to win the power game in Rome by a combination of force and persuasion, but he was outfoxed and outmuscled by Antony. Like any good Roman aristocrat, Brutus now turned to the one certain haven in a heartless world—his family. Or, as a Roman might have put it, his *familiares*—a broad term including friends, servants, and even property as well as relatives.

Brutus was hardly passive. He was well aware that money was the mother's milk of politics. His friend the Roman knight Gaius Flavius tried to organize a group of wealthy knights as contributors to a fund for Caesar's assassins. Brutus did his part by wining and dining Atticus, the prince of Roman political financiers. Atticus was an old friend of the family but he was a pragmatist and a survivor. Atticus was Antony's friend, too. Rather than take a chance, Atticus had declined and so torpedoed Brutus's fund. Perhaps this is what Brutus and Cassius were referring to when they wrote to Antony a few weeks earlier and said they had dismissed their friends from the cities of Italy at his advice. But Brutus looked for other ways of building a power base.

He called Cicero for advice and on June 7, the orator went to see Brutus in his villa at Antium, a scene later described by Cicero in a letter to Atticus (who was also a friend of Cicero). The other people present were Cassius (who arrived late); Brutus's wife, Porcia; Cassius's wife, Junia Tertia (in some sources called Tertulla), who was also Brutus's half sister; and Servilia, mother or mother-in-law to most of the people in the room. Rounding out the group was Marcus Favonius. Like Cicero, Favonius was left out of the conspiracy to kill Caesar but showed his support for it right afterward.

The fiasco at the Lupercalia on February 15, the dinner party at Lepidus's on March 14, the funeral of Caesar, and, of course, the assassination itself—these are all events that make the historian wish he could be a fly on the wall. But for the combination of fear, spite, and theater of the absurd, nothing matches the scene in Brutus's villa at Antium on June 7, 44 B.C.

The purpose of the meeting was to consider an offer from the Senate, made at Antony's prodding, to put Brutus and Cassius in charge of collecting grain in Sicily and Roman Asia (western Turkey). The decree also gave them permission to leave Rome, where, as praetors, they were supposed to serve. It was a graceful out and Cicero advised them to take it. Brutus wanted to go back to Rome and preside at the games that he was giving as urban praetor. Cicero pointed out that Rome wasn't safe for Brutus, and he flattered Brutus by saying that his safety really mattered because Brutus was the Republic's only defense. Brutus eventually agreed that Rome was dangerous.

Then Cassius entered and angrily refused the job of grain commissioner, which he considered an insult. He said that he was going to Greece and from there to Syria, where he was scheduled to serve as governor in 43 B.C. Cicero had the impression that Brutus was going to go to Roman Asia, where he could join Trebonius, who was governor. Although it was Brutus who called the meeting, Servilia was not shy. She spoke as if she had real influence in the Senate and she promised to get the grain commission withdrawn from the Senate's decree.

Then the talk turned to lost opportunities. Everyone was bitter, especially Cassius. They heaped the most blame on Decimus, probably for not using his troops in Italian Gaul against Antony. This was just talk because Decimus's troops were untested and no one, least of all Brutus, would begin a civil war lightly. Cicero said they shouldn't dwell on the past, and then proceeded to blame the conspirators for their passivity after killing Caesar on the Ides of March and the next few days. Servilia proceeded to cut him off.

"I've really never heard anyone say that!" Servilia exclaimed. Cicero told Atticus that he now stopped her, but it was the other way around. Cicero was still rehashing past politics while Brutus and his family had moved on to the clash of armies in addition to the funds needed to raise and outfit them.

Wheels began to turn after the meeting. By summer's end, the Senate assigned Brutus and Cassius new provinces, Crete and Cyrene (in modern Libya). If Servilia had worked her magic, it wasn't a potent spell, since these provinces were still relatively small and unimportant. Brutus and Cassius had much bigger things in mind.

In letter after letter from this period Cicero calls Brutus depressed, but if Brutus was down he was not yet out. With the help of family and friends he was actively building a new power base. Yet Brutus had good reason to be depressed. He had wanted peace and reconciliation but both sides were digging in their heels. Caesar's veterans wanted loot and vengeance. Caesar's enemies wanted their confiscated lands back.

In July, for instance, Brutus and Cicero met a very important envoy on Brutus's estate on the little island of Nesis (modern Nisida) on the Bay of

Naples. A former praetor, he was Sextus Pompey's father-in-law and he brought news of Pompey's continued military success in Hispania. No deal was made but the door was open to an alliance between Sextus and Caesar's assassins.

On August 4, Brutus and Cassius wrote a letter to Antony from Naples. First they blasted him for writing them an abusive and threatening letter. They were praetors after all, and men of dignity. In his letter, Antony denied ever accusing them of raising troops and money or of tampering with the soldiers and sending ambassadors overseas. For their part, Brutus and Cassius said that they knew nothing about any of these charges. They cattily added that they were amazed by Antony's restraint, considering his inability to keep from angrily taunting them with Caesar's death. They couldn't resist a warning before closing: "Bear in mind not only how long Caesar lived but how briefly he reigned."

That surely did little to ease Antony's suspicions about Brutus and Cassius. Their fellow assassins had already laid a bridgehead in the East. Probably in April, Trebonius went to Roman Asia and Cimber went to the nearby province of Bithynia, both as provincial governors. Other assassins and their friends also took up important civil and military positions in the eastern provinces. Meanwhile, the long, slow courtship of Sextus Pompey went forward. Decimus held Italian Gaul while Cicero remained in Rome to anchor the cause in the capital.

In mid-August, Brutus left Italy for the East. Before his departure, he and Cassius issued edicts saying that for the sake of the Republic and to avoid civil war, they were going into exile. But Brutus's actions said otherwise; they bespoke armed conflict. He and Porcia had a tearful farewell in the city of Velia, south of Naples. This was the Roman equivalent of a photo op. Velia had formerly been the Greek colony of Elea, famous for its philosophers. Brutus and Porcia let it be known that they parted in front of a painting of Hector and Andromache, the doomed couple of Homer's *Iliad*. No doubt they felt deep emotion, but it was also a message for the Greek East: Brutus is coming and he is one of you. He spoke Greek, he loved philosophy, and he would be polite as he shook down city after city for the money needed to fund the war for the Republic. Cassius, who followed shortly afterward, would be less diplomatic.

DECIMUS UNDER SIEGE

From the day that Decimus left Rome in April 44 B.C. to the moment he stepped into a trap in a pass in the Iura (modern Jura) Mountains on the modern French-Swiss border, his post-assassination life was an epic. Actually, it had been an epic from the day he first served in Caesar's army. The last phase was merely the most dramatic.

If ever there was a man suited to the province he governed, it was Decimus in Italian Gaul. He was, once again, among Celts. From boyhood he heard about his grandfather's exploits among the Celts in Hispania. He spent much of his adult life among Celts in Transalpine Gaul, what is today France and Belgium. He even spoke the Gaulish language. Rome had begun colonizing Italian Gaul in the third century B.C. By Decimus's day, Latin was mandatory for the local elite. Yet there was still a heavy Celtic flavor to the region, especially in the foothills and mountains of the Alps. Decimus would have felt at home.

As governor, Decimus had two legions, one composed of veterans, the other men with one year's experience. Decimus spent the summer of 44 B.C. attacking the Alpine tribes. He claimed to have fought exceptionally fierce enemies, laid waste to many strongholds, and captured a great deal of loot to distribute to his men. They, in turn, saluted him as imperator, great commander, the title customarily given to a general after a successful battle. The experience honed his two legions and made them more attached to their commander. Decimus wrote to Cicero in Rome to help him get formal recognition from the Senate. Cicero promised to take care of Decimus's dignitas—it was dearer to him than his own, said Cicero.

No doubt Cicero had better things to do with his limited resources in the Senate but he knew to whom he wrote. He refers in other letters as well to

Decimus's dignitas. He assures Decimus how much the Roman people love him for freeing them from tyranny. He ends one letter with the firm hope that Decimus will be the greatest and most famous man of all.

In any case, by then, Decimus's actions in Italian Gaul were illegal. On June 1, Antony got the people to vote him command of Italian Gaul, for a term that was soon extended to five years. Antony protected his dignitas and attacked that of the assassins. It was a blow to Decimus, who was to lose his governorship of the province, and he refused to accept this insult and threat. He disobeyed the law and stayed in command in Italian Gaul. Then in October, Antony's friends arranged for the execution of a slave named Myrtilus for allegedly aiming to assassinate him. They claimed that Decimus was behind the whole thing.

If Decimus led the republican cause in Italian Gaul, Cicero led it in Rome. He never trusted Antony and, by September 44 B.C., he made his opposition public. He gave a series of speeches against Antony that he called *Philippics*, after a famous set of speeches against King Philip of Macedon by the Athenian orator Demosthenes in the mid-fourth century B.C. Cicero's speeches savaged Antony and praised Octavian. He hailed Decimus as a defender of the Republic, a member of a family (the Brutus family) with a divine mission to protect Roman liberty. Cicero could only hope for more success than Demosthenes, who rallied the public to a losing cause—Philip won and conquered all of Greece.

Whatever happened, Cicero could be sure of one thing. Never again would he have to say that he lacked courage. By taking his stand, particularly at the age of sixty-two, Cicero risked everything for the Republic.

At first, Cicero helped to push Antony out of Rome. In October 44 B.C., three of the Macedonian legions chosen for Antony landed in Brundisium, with a fourth on the way. Antony went to meet them and got an angry reception for his policy of reconciliation with Caesar's killers—the soldiers wanted vengeance. Antony offered the men a small sum of money to appease them, but Octavian's agents had already promised more and they refused. Finally, Antony ordered that some of the troops be executed in order to restore discipline.

Octavian had already recruited three thousand veterans of Caesar in Campania. This private army was illegal but that did not stop the young man whose name was now Caesar. Years later, Octavian boasted of his action, which he brilliantly rebranded as a way of saving the Republic:

> At the age of nineteen I raised an army at my private initiative and private expense by means of which I set free the Republic that had been oppressed by the unrestricted power of a political faction.

In November, Octavian marched his new army to Rome but quickly left again as Antony approached. After regrouping, Octavian learned that two of the Macedonian legions had mutinied and would now join him. They were veterans, which made them valuable. Many of the legions of this period were inexperienced or undersized. Octavian mustered his army in a hill town in Central Italy. He promptly paid each man 500 denarii and promised them much more if they defeated Antony—an additional 5,000 denarii each, almost as much as Caesar had paid his men at his Triple Triumph in 46 B.C.

Decimus was bold, courageous, and stubborn. From his base in northern Italy he jeopardized Rome. Both Antony and Octavian knew it and they both courted Decimus. Either would be a dubious ally but Decimus chose Octavian, no doubt because the youth seemed less threatening than a senior leader like Antony. Cicero championed this course, risky though it was. Besides, Octavian was a very good salesman. And so Decimus stayed and fought, although many considered that a fool's errand. Behind the heroics of Cicero's *Philippics* lay a leap in the dark.

Antony now marched his men, including the remaining Macedonian legions, to Italian Gaul. He made a similar promise of booty in the event of victory. First, he had to deal with Decimus. It was late November in 44 B.C. Antony could count on four veteran legions as well as bodyguards, auxiliaries, and new recruits. In December, he demanded that Decimus surrender his province but Decimus refused. Cicero and other senators wrote to Decimus from Rome and urged him to resist. Finally, on December 20, Cicero managed to get the Senate to decree that Decimus and all governors should keep their provinces. The Senate sent ambassadors to Antony to negotiate his withdrawal from the province but he refused. Instead, he made ready for war with Decimus.

Safe in Greece, Brutus was not impressed—he feared Octavian, as he said, and he refused Cicero's requests to come to Decimus's aid with troops from Macedonia. Sextus Pompey also declined to come to Decimus's aid, saying he didn't want "to offend" Caesar's veterans by the presence of their old enemy's son. The smart money, in short, was on getting out of Italy. But Decimus stayed. If he wanted to be a leading figure in Rome he had no choice. Sextus Pompey had a base in Hispania and was able to find a second one in Sicily. Brutus and Cassius had long histories in the Roman East. Decimus had spent his career in Gaul and so it made sense to stay there. The rewards of victory south of the Alps were so great that he preferred to stay there and fight. There would be time later, if need be, to cross the Alps and seek refuge in his former province.

He went to Mutina (modern Modena), a wealthy agricultural city in the Padus (Po) River Valley of Italian Gaul. He occupied the place, closed the gates, confiscated the property of the inhabitants, slaughtered and salted all his transport cattle, and generally prepared for a long siege.

By now, Decimus had raised a third legion, but they were new recruits and inexperienced. He could put more trust in his gladiators. Like several other commanders of this era of civil war, Decimus used gladiators for his bodyguard. They replaced or formed a large part of the Roman general's traditional bodyguard, the 500-man-strong praetorian cohort. Appian says that Decimus had "a large number of gladiators" with him in Mutina. Perhaps they—or at least some of them—were the same gladiators who had been with him on the Ides of March.

In December, Antony laid siege to the city. Decimus's forces were no match for Antony, who would soon have six legions as well as a praetorian cohort and cavalry. Antony surrounded the city with a wall. It was like Caesar's siege of Alesia, except that this time, the two generals who had served Caesar there were on opposite sides. In a poignant moment in Rome the next month, Decimus's wife, Valeria Paula, asked Cicero to include her let-ter with his next one to her husband.

In January 43 B.C., things moved rapidly. There were two new consuls, Hirtius and Pansa. Although friends of Caesar, they were political moder-ates with respect for the Republic. Like Cicero, they had decided to throw in their lot with Octavian. The hope was that they could keep the young man under control. The Senate demanded that Antony withdraw from Ital-ian Gaul; they gave Octavian the rank of substitute high official (proprietor) and sent him along with the consul Hirtius to help Decimus. The three men had seven legions among them.

While a private citizen Octavian raised an army. That was illegal but the Senate dealt with that by giving him a public office. Yet Octavian was not fooled. He knew that the Senate was using him only until Antony was de-feated.

In February 43 B.C., news arrived in Rome from Asia that Dolabella had executed Trebonius the month before. Few people changed sides as often as Dolabella. A follower of Caesar in 45 B.C., he supported the assassins after the Ides of March but then turned against them. Now Dolabella killed Trebonius in Smyrna (modern Izmir, Turkey) and placed his head in the marketplace at the foot of a statue of Caesar. Trebonius had told Cicero that he was proud of his part in the death of Caesar but now he had to pay for it. He was the first of Caesar's assassins to die. The Senate condemned Dola-bella and named him an enemy of the state.

Like Decimus, Trebonius had been part of Caesar's old guard and yet he had turned on his chief. He was enough of an old Roman that, like Cicero, with whom he corresponded, Trebonius couldn't bear Caesar's violence to the republican form of government and to the honor and power that sena-tors like him possessed. On the Ides of March he had played the vital role of detaining Antony.

Back in Italy, Decimus became something of a legend for his masterful control of his army during the siege of Mutina. He and his allies carried out several grand gestures. Before Antony shut off the city he sent in spies to try to corrupt Decimus's soldiers, but Decimus suspected this and managed to smoke them out. After Hirtius and Octavian approached Mutina, they made their presence known to Decimus by sending divers to swim across the river at night with messages on rolled-up lead tablets attached to their arms. Decimus got the messages and sent one back; the two sides continued to communicate this way. Hirtius and Decimus also communicated by carrier pigeon. In February, Decimus got word that a certain senator in Mutina had defected to Antony. Decimus magnanimously sent the man his baggage. This gesture supposedly convinced some of the neighboring towns supporting Antony to switch sides.

The main problem for the men in Mutina was food. At one point Decimus's allies managed to float salt and sheep down the river to a place where they could be brought into the city undetected, but this was a one-time measure. Conditions in Mutina were, in general, dreadful. The remarkable thing is that nobody opened the city gates to Antony. That is surely a tribute both to Decimus's vigilance and to his skill as a leader of men. He evoked loyalty, either to himself or to the cause, or both.

The fate of Mutina was decided in April 43 B.C. On April 14, Antony defeated the consul Pansa at the battle of Forum Gallorum ("Forum of the Gauls"), a small place on the Via Aemilia, the Roman road that ran from the Adriatic coast northwestward to Placentia (modern Piacenza) on the River Padus. If Appian is right about the battle, the veterans slammed into each other in silence, where they fought locked together like wrestlers. Galba, one of Caesar's assassins and formerly a legionary commander in Gaul, commanded one of Pansa's legions. Galba sent Cicero a memorable account of the fierce fighting where he was in the thick of things and barely escaped being killed mistakenly by his own men. This would not have surprised any reader of Caesar's *Commentaries*, which chronicle Galba's military missteps in Gaul.

Pansa was not as lucky and received a mortal wound. Still, Antony had no chance to savor his victory. Reinforcements led by the other consul, Hirtius, arrived later in the day and crushed Antony's troops, forcing him to retreat. A week later, on April 21, a second battle took place outside Mutina.

Octavian was now present with his legions to reinforce Hirtius. Decimus too participated in the battle by sallying out from the city with at least some of his men. Mutina was free. Ironically, it was Decimus's birthday.

The combined forces defeated Antony but at the cost of Hirtius's life. Octavian survived. Antony claimed that Octavian ran from the battlefield at Forum Gallorum and lost his military cloak and his horse—to the Romans, a disgrace. Whether that was true or not, it appears that the sources agreed that Octavian was a hero at the second battle at Mutina. When the eagle-bearer of his legion received a bad wound, Octavian shouldered the eagle and carried it himself for a while.

Another fallen soldier at Mutina was Pontius Aquila, Decimus's lieutenant. Earlier, when the city was still under siege, Pontius was in northwestern Italy, where he defeated one of Antony's lieutenants. He came back to Mutina to fight. It was the end of a courageous man. Pontius was the second assassin of Caesar to die. As People's Tribune in 45 B.C., he had defied Caesar during his triumphal reentry to Rome. Cicero moved successfully that a statue be erected in Pontius's honor.

Although he had lost the battle, Antony still had most of his forces intact. He decided on an orderly retreat westward to meet up with his allies elsewhere in northern Italy and his potential allies over the Alps in Gaul. Lepidus was governor of Narbonese Gaul and Nearer Hispania, Plancus was governor of Gallia Comata, and Pollio was governor of Further Hispania, with many legions among them. All had promised to support Decimus and the Senate, but all had been supporters of Caesar and none could be trusted not to switch to Antony.

Antony began his march almost immediately, on April 22. Decimus prepared to pursue him but his army was weak and depleted in numbers. He had no cavalry or pack animals. What he did have, however, was some of Hirtius's and Pansa's newly recruited legions; Octavian kept the rest, plus his veterans. Decimus had political capital, too, for what it was worth—the enthusiastic support of the Senate. It named Antony and his allies as public enemies.

HIS FATHER'S MURDERER

Octavian was a question mark. The death of Hirtius and Pansa, the two consuls, left him great freedom as a commander. It was a boon for his career but a blow for the republican form of government. The question was, how big a blow?

Now free from the siege, Decimus met with Octavian. It would be hard to imagine a less comfortable encounter. Two years earlier Decimus and Octavian had ridden together in Caesar's victorious entourage. Since then, Decimus had become Caesar's murderer while Octavian had become Caesar's son. Now, according to Appian, Decimus tried to smooth the way by sending word to Octavian before the meeting. An evil spirit, said Decimus, had deceived him; others had led him into the conspiracy. The report is plausible but can't be trusted because Appian also states that Octavian refused to meet Decimus—which was untrue—saying that it was unnatural for him even to look at his father's murderer, let alone hold a conversation with him.

However Octavian might have felt about Decimus's betrayal of Caesar, Octavian received him anyhow—and Octavian was more than civil. In a letter to Cicero on May 9, 43 B.C., Decimus states plainly that he met with Octavian and came away trusting him, although he hadn't trusted Octavian before. Decimus told Octavian that he planned to cross the Apennines to pursue Antony and urged him to do the same, but Octavian refused to commit himself. He also refused to turn over the dead consuls' legions that he still commanded.

Decimus was a powerful person, and Octavian wanted to be a player, so it makes sense that Octavian behaved as he did. It also makes sense that he later denied that the meeting ever happened. That is surely the reason why Appian states this denial as fact. Octavian did not agree to help Decimus against Antony because it served Octavian's purpose to wound Antony but no more. Octavian did not want to help Decimus win.

A letter of Decimus to Cicero on May 5, 43 B.C. tells the tale. Decimus expressed frustration at Octavian's inaction:

If Caesar [Octavian] had listened to me and crossed the Apennines, I would have forced Antony into such dire straits that he would have been destroyed by lack of supplies rather than by iron. But Caesar cannot be ordered about, nor can he get his own army to obey his orders—both of which are very bad things.

Better for Decimus to blame Octavian than himself. Proud Decimus was not the sort of man ever to blame himself.

Decimus worried about Octavian's loyalty. He wrote to Cicero at the end of May with a report that the young man's veterans were cursing Cicero and urging their commander to force him to give them a better deal. Decimus also wrote that Octavian had gotten wind of a remark by Cicero that angered him. Supposedly, Cicero had said "the young man should be complimented, honored and lifted up—and out." Octavian had no intention of being forced out of power.

Decimus was right to worry. Far from helping Decimus destroy Antony, Octavian adopted a position of neutrality. Was he thinking of changing sides and joining Antony? That would have been a cold-blooded move but it suited an unfeeling era. Even Shakespeare's hero, Brutus, was a serial betrayer—of his father's memory; his chief, Pompey; his uncle, Cato; and his patron, Caesar. Besides, the Senate had made its opinion of Octavian clear. Not only did it refuse to grant him equal power or honor to Decimus, but it also cut the payments it had promised to Octavian's troops. Decimus was voted a triumph while Octavian had to settle for the lesser distinction of an ovation. Decimus was put in charge of the war against Antony and given the dead consuls' troops. But Octavian had no intention of dancing to the Senate's tune.

Octavian knew that as soon as the threat of Antony was removed, the Senate would drop him altogether. Although it was risky for him to support Antony, it was certain failure to continue supporting the Senate. And so Octavian stayed out of the fight against Antony and contemplated a change of course. Like Caesar before him, he savored risk.

In early May, three legions recruited in Central Italy by one of Antony's associates joined Antony in northwestern Italy, not far from today's Genoa. Antony and Decimus each now had seven legions, but Antony's were veterans and he had five thousand cavalry to boot. Decimus could not compete, especially because he had run out of money. He wrote Cicero that, to feed his troops he spent not only his own fortune but asked his friends to lend him money.

Cicero was not impressed. He criticized Decimus for failing to pursue a wounded enemy and letting Antony escape. That hardly seems fair, not with Decimus's troops exhausted and inexperienced and with him lacking cavalry and pack animals, and not with Octavian refusing to fight further against Antony.

Antony planned to cross the Alps, after which, as Decimus feared, he would join forces with Lepidus and Pollio—a prospect that Lepidus vehemently denied, not that Decimus believed him. He thought that Lepidus was unreliable.

Another man might have given up the chase, but not Decimus. He was very ambitious and he wanted nothing less than to rid himself of his greatest military threat in Italy—that is, to rid himself of Antony. At stake was the future of Italy. Defeat Antony and the Senate would rule Rome again and Decimus would be a prince of the Senate.

Decimus knew that the only way to defeat Antony was to cross the Alps himself and to meet up with the forces of Plancus in Gallia Comata. Plancus had four legions and allied cavalry but Decimus and Plancus could not defeat the combined forces of Antony and Lepidus. Still, Decimus plunged ahead, reckless and fearless, just as Caesar might have done. Decimus did not lack self-confidence. Gaul was his comfort zone, the area of his past military triumphs. So he took a pass through the Graian Alps (today's Little St. Bernard Pass), somehow coming up with the money for the tolls demanded by the local inhabitants.

Decimus might also have expected to find native allies in Gaul. Around June 10, he met Plancus at Cularo (Grenoble), a town of the Allobrogian Gauls—the same tribe that had allied with Catiline twenty years earlier. Decimus's mother, Sempronia, had opened her house to a group of

Allobroges during the revolutionary days of 63 B.C. Decimus was in contact with the Allobroges so he might have had reason to think they could provide men, money, and supplies.

Although Decimus and Plancus had a large number of troops—but few veterans—bad news from southern Gaul kept them from acting and surely discouraged any Allobrogian support, if that had ever been possible. Antony had arrived in Narbonese Gaul (modern Provence) in mid-May. He borrowed several leaves from Caesar's book by camping near Lepidus's army, allowing the men to fraternize, and growing a beard in mourning for his fallen men—all ploys that Caesar had used. Lepidus's men were charmed and defected as a group, and Lepidus soon followed. On May 29, the two armies were one.

They had as many legions as Decimus and Plancus, more veterans, more cavalry, and better equipment. Cicero asked Brutus and Cassius to send help to Decimus but none came. For more than two months, the armies of Decimus and Plancus stayed put. Then, disaster struck.

At the end of August, first Pollio and then Plancus deserted Decimus, announcing for Antony. By then, a revolution had shaken Rome.

12

VENGEANCE

I N SUMMER 43 B.C. WHILE DECIMUS CAMPED WEST OF GAUL'S ALPS
and trained his men to work with Plancus's troops, he was suddenly out-
flanked. Antony and Lepidus had just combined forces. Beyond the Alps, in
Rome, an even more dangerous beast was stirring.

LOOK EASTWARD

After Brutus and Cassius left Italy in August 44 B.C., only scattered reports
of their activity reached the capital. Like a spymaster, Servilia sat in Rome
and dished out news from the East. In October 44 B.C., she received a slave
of Caecilius Bassus, the rebel governor of Syria. The slave told her that the
legions in Alexandria were rioting, Bassus had been summoned, and meanwhile, Cassius was due to arrive in Syria. She was expecting a secret visit
from Marcus Scaptius, who was Brutus's long-standing agent in the East.
When Servilia passed on the information to Cicero, he wrote to Atticus
with a mix of excitement about the progress in the East and worry about the
"villainy and madness" of Antony and his followers in the West.

Meanwhile, Brutus was building up his power from a base in Athens. He was hailed as a hero there and his statue was put up next to the statues of famous Athenian tyrant slayers. He gathered supporters and potential officers, and made deals and threats. He talked his way into control of the provinces of Macedonia (roughly northern and central Greece as well as parts of Albania and the former Yugoslav Republic of Macedonia) and Illyricum (roughly modern Albania and much of the former Yugoslavia). He was a usurper at first with no legal authority until February 43 B.C., when the Senate confirmed him as legitimate governor of these provinces. Brutus captured Mark Antony's brother, Gaius Antonius, who was supposed to be governor of Macedonia. Brutus was careful to treat Gaius Antonius well. Unlike Cicero, Brutus still hoped that it would be possible to reach agreement with Mark Antony, a follower of Caesar but a moderate. He had no faith in Octavian and he took Cicero to task for trusting him. "I only wish you could see how much I fear him!" Brutus wrote of Octavian to Cicero.

Cassius, for his part, was even busier. By late February 43 B.C., the news reached Rome that he had taken over Syria as well as legions stationed there and nearby. Again, Cassius acted without legal authority.

From her base in Egypt, Cleopatra watched with concern. Caesar had left four legions in Egypt, and both Dolabella and Cassius asked for them. The queen chose Dolabella and sent the legions, but Cassius captured them en route to Syria. He put together a twelve-legion army and defeated Dolabella, who committed suicide.

But Cleopatra was not done. She decided to help the opponents of Brutus and Cassius, opponents who were then in western Greece. She equipped a fleet and took command of it herself, making her a female admiral like Artemisia of Halicarnassus (modern Bodrum, Turkey), who had fought at the battle of Salamis in 480 B.C. or the pirate queen Teuta of Illyria (modern Montenegro and Albania), who battled the Romans in the 220s B.C. Cassius sent another supporter of the assassins, Murcus, to ambush Cleopatra off southern Greece, but the Egyptian fleet never got that far. A storm off Libya damaged it so badly that it had to turn back. Cleopatra herself had a bad case of seasickness. Cassius considered invading Egypt until Brutus reminded him that they needed to save their resources.

From their base in the East, Brutus and Cassius put together the components of a Mediterranean-wide strategy. They would win by fighting the war in the empire, not in Rome or Italy. That had been Pompey's strategy against Caesar and now they returned to it. Either they felt confident that this time things would be different or they accepted Pompey's strategy as the best among several bad alternatives.

In April 43 B.C., after the victory at Mutina, the Senate entrusted the Republic's fate to three commanders in addition to Decimus. They confirmed Brutus as governor of Macedonia, Cassius as governor of Syria, and Sextus Pompey as admiral of the fleet.

Cassius was a better strategist than Decimus. He planned to build up an army and navy in the east and to combine it with Sextus's naval forces in the west. By the summer of 43 B.C., Sextus moved his base to Sicily.

Sextus Pompey brought sea power. That was immensely useful but not decisive. As in the civil war between Pompey and Caesar, so in the new struggle, strategists hoped to strangle the enemy by sea. They meant to cut off the enemy's supplies of food and to cripple his transport of men. But with roads available along most of the coastline, a determined and supple enemy could travel overland. Sea power alone could not win the war; it would take an army to deliver the decisive blow. Cassius knew that, and he and Brutus worked mightily to build one.

Brutus had no time to stop, even for grief. In the summer of 43 B.C., Porcia died after an illness; the details are unknown. She was in Italy, Brutus was in Greece, and the two had no chance for a last farewell. Cicero wrote a mourning Brutus to be strong. His country needed him, said the orator: "Not only your army but all citizens and nearly all people have their eyes on you."

Brutus was active in Thrace (modern Bulgaria) and western Anatolia. Deiotarus sent him troops. Brutus extorted money here and there, winning a minor victory over a Thracian tribe, which earned him an acclamation as imperator by his troops. He put the title on his official statements and his coins.

Like a lioness, Servilia defended Brutus's and Cassius's interests in Rome while they were away. Or like a senator, since Servilia ran her family conferences like a Senate meeting. On July 25, 43 B.C., she convened a meeting at one of her houses. Cicero was there as well as Casca and Labeo, two of the assassins on the Ides, and Marcus Scaptius, Brutus's agent in the east, first in 50 B.C. and now again. Servilia asked if they should send for Brutus now or tell him to stay where he was. Send for him now, said Cicero, but Brutus stayed put. Servilia no doubt kept Brutus informed about the meeting, as she did about her grandchildren. That same summer, Cicero spoke up in the Senate for them, the children of Lepidus, who was married to another one of Servilia's daughters. Now that Lepidus had defected to Antony, Brutus worried about the children as well as their mother and Servilia.

Servilia worried in turn about Brutus and her son-in-law Cassius but they were doing well on their own. Most of the Roman commanders of the East came over to them. Some of those commanders were convinced opponents of Caesar or believers in the Republic, some were repelled by the brutal methods that Antony and Octavian would each soon employ. Some reasoned that anyone who managed to kill Caesar was an effective soldier indeed—and they wanted to be on the winning side. And some liked the jingle of the assassins' money.

Meanwhile, in Italy the world was about to turn upside down. Soon it was Servilia who was in danger, not Brutus or Cassius.

ELECTED BY THE SWORD

In July 43 B.C., Octavian made his move. He demanded that the Senate give him one of the two vacant consulships. It was a disrespectful demand on the part of a nineteen-year-old, especially since the Senate had already knocked ten years off the minimum age requirement of forty-three for consul and said he could hold the position at age thirty-three. But Octavian did not lack gall. He sent an embassy of soldiers to the Senate but the senators refused his request. As he left the chamber, one of the soldiers retrieved the sword he had left outside and angrily said, "This will make him consul, if you won't." And so it did. Octavian crossed the Rubicon and marched on Rome, using the same road that Caesar had taken six and a half years earlier. He had eight legions, including new recruits.

Octavian had himself and his cousin Quintus Pedius named co-consuls. The senators acquiesced and the people held elections to rubber-stamp the choices. Then he had Pedius pass a law to rescind the amnesty for Caesar's killers. The Lex Pedia, as it was called, set up a special court that promptly condemned the assassins and many of their associates. Even Sextus Pompey, who sympathized with the assassination but had had nothing to do with it, was condemned. Only one judge voted to acquit Brutus. Just like that, the compromise hammered out by the Senate in the days following the Ides of March was abolished.

When it came to Antony and his allies, however, peace was the order of the day. Octavian lifted the decree outlawing Antony and began negotiations. In September 43 B.C., Antony reentered Italian Gaul with about eighteen or nineteen legions. The next month, Antony, Lepidus, and Octavian met near Bononia (modern Bologna) and formed a triumvirate, a three-man commission with dictatorial powers for five years. They had over forty legions. They divided up the western part of the empire among them, with Antony taking most of Gaul, Lepidus taking Narbonese Gaul and Nearer Hispania, and Octavian taking Sicily, Sardinia, and Roman Africa. They were the supreme authority in the state.

On November 27, 43 B.C., a law was passed to make the triumvirate legal. If that wasn't the death notice of the Roman Republic, it was a declaration that only heroic measures could save it.

Blood, money, and real estate were the first orders of business for the triumvirs. They had no interest in the clemency that, in their judgment, had killed Caesar. Instead, like Sulla, they chose proscription, that is, a purge—the public decree of enemies condemned to death and property confiscation. Three hundred senators and two thousand Roman knights were on the list. One of the senators executed was the judge who had voted to acquit

Brutus earlier that year. Gangs of executioners now fanned out in search of loot and bounties. Most of the victims escaped by fleeing Italy but they lost their property nonetheless. It was confiscated and sold. Like so much of Rome's violent politics in these years, much of the action came down to real estate.

The proscriptions served several purposes, from settling scores to instilling obedience to the new regime, but the main one was raising money. War was expensive and a new conflict loomed against Brutus, Cassius, and Sextus Pompey. The proscriptions could not raise enough money, though, so the triumvirs instituted new taxes as well.

The triumvirs also announced their decision to confiscate the land of eighteen of the richest cities of Italy in order to settle their soldiers. For the inhabitants of those towns, it was a virtual declaration of war. For Brutus and Cassius, it was a recruiting tool.

Caesar's assassin Galba was one of the senators whose name appeared on the proscription list. We don't know if he was killed, but in any case he did not survive the wars of these years.

Servilia fared better. She found asylum with Atticus. The careful Atticus had friends in every faction, and earlier he had helped Antony's wife, Fulvia. Servilia made it through the storm. Not so Cicero. He was the most famous victim of the terror.

On December 7, 43 B.C., Cicero was caught trying to escape from his villa on the coast north of Naples to a ship waiting to take him to safety in the East. He could have escaped earlier but he waited too long. Cicero died with dignity and without offering resistance. His head was brought to Rome and nailed to the Speaker's Platform in the Roman Forum, echoing Marius's and Sulla's treatment of their victims. But Cicero's hands were cut off and displayed as well in vengeance for the bitter denunciations of Antony that he had written in his *Philippics*. One source claims that Antony's wife, Fulvia, pulled out Cicero's tongue and stabbed it with a hairpin.

Cicero's death is not just an event in Roman politics but a milestone in Western civilization, of which he is one of the founders. Our purview is narrower; we esteem Cicero as the most famous, the most eloquent, and the most entertaining observer of politics in the age of Caesar. Indeed, no one in all of ancient history has left such a quantity of political commentary. He was also a key actor in the events of 44 B.C. and 43 B.C.

Cicero survived the Ides of March by twenty months. During that time he became the heart and soul of what might be called the Italy First policy. Others fought for the Republic but they did so from abroad. Not Cicero. He was vigorous and courageous, but he was wrong. Octavian was unreliable. Octavian agreed to proscribe his ally Cicero as a favor to Antony. Antony was unbeatable—not by the scanty forces available to the anti-Caesar faction in Italy. The Republic would be saved from outside Italy or not at all. If not for Cicero, Decimus might have evacuated Italy and any remaining republicans might have evacuated Rome to join the armies in the East. A good general like Decimus could have made a major contribution to the republican cause there.

After Cicero's death, a friend of Antony's was allowed to buy Cicero's town house on the Palatine Hill on Rome. It was none other than Censorinus, who had tried to save Caesar in the Senate on the Ides of March.

While Cicero was killed, Caesar's memory was exalted. The triumvirs passed a law to build a temple and institute the public worship of *divus Iulius*, the Deified Julius Caesar. Within a few years, when Antony accepted consecration as High Priest of the cult, Caesar's deification was official. This entitled Octavian to call himself *divi filius*, the Son of a Man Made God. Acclaimed as an Imperator, Octavian became IMPERATOR CAESAR DIVI FILIUS.

THE END OF DECIMUS

Meanwhile, Decimus decided to save his army and join Brutus in Macedonia. The easiest route, through northern Italy, was closed because of the presence of Octavian and his army. Decimus proposed to his men a much more difficult route, a journey through the Alps. His legions immediately deserted—the veterans and auxiliaries went to Antony while the new recruits went home to Italian Gaul and Octavian. After Mutina, we hear nothing more of Decimus's gladiators but he still had a bodyguard of Gallic horsemen, perhaps dating back to his days as governor of Gaul. He let those who wanted to go home do so with generous pay for their services while he headed for the Rhenus (Rhine) River with three hundred followers. They probably skirted the Iura Mountains to the east and south, reaching the river in the vicinity of today's Basel, Switzerland. But the sight of the mighty Rhenus frightened most of them away. Decimus was left with only ten men, of whom at least two were Romans.

Undaunted, Decimus decided to travel through Italian Gaul after all, but in disguise as a Gaul. He knew the language. In hooded coats, breeches, and clogs, he and the non-Gauls among them could look the part. Decimus was not the first Roman to go native, but it was rare to see one in such extreme conditions.

The desperate men probably retraced their steps toward Vesontio (Besançon, France), and then they possibly took the narrow Jougne Pass through the Iura Mountains from today's France to Switzerland. This was the territory of the Sequani Gauls. Armed locals policed the pass and collected tolls. Their suspicious eyes noted Decimus and his party and arrested them. Decimus was relieved to learn that their leader was a local bigwig named Camilus. As governor, Decimus had done many a favor for Camilus, so he demanded to be taken to him. Camilus fawned over Decimus, apologizing for the mistaken imprisonment, but he secretly sent word to Antony. There was a reward for capturing Decimus, and besides, Antony, and not the former governor, was the man who mattered now.

The sources agree that Antony ordered Decimus's death. They disagree as to how Decimus died. Some say that Camilus carried out the execution while others say that a group of knights sent by Antony did the job. Several sources claim that, at the end, Decimus forgot about his vaunted prowess and started bemoaning his fate. But Decimus was never anything but brave and this sounds like slander put out later by his enemies. In any case, a sword blow to the neck killed Decimus. Camilus sent his head to Antony, who then had it buried. It was about mid-September 43 B.C.

So died one of the three main conspirators against Julius Caesar. In the last fifteen months of his life, Decimus displayed courage, leadership, determination, energy, and suppleness. He raised new troops and held his army together through a siege. He led his men over the Alps but he could not talk them into trusting their lives to a nearly trackless wilderness. To save the Republic and advance his career, he flouted the law and he was rewarded with the glittering, long-sought prize—a triumph. But he never lived to celebrate it. Had he defeated Antony he would have been one of the very top figures in the Roman state. He would have been the military hero of reestablishing the Republic. For that matter, he would have been in a position to undermine it and make himself the next Caesar, if he so chose.

Decimus demonstrated a taste for risk taking that would have put Caesar to shame, except that Caesar usually took only carefully calculated risks. By choosing to defend Italian Gaul instead of retreating to Macedonia while there was still time, Decimus took as big a gamble as Caesar did by going into the Senate House without a bodyguard on the Ides of March. Decimus displayed everything, in short, except strategic caution.

No doubt Decimus would have preferred a hero's death in battle to his execution, but on one thing he might have been satisfied. He died on the scene of nearly all his military triumphs—in Gaul.

THE SINEWS OF WAR

Money, said Cicero, is "the sinews of war." He made this remark in his Fifth Philippic, delivered in the Senate on January 1, 43 B.C. It might have served as a mission statement for Brutus and Cassius in the East. They committed themselves to fighting for the freedom of the Roman people, but the people of the empire were another matter. They squeezed the provincials very hard indeed in order to raise money, but they knew as well as anyone that war was expensive.

At the news from the west, Brutus ordered the execution of his prisoner, Antony's brother Gaius, in revenge for the deaths of Cicero and Decimus—the latter his kinsman, said Brutus, and the former his friend. As often, Brutus mixed his sentiment with steel and ice; he said that he felt more shame

at the cause of Cicero's death, which he blamed on Roman softness, than he
felt grief at the event itself.

In the spring of 42 B.C., the two leaders attacked various centers of resistance. Cassius made war on the island of Rhodes, a small naval power that
had supported Dolabella. After two naval defeats and a threatened siege,
some Rhodians opened the gates of their city to the Romans. Cassius had
fifty leading men put to death and plundered the town's gold and silver.

For his part, Brutus assaulted the cities of Lycia in southwestern Anatolia. He laid siege to the well-fortified city of Xanthus. When the Romans
finally broke in, large numbers of citizens preferred suicide to surrender.
Plutarch tells a pretty story about how Brutus cried tears over them, but
that sounds unlikely. Next, a neighboring city preferred to accept Brutus's
terms and give up all their coin and treasure. Liberty might have been Brutus's motto, but it meant the free exercise of Rome's republican government,
not freedom for the cities of the empire.

Around June 42 B.C., Brutus and Cassius met at the city of Sardis in
western Anatolia. They resolved various differences and decided to head to
Macedonia. After leaving Lepidus behind to hold Italy, Antony and Octavian had crossed the Adriatic Sea with nineteen legions. On paper, that
meant 95,000 men, but the real number was probably only about half as
much. They were also supposed to have had 13,000 cavalrymen. For their
part, Brutus and Cassius had seventeen legions—supposedly 85,000 men
but, again, the real number was probably only half. In addition, they are
said to have had 20,000 horsemen. Even with the figures cut in half, a massive number of legionaries—around 90,000 all told—were preparing to
meet. The largest showdown of the era loomed.

Various eastern allies sent troops to help Brutus and Cassius, primarily
cavalry. Deiotarus sent both infantry and cavalry. The king of Parthia sent
a contingent of archers. This was a tribute to Brutus's and Cassius's diplomacy. In late 43 B.C., they had sent the son of Caesar's old friend-turned-enemy, Labienus, to Parthia. He negotiated the support.

In the summer of 42 B.C., outside the city of Cardia on the Gallipoli Peninsula, Brutus and Cassius gathered their combined forces. These very large armies had to be fed, housed, exercised, inspired, and, above all, paid.

The commanders did not disappoint. For a year or more they had been raising money by diplomacy or force. Now they had a variety of coins issued by their officials, probably using one or more of the mints of Macedonia.

Brutus had learned his lesson. Unlike in the days following the Ides of March, he would not stint the soldiers. As Appian says, he and Cassius had raised plenty of money to pay them. They worried especially that the large portion of their soldiers who had fought for Julius Caesar might now defect to his adopted son, Octavian. According to Appian, Cassius addressed this point in a speech to the assembled troops. He told them that, whoever the general, they were always fighting for the same cause—Rome. But Brutus and Cassius were not so naïve as to rely on words. Every legionary got 1,500 denarii, every centurion 7,500, and every military tribune 15,000. These were generous sums. They didn't match the amount that Antony and Octavian promised their men in the case of victory—5,000 denarii (20,000 sesterces) each. They were outdone by the sums at Caesar's Triple Triumph in 46 B.C., where the payout began at 6,000 denarii per legionary. Brutus and Cassius paid their men *before* the battle. They already had the money while Antony and Octavian Caesar only promised to get it—they didn't have it yet, a point that, according to Appian, Cassius emphasized to his soldiers. Even Caesar paid his men only after they had fought for him in Gaul and the Civil War. It's often risky to pay someone in advance but no doubt Brutus and Cassius felt they had to do so to win over Caesar's former soldiers. Perhaps as well the two assassins were overcompensating for the mistake of not wooing the soldiers after the Ides of March. In any case, now they surely pointed out that victory would bring even more loot.

The gorgeous array of money illustrated a variety of themes, among them, heroes of the Roman past, gods, and eagles. One coin, issued by Brutus and Casca, shows Neptune with a trident on one side as a symbol of republican sea power. The other side shows a winged victory holding a palm and a broken diadem with a broken scepter under her feet—symbols of success over Caesar's would-be kingship. The inscription says "BRUTUS IMP," Brutus Imperator.

One coin, however, stands out from the rest. Issued by Brutus, it is a small, silver denarius, and it may well be the most famous coin of ancient Rome. A gold version, an aureus, exists as well. On its obverse the coin shows Brutus in profile. He wears a beard as a sign of mourning for the Republic. Still, it is a strange image considering that Caesar had been criticized for breaking with precedent and becoming the first Roman ever to depict himself on coins. Now, Brutus, identified as an IMPERATOR, strikes a very unrepublican pose. Yet there was a war to be won. That came first—constitutional niceties could wait for later.

The other side of the coin is even more surprising. The coin shows on its reverse a *pileus* or freed slave's cap above the inscription EID MAR—that is, an abbreviation of "IDES OF MARCH." On either side of the cap stands a military dagger, point facing down. It is an arresting image.

With the prospect of a great battle against the armies of Antony and Octavian looming, the military imagery makes sense. But that, of course, was not the primary meaning of the daggers on this coin, at least not for those who issued it.

Writing centuries later, Dio offers an identification of the two military daggers, making this one of the few coins mentioned by an ancient writer:

> In addition to these activities, Brutus stamped upon the coins which were being minted in his own likeness with a cap and two daggers, indicating by this and by the inscription that he and Cassius had liberated the fatherland.

In short, the two military daggers are meant to represent the weapons used by the two leaders of the anti-Caesar movement on the Ides of March. Even for a gathering of soldiers, this was blunt.

As noted earlier, each of the two daggers on the coin has a different hilt. The cruciform hilt might have been Brutus's dagger, and the two-disk hilt might have been Cassius's. A less speculative point comes from noticing what the daggers have in common. They are both precisely military daggers—*pugiones* (singular, *pugio*) in Latin. The Romans distinguished the military dagger from the *sica*, a curved dagger of Thracian origin, which was not normally carried by Roman soldiers. The sica, in Roman eyes, was a weapon for cutthroats; a word for "murderer" or "asssassin" is *sicarius*, literally, "a sica-man."

After the Ides of March, Caesar's friends claimed that the assassins were mere murderers. But through imagery this coin argues that the Ides of March was an honorable act carried out by the tools of Roman soldiers, as the military daggers show. It was an act not of murder but of liberation, as the freed-slave's cap shows.

Of course the soldiers who took Brutus's coin in 42 B.C. knew that their commanders' daggers had killed Caesar. They understood the symbolism of the military dagger as a tool of tyrannicide. They were already familiar with the gruesome reality of the weapon. They understood that they were getting paid to use the military dagger, along with the sword and the spear, to finish what Brutus and Cassius had started.

PHILIPPI AND AFTERWARD

The great confrontation took place outside of Philippi, a city in eastern Macedonia, on the Via Egnatia and near the Aegean coast. The number of combatants was huge. The site bespoke destiny. A famous warrior, King Philip of Macedon, the father of Alexander the Great, had founded the city and named it after himself. Even the spirits played their part. One night before he took his army across the Hellespont, Brutus saw a vision of his evil genius—the bad fortune or bad judgment that the Romans believed each person has. The vision warned Brutus, "you will see me at Philippi." The vision supposedly appeared again on the night before the final battle. In the heat of combat at Philippi the next day, Cassius supposedly saw Caesar's ghost dressed in his reddish purple commander's cape.

As the great clash approached, Brutus wrote with courage and acceptance to Atticus. Either they would free the Roman people, Brutus wrote, or they would die and be freed from slavery. Everything was safe and secure, he added, except for the knowledge of whether they would live free or die.

The odds were good for Brutus and Cassius at Philippi. Their numbers were strong and they had an excellent position on the high ground straddling the Roman road. Mountains protected their northern flank and a marsh protected their southern flank. In Cassius they had a very good commander, and in Brutus, a competent one. They controlled the sea and had their fleet nearby on an island from which it could bring supplies to a port not far from their camp. Octavian and Antony, by contrast, were short of food. So the pressure was on them, while Brutus and Cassius could sit back and let the enemy starve.

They had the help of several of their fellow assassins. Cimber—the drunkard and brawler—had helped them seize this position from an advance guard of the enemy. Publius Servilius Casca, the first man to strike Caesar on the Ides of March, served under Brutus as a commander. There was also a veritable roll call of Roman nobles, including the son of Cato.

Antony was a resourceful general. He was by far the most experienced of the four commanders present. He managed to sneak around Brutus and Cassius's position and threaten their supply route. Then he started building fortifications to cut the enemy off from the sea and their supplies, so Brutus and Cassius had to begin a counterfortification to stop him. On or around October 3, Antony attacked, and with such success that he took not only the counterfortifications but also Cassius's camp. Cassius's men fled in a rout. Meanwhile, to the north, Brutus's men managed to take Octavian's camp, even though they were poorly disciplined and failed to listen to Brutus's orders.

Octavian himself was ill and was not there. His main contribution to victory was to survive unharmed. Afterward, reports credited him with paying careful attention to divine signs. They said that in response to one person's vision, he put on Caesar's ring as a good luck charm. In response to another vision, he left his tent beforehand and so avoided harm.

Forced to withdraw to a hill for safety, Cassius mistakenly thought he saw Brutus's army routed as well. He preferred suicide to capture, so Cassius had a freedman decapitate him. Some ancient writers said that the man killed him without orders. It was Cassius's birthday.

Cassius was a politician of conviction, one of the Best Men through and through, hostile to Caesar and to anything that smacked of one-man rule. If Plutarch is right, Cassius spurred on the plot to kill Caesar. Given his military background, Cassius surely played a major role in working out the details of the assassination. He pushed consistently for a hard line, both for killing Antony and for denying Caesar a public funeral, but Brutus overruled him. But killing Antony might have unleashed Lepidus and his legion on the assassins on the Capitoline Hill and denying Caesar a public funeral might only have furnished a grievance for the riot that was probably inevitable. Cassius demonstrated strategic insight in the two years after the assassination, back in the eastern Mediterranean that he knew well. His methods were brutal at times but he did a superb job of putting together an army to challenge Antony and Octavian.

Brutus had Cassius buried in secret, so as not to depress the army. He mourned Cassius as "the last of the Romans," a man whose prowess would never be seen again. It would certainly not be seen in Brutus's camp. Even if Cassius had lived, it is unclear that he could have outfought Antony. With Brutus in command, his army's chances plummeted because Brutus was no general. Decimus was—and the army's chances would surely have improved if Decimus had survived and reached them to hold a position of command.

Brutus distrusted the loyalty of Cassius's men and he suffered at least one notable defection. Deiotarus's general, noticing which way the wind was blowing, switched to Antony. One wonders if the old king, with his usual ruthlessness, had ordered his commander to pick the winner. Brutus also knew that the enemy was still trying to cut him off. So, three weeks later, on October 23, he attacked. After a long, fierce fight, the enemy broke Brutus's line.

Antony was the architect of victory at Philippi—a thorough, decisive victory. Brutus and Cassius's stand for the Republic was over. Now, if not earlier, Brutus might have reconsidered his decision to spare Antony on the Ides of March.

Brutus managed to escape the battlefield. Traveling in the hills with a few friends, he quoted Greek poetry that night under the stars. After some time passed, he decided to end it all. He told his friends that he blamed fortune but he would die happy. Unlike the victors, he said, he left behind a reputation for virtue, while his enemies were unjust and wicked. So Plutarch tells the story, relying on the eyewitness account of Brutus's friend and fellow student Publius Volumnius. For once, Plutarch is more credible than the other versions.

Philippi devastated the ranks of the assassins and their supporters. Neither Publius Servilius Casca nor Cimber is ever heard from again. They are presumed either to have fallen in battle or committed suicide afterward. Other nobles joined the ranks of the fallen, including the son of Cato.

The poet Horace made his peace with the new regime after fighting against it at Philippi. He criticized Brutus's poor generalship and described the battle as "when virtue broke." "Virtue" in Latin is *virtus*, a word combining manly prowess with moral excellence. In his own lifetime, Brutus was famous for virtus and proud of it, but now it came into question. Why hadn't he been a better general at Philippi? Why did he kill himself instead of fighting on? So men asked at first.

In the long term, though, an afterglow of glory attached itself to Brutus. He was remembered not as the Loser of Philippi, but instead as the Man of Virtue, as he is in Plutarch. Brutus had a good press, and that owed something to his connections and to Servilia's, but there was more to the matter than that. Brutus appealed to the Romans. He was both a figure out of their steely, Central Italian past and a suppler, more forward-looking practitioner of Greek wisdom. Make no mistake about it—if Brutus's action on the Ides of March horrified the people of Rome, it also electrified them. By drawing his dagger and stabbing Caesar, Brutus proved his courage. As Plutarch says, even those who hated him for killing Caesar couldn't help but find something noble in him.

Brutus was not the woolly-eyed idealist that he is sometimes portrayed as. Although Antony's generalship destroyed Brutus, Brutus was not wrong to have spared him on the Ides of March. Without Antony's moderating hand it's not clear that the assassins could have survived the vengeance of Lepidus and his men. Nor could Brutus have predicted Octavian's effectiveness and how that would push Antony into destroying Decimus. In any case, Brutus had warned Cicero not to trust Octavian. If Brutus had had his way, Decimus would have allied with Antony against Octavian. The world might have looked very different if that had happened. Brutus might just have saved the Republic.

And yet the ancients couldn't resist a series of ghastly, comic anecdotes about the fate of Brutus's corpse. For example, the story goes that when Antony found Brutus's dead body, he had it wrapped in his most luxurious reddish purple robe—the mark of a Roman commander. Then some thief stole the robe and Antony had him executed.

After having Brutus's body cremated, Antony sent the ashes home. And so, late in 42 B.C., a messenger arrived at Servilia's villa, either a town house in Rome or one of her country places in Antium or near Naples. He brought an urn. It carried all that was mortal of her only son—all, that is, except his head, if we can believe the source that says that Octavian had it cut off just as Decimus's head was cut off. According to the source, Brutus's head was sent to Rome to place at the foot of a statue of Caesar as revenge. But the head never made it there, because during the sea voyage to Rome, the sailors tossed it overboard as bad luck during a storm, like the biblical Jonah. As Servilia looked at the urn containing the remains of Brutus, what did she think? Did she tote up the corpses? In addition to her son and his wife, Porcia, her son-in-law, Cassius, also lay dead. Or did Servilia take comfort in the thought of her son's glory? Of Servilia, not another word is heard. The sources do not mention her again.

"This was the noblest Roman of them all," says Shakespeare's Antony on finding Brutus's body. He is echoing the sentiments about Brutus that Plutarch ascribes to him in another earlier context. In the earshot of many, says Plutarch, Antony once declared that Brutus was the only conspirator against Caesar who was motivated by the splendor and nobility of the deed; as for the others, only hate and jealousy moved them.

In truth, Antony was a noble Roman as well, a man of the old school.

He belonged to Brutus's generation. Like Brutus, he took his bearings from a world that was disappearing around him. Not so Antony's twenty-one-year-old co-commander at Philippi. Octavian treated the Roman past with breezy insincerity.

Brutus said that Antony would pay the penalty for his folly. Instead of standing up to be counted with the likes of Cato, Cassius, and Brutus himself, Antony had made himself Octavian's accessory. Brutus predicted before the decisive encounter at Philippi that if Antony wasn't defeated with Octavian, then the two men would soon be fighting each other. He was right.

THE LAST ASSASSIN

Philippi was a massive victory for Antony and Octavian, but there was still work to do to bring the Roman world under their thumb. The republican fleet, led by Sextus Pompey from his base in Sicily, still controlled the sea. In the following years, Sextus Pompey first brought the triumvirs to the bargaining table and then destroyed two of Octavian's fleets before finally losing decisively at sea in 36 b.c. Afterward he fled to Anatolia, where he was caught and executed.

Lepidus suffered a steady decline. In 40 b.c. he had to trade Nearer Hispania and Narbonese Gaul for the less strategic province of Roman Africa. From there he helped Octavian against Sextus Pompey—and only too well, as Pompey's troops eventually defected to Lepidus. He wanted to add Sicily to his portfolio, but Octavian was strong enough to push Lepidus aside. In 36 b.c. Lepidus was forced into permanent exile south of Rome at Circeii, a beautiful but lonely seaside spot, famous only for its oysters.

Antony and Octavian divided the Roman Empire between them. Antony took the East and Octavian the West. That left Octavian the unpopular job in Italy of confiscating land for veterans. The result pleased the ex-soldiers but meant ruin for many other Italians. Military gravestones around Italy record the new prosperity, while contemporary poetry echoes the misery of the dispossessed. Fulvia, Antony's formidable wife, and Lucius, his surviving brother, stirred up so much opposition to the land grab that it came down to war around the Central Italian town of Perusia (modern Perugia). Octavian's forces won. If the report is not just propaganda, they then massacred a large number of enemy senators and knights on the altar of the Deified Julius on the Ides of March. It was virtually a human sacrifice for Caesar's ghost. They let Fulvia and Lucius go free.

In the East, Antony picked up Caesar's mantle of opposition to the Parthians. Astoundingly, the Parthians had the help of Quintus Labienus, the son of Caesar's old friend-turned-enemy Titus Labienus. The Parthians conquered much of the Roman east after Philippi. Now Antony's deputy pushed them back and captured and executed Quintus Labienus. Then Antony pushed too far—he tried to invade Parthian territory via Armenia, only to end in utter failure. But history remembers Antony for something entirely different during his time in the East—his relationship with Cleopatra, a political and military alliance as well as a love affair. It wasn't his first move. After Fulvia died in 40 B.C., Antony married Octavian's sister, Octavia. They had two daughters together, but it was not enough to keep him from Cleopatra.

If Octavian had Caesar's name, Antony had Caesar's mistress. There are many fascinating stories to tell about history's most famous power couple, but they are not our subject. Cleopatra was once again the lover of a man like Caesar. He was one of the two most powerful men in the Roman world. But the world could not stand two Caesars. Eventually, there was war between Octavian on the one side with Antony and Cleopatra on the other.

Now master of the sea at last, Octavian had the winning fleet at the Battle of Actium in western Greece in 31 B.C. It was a decisive victory. Within the next year, Antony and Cleopatra each committed suicide in Alexandria. At last, Octavian really was the one and only Caesar, the sole master of the Roman Empire. But there were still scores to settle over the Ides of March.

Suetonius writes that within three years of Caesar's assassination, all the participants in the conspiracy were dead. That's not correct. At least two of the assassins lived on for another decade. They were both obscure characters, which is probably not an accident. The triumvirs cut off the tallest heads as quickly as they could. The more obscure were able to escape vengeance longer.

Decimus Turullius was one survivor. After Philippi, Turullius escaped with his ships and a large sum of money to Sextus Pompey in Sicily. Several years later, after Sextus's eventual defeat, Turullius went over to Antony. He supported his former enemy with gusto, building Antony a fleet and even minting coins for him. Turullius fought for Antony at Actium in 31 B.C. The next year, Octavian caught up with Turullius on the Greek island of Cos. He had Turullius executed on the grounds of having cut down wood from a sacred grove in order to build warships. Why not a charge of having assassinated Caesar? Perhaps by now Octavian wanted to change the subject.

The next of Caesar's assassins to die was Turullius's colleague Cassius of Parma. He was a poet, and a good one, to judge from the great Roman poet Horace, who praised Cassius of Parma's "little works," probably elegies—that is, short, epigrammatic and learned poems. None of Cassius of Parma's pieces survive. Cassius of Parma was an officer at Philippi, and Horace too fought in the republican army there. Perhaps the two men exchanged lines of poetry while waiting for the battle.

After Philippi, Cassius of Parma gathered the remaining troops and went over to Sextus Pompey. Six years later, in 36 B.C., he switched his loyalties to Antony. While associated with Antony, Cassius of Parma wrote satire insulting Octavian's ancestry. He fought for Antony at Actium in 31 B.C. Once again, Cassius of Parma escaped defeat, this time fleeing to Athens, but his nemesis was on his heels. At Athens, he had a recurring nightmare of a dark and disheveled man coming for him, telling the poet that he was his evil genius. Not long afterward, in 30 B.C., Cassius of Parma was executed on Octavian's instructions.

If the sources are right, Cassius of Parma was the last of Caesar's assassins to die. We cannot document the fate of all of Caesar's known assassins but none appears in the sources after 30 B.C. It seems likely that fourteen years after the Ides of March, they were all dead. Octavian had his revenge. But Rome, Italy, and indeed places around the Roman world had all paid a price.

13

AUGUSTUS

Summer 29 B.C. was a time for celebration. After fifteen years of civil war there were no more enemies. Octavian returned to Rome from his victories overseas and he returned in peace.

Decimus did not trouble Octavian for long. Brutus and Cassius had been more formidable foes but they were gone within three years of the Ides of March. Sextus Pompey held out for another seven years and then he too succumbed. Antony provided Octavian's greatest challenge, but Octavian prevailed in the end.

After Actium and the deaths of Antony and Cleopatra, Octavian was the master of the Roman world. He had won a civil war but the Roman public didn't like being reminded of citizens killing each other, so Octavian shrewdly rebranded his success. It was, he said, victory over a foreign foe, the defeat not of Antony but rather of the Egyptian queen, Cleopatra. Horace, the politically savvy poet, agreed, writing a poem that savaged Cleopatra without mentioning Antony. Octavian did something more—he sealed his victory with the approval of the man who spelled success in Roman eyes. He claimed the blessing of Caesar.

Octavian held a triple triumph—three triumphs on successive days. On the first day he celebrated victories in the Balkans. The second day marked his naval victory at Actium. On the third day, he celebrated the conquest of Egypt, the last independent major Greek state, now finally a Roman province. Egypt was one of the richest countries in the ancient world and Octavian was proud of having conquered it for Rome. Appropriately, the Egyptian triumph was the most magnificent of the three. Cleopatra was dead and she couldn't be forced to march, but she appeared in effigy, lying on a couch while two of her children by Antony walked behind. Not Caesarion, though—he wasn't there. Octavian had executed him on the advice that "Too many Caesars is not a good thing." Caesarion was only seventeen but Octavian had been dangerous at that age, as he might have remembered. Octavian entered last, riding in a chariot, followed by senators and other leading public officials.

Victory at Actium meant peace. Octavian now demobilized about half his legions. Egypt meant wealth. Octavian was able to buy land in Italy and around the empire for new colonies to settle his veterans. There were no more property confiscations to settle former soldiers, as there had been in 46–45 B.C. and 41 B.C. Octavian managed to resolve one of Rome's biggest causes of conflict—real estate.

On the eighteenth of the month Sextilis, the day after the third triumph, Octavian continued the pageantry. He dedicated the Temple of the Deified Julius, an event followed by days of spectacular public games and banquets. The building had been planned in 42 B.C. and construction had begun in 36 B.C. One might have thought the temple would be dedicated in the month of July—that is, the month of Caesar's birthday, formerly known as Quintilis. But the point of the ceremony was less to commemorate Caesar than to consecrate Octavian. Octavian wanted to tie the dedication to his triumphs. (In 8 B.C. Sextilis would be renamed August in memory of the three triumphs and in recognition of the title that Octavian had taken by then: Augustus, "revered.")

The architecture and decoration of the new temple seemed to give Caesar's blessing to the new regime. The columned structure stood on a high podium. Inside the temple stood a statue of Caesar in his robe as Chief Priest. Octavian decorated the building with the spoils of war from Egypt. Perhaps one of those was a masterpiece of Greek painting showing Venus—Caesar's patron goddess and alleged ancestor—emerging from the ocean. Symbols of the comet that proclaimed Caesar's divinity were also carved in the marble that lined the interior.

In addition to the temple proper, the structure consisted of a rectangular platform that was decorated with the prows of ships captured at Actium. The message was that Caesar's mistress, Cleopatra, and Caesar's right-hand man, Antony, were now public enemies. Only Caesar's son, Octavian, was true to Caesar's memory. Only Octavian had built Caesar's temple.

In the center of the front of the platform before the temple was a niche with an altar to mark the spot of Caesar's cremation. The platform served as a Speaker's Platform, just like the other, older Speaker's Platform at the opposite end of the Roman Forum. From now on, funerals for the Roman emperors were held on this new Speaker's Platform in front of the deified Caesar's temple.

The celebrations for the new temple looked backward and ahead. As at Caesar's dedication of the Temple of Mother Venus in 46 B.C., they included the "Games of Troy." These were equestrian exercises by young nobles, exercises supposedly going back to Troy, the place where Caesar claimed his family began before immigrating to Italy. There were hints of Egypt with the appearance of a hippopotamus and rhinoceros for the first time ever in Rome. There were gladiatorial games and public feasts as well.

The new religion had its own sacred days. Caesar's birthday was to be celebrated every year on July 12. After Antony's death in 30 B.C., his birthday, January 14, was marked as a day when normal public business was prohibited. Antony's death was to be remembered negatively. The Ides of March was called Parricide Day, the day of murdering a close relative. It was an inauspicious day, one on which no courts could convene or legislation be passed. Pompey's Senate House would never be used again for meetings of the Senate. In 42 B.C., the Senate had voted to wall up the structure. Later, public toilets were constructed outside the building. It is also possible that a monument was erected inside the building to mark the spot where Caesar fell.

Romans had glorified great leaders before, but only Romulus, the semi-legendary founder of Rome, had a temple in Rome (and even he was worshipped under another name, Quirinus). The cult of Caesar was something new.

Caesar's name became a category. After Augustus, it became clear that every ruler of Rome would be called Caesar. A "Caesar" was an emperor, and so it would continue through modern times. The German *kaiser* and the Russian *tsar* (or *czar*) derive from Caesar.

Caesar became, in short, a kind of saint: St. Julius, the patron of the Roman Empire. His assassination did not herald the restoration of republican liberty but its burial. The Ides of March, the day of Caesar's martyrdom, might have become a saint's day, except that Caesar got an entire month instead. His temple on the edge of the Roman Forum, on the site of his cremation, was his shrine.

Caesar's blood sanctified the Roman Empire. Where Caesar rose to heaven, Octavian came to earth. We call him Octavian but he called himself Caesar. He was also an imperator, a conquering general, and the Son of the Deified One. Octavian or, more accurately, the new Caesar, was well on his way to becoming Augustus. Two years later, in 27 B.C., he accepted that title from the Senate. He would rule the Roman Empire for forty-one more years, until A.D. 14. Historians refer to Octavian from 27 B.C. onward as Augustus. He was the first Roman emperor. Sometimes referred to as the Augustan Age, his reign is thought of as one of the high points of Latin literature, a classical period in which the poets Virgil, Horace, and Ovid and the historian Livy were all writing.

What Caesar had hinted at, Augustus carried out. Augustus created a dynasty. When he died, his adopted son Tiberius replaced him. After Tiberius's death in A.D. 37, other members of their extended family served as emperor. Ironically, three of those emperors were descended from Antony through his marriage to Octavia, Augustus's sister. Eventually the family was forced out of power and, in A.D. 69, a new dynasty replaced it. And so it went on for centuries, through wars and revolutions, invasions and revelations, plagues and upheavals. An emperor ruled in Italy until 476 and, in Constantinople, in the Eastern Roman or Byzantine Empire, emperors lasted for another millennium, until 1453. So mighty were the foundations of the system that Caesar and Augustus put into place.

Augustus himself denied being a monarch. He maintained that he had restored the Republic. He officially returned control of the state to the Senate. True, he held the powers of consul, tribune, and Chief Priest, which would have been anathema to Cato or Cicero. He controlled enough of the army to put down any would-be rival. He lived in a great mansion on the Palatine Hill overlooking the city to which he descended and which he graced with his presence from time to time when needed. Behind the scenes, he manipulated the system. It was monarchy with a friendly face.

The ruins of Caesar's temple still stand. Even today, someone regularly leaves flowers at the site of the altar there in memory of Rome's last dictator. Far from condemning Caesar as a tyrant, people mourn him as a martyr. Caesar's genius and his sympathy for the poor live on while his war against the Republic in favor of one-man rule and his murderous rampage in Gaul, which killed or enslaved millions, are forgotten. It is the opposite of what Shakespeare said:

> *The evil that men do lives after them;*
> *The good is oft interred with their bones.*

And so, is that what they were reduced to, the most famous assassination in history and the titanic civil war that followed? Were they all just detours on the road to monarchy and canonization of a dictator? Did men wield their daggers and risk their lives in vain?

In fact, they fought the good fight. It would take more violence to save the Republic but it could have been saved. That was the lesson of the years after the Ides of March. If the assassins had prevailed on the battlefield they could have restored the Republic as long as they made some concessions. To begin with, they would probably have had to purge their opponents and to accept a period of dictatorship to reform the regime. Then they would have had to adopt certain additional reforms to prevent the instability that had plagued Rome in the years of Pompey and Caesar. Rome needed a stronger executive in order to introduce continuity into imperial administration; it needed strict term limits on governorships to keep a new Caesar from arising; more power-sharing with the provinces in order to prevent revolts; higher taxes on the rich in order to pay for the military; and a limit on military expansion in order to keep costs down and to prevent the emergence of future military strongmen. Would the result still be a republic? Certainly. Unlike in Augustus's Rome, the government would not belong to just one family. A reformed Republic would have had constitutional government, free elections, term limits in the executive, freedom of speech, and rule by a public-spirited elite. But in order to survive the Republic would have had to evolve far more than Cato, Brutus, or Cicero would have liked. History respects tradition but it is hard on institutions that don't evolve with the times. In the words of the classic Italian novel *The Leopard*: "If we want everything to stay the same, everything has to change."

Most of the assassins faded into oblivion. Decimus's memory did not age well. Decimus was no intellectual. He had no philosophical friends to canonize him after his death, as Brutus had, nor any famous son to praise his memory as Sextus praised his father Pompey. Augustus portrayed Decimus as an archvillain, but a half century later, Decimus's fate was not merely oblivion but ridicule.

Decimus was destined to become Imperial Rome's poster child for a bad death. By the time Seneca the Younger wrote in A.D. 64, the anti-Decimus version of his execution was ready to hand. If Cato epitomizes the good death, writes the moralist Seneca, then Decimus stands for a death that is unseemly and shamefaced. When ordered to bare his throat, writes Seneca, Decimus said, "I'll do it but only if I live." Decimus was reduced to a mockery; so much for the courageous man who braved the tides of Brittany, the siege of Mutina, and the privation of an overland route through the Alps.

Poor Decimus became a diminished thing for all his importance on the

Ides of March. Not so for Brutus and Cassius. They failed as men of action but, as martyrs, they succeeded beyond their wildest dreams.

"When the legend becomes fact, print the legend." This cynical remark of a newspaper editor in the movie *The Man Who Shot Liberty Valance* applies to the men who stabbed Julius Caesar. Brutus, in particular, turned into myth. At least three or four friends of Brutus—including philosophers, historians, or fellow soldiers—wrote books or gave speeches that revered his memory. Cassius, Brutus's brother-in-law and comrade-in-arms, shared in the reflected glory, but Brutus was the star.

Like Caesar, Brutus became a cult figure, virtually the patron saint of nostalgia for the lost Republic. Unlike Caesar he had no temple but he lived on in men's hearts—and in words and images. Senators who chafed under the pressure of the ruling dynasty, philosophers who dreamt of liberty, orators who ached for the eloquent days of the Republic and its free speech— all called on Brutus (and sometimes Cassius, too). Even Augustus allowed a certain amount of revisionism on the subject of Brutus. The story goes that when Augustus saw a statue of Brutus in Mediolanum (Milan), he called not for its destruction but its preservation.

Brutus, Cassius, and Decimus didn't maintain their offices or honors. They didn't prevent Octavian from ruling Rome; in fact, they opened his road to power. They didn't save their own skins. On the contrary, they hastened their own ends—violent and untimely deaths. And yet, if they didn't save the Republic, they saved republicanism.

The Ides of March changed the world, but not as the men who held the daggers that day planned. If Caesar had lived, won at least a grain of success against Parthia, and then marched back to Rome in triumph, things would have been different. By their subservience, the Roman nobility would have proved themselves ready for tyranny. Like Alexander before him, Caesar would have sampled the trappings of eastern despotism, and it is hard to believe that he wouldn't have liked them. With his mistress Cleopatra, Queen of Egypt, beside him, and with dozens of new noble Parthian clients in tow, no doubt bowing low to him as their ancestors did to Alexander, Caesar would have come back to Rome as king of Asia. In short order, Rome would have become an absolute monarchy.

Of course, Rome did eventually become an autocracy, but not for another three hundred years until the reign of Diocletian (ruled A.D. 285–309). Not under Augustus. When Octavian defeated Antony and became the ruler of Rome, he did not call himself dictator, much less king. Instead, he called himself *Princeps*—First Citizen. Unlike Caesar, he wore no purple toga or golden crown. He even claimed to turn power over to the Senate and to have restored the Republic—claims that no one believed. Yet, if Augustus was a king, it was a limited monarchy. Augustus carefully justified his very powers by reference to Rome's traditional form of government. For much of his reign he let senators hold the consulship. He controlled the most strategic provinces and the bulk of the legions, but he let the Senate run a few important provinces and a small number of legions.

Augustus showed a certain fear and a healthy respect for the Roman nobility. He remembered what had happened on the Ides of March and he knew that it could happen again. Nor was he the only person in power who thought so.

Early in A.D. 23, on a winter's day in the reign of Emperor Tiberius Caesar, a magnificent funeral was held in the Roman Forum with all the splendor that the old nobility could still muster. A funeral oration from the Speaker's Platform was given for the deceased, who had lived into her eighties. She was a great lady and a wealthy widow with a vast fortune. There was the traditional parade of mourners and musicians. Twenty men marched wearing beeswax masks of her noble ancestors, boasting such famous names as Manlius and Quinctius. The only thing missing were the masks of her late husband and her late brother. The emperor forbade them. Tiberius forgave the deceased for not mentioning him in her will although she rewarded many other noble Romans. He would not forgive her family for resurrecting memories better left dead.

The deceased was Junia Tertia, daughter of Servilia, niece of Cato the Younger, half sister of Brutus, and widow of Cassius. Long ago, rumor had linked Tertia to Julius Caesar, claiming she was his mistress. She died on

December 31, A.D. 22. With her gone, Rome's last living link to the men who killed Julius Caesar was cut. By leaving the emperor out of her will, Tertia was not just insulting Tiberius. By saying no to Caesar, she was giving a final salute to the generation that fought to the death rather than surrender the Republic to one-man rule.

That their images were too controversial to display in the Forum says it all about the passion that Brutus and Cassius still inspired, sixty-six years after the Ides of March. They were legends now. Their petty personal motives—their greed, their brutality, and their ambition, their partnership with a turncoat whose act of betrayal dwarfed their own, and their murderous mistreatment of the civilian inhabitants of the provinces were all forgotten. They had been transformed, rendered powerful reminders that as long as men and women remember the names of those who killed Julius Caesar, dictators will not sleep safely.

Acknowledgments

The word *gratitude* doesn't begin to express my feelings toward the many people whom I begged, bothered, or buttonholed for help. Thanks to them the book is infinitely better. The faults, of course, remain my own.

I'm deeply indebted to the friends, students, and colleagues who read all or part of the manuscript: David Blome, Judith Dupré, Michael Fontaine, Christopher Harper, Adrienne Mayor, J. Kimball McKnight, Adam Mogelonsky, Jacob Nabel, Iddo Netanyahu, Joel Rudin, Matthew Sears, Timothy Sorg, and Jacob Vaughan. Their advice proved invaluable.

Lieutenant Colonel (Ret.) Timothy Wilson RA (Royal Artillery) provided expert military advice, which he modestly described as "playing Watson to my Holmes." It was far more than that.

Of the many scholars who graciously took time from their busy schedules to meet with me and discuss in detail aspects of their work, I would like particularly to thank Annetta Alexandridis, Margaret Andrews, Elizabeth Bartman, Arthur Eckstein, Harriet Flower, Kathryn Gleason, Elizabeth Macaulay-Lewis, Sturt Manning, Josiah Ober, James Packer, and Barry Weingast. Professor Antonio Monterroso, University of Córdoba, was kind enough to meet with me in Rome and to discuss his work on the place where Caesar was assassinated. Dr. Carl Bazil, M.D., Ph.D., Director, Division of Epilepsy and Sleep, Columbia University, graciously answered my questions about epilepsy and Caesar's possible medical condition. Brook Manville took part in many stimulating conversations about leadership, ancient and modern. David Blome offered expert advice about battle blades. I am very grateful to Professor Mark Toher, Union College, for sharing unpublished material.

Jacob Nabel and Serhan Güngör were stout-hearted traveling companions to Caesar's battle sites in France, where we also had the assistance of André Bigotte, and in Turkey. Lorenzo Gasperoni, Giancarlo Brighi, and the Terre Centuriate association of Cesena, Italy kindly arranged a visit to three possible sites of the Rubicon River (whose identification is still debated) as well as to the square grid of territory laid out by Roman surveys outside today's Cesena which—who knows?—might just be the place where Caesar lost his way in the night before crossing the Rubicon (Suetonius, *Julius Caesar* 31.2). Steven Ellis joined me on a visit to the basement of Rome's Teatro Argentina and, thanks to his archaeological expertise, helped make sense of the foundations of the Portico of Pompey. John Guare, Daniel P. Jacobson, and his wife, Lou Jacobson, took part in a memorable visit to the ruins of the Largo Argentina. Carol Warshawsky offered generous hospitality.

Over coffee, on the phone, in emails and even in letters, many friends, students, and colleagues shared their expertise and wisdom, in particular: Stephen Ashley, Patrick Baker, Sandra Bernstein, Emma Blake, Jeffrey Blanchard, Nikki Bonanni, Giovanni Brizzi, Michela De Benardin, Anna Celenza, Adele Chatfield-Taylor, Christopher Christoff, David DesRosiers, Rabbi Mordechai Dinerman, Laurent Ferri, Giovanni Giorgini, Shawn Goldsmith, Stephen Greenblatt, Elizabeth Harper, Richard Hodges, Allegra Iafrate, Donald Kagan, Karl Kirchwey, Eric Kondratieff, Brenda Longfellow, Dwight McLemore, Kathryn Milne, Ian Morris, Claudia Moser, Waller and Jackie Newell, Jan Parker, Catherine Penner, Eric Rebillard, Andrew Roberts, Courtney Roby, Claudia Rosett, Robert Schon, Elizabeth and Jeff Shulte, Rabbi Eli Silberstein, Ramie Targoff, David Teegarden, Rob Tempio, Christian Wendt, Lila Yawn, Bill Zeiser, and M. Theodora Zemek.

I am fortunate to work with wonderful students, colleagues, and staff in the Departments of History and Classics at Cornell University. I gratefully acknowledge the help of Cornell's John M. Olin Library.

I am deeply grateful to the American Academy in Rome and, in particular, to its current and former directors, Kimberly Bowes and Christopher Celenza, for hosting me as a resident and visiting scholar in 2012 and 2013. The Academy was an ideal community in which to work on this book. With the help of the Academy and thanks to the Soprintendenza Speciale per i beni archeologici di Roma, the Vatican Museums, and Rome's Teatro Argentina, I was able to visit sites and see objects that would otherwise have been closed to me. I would also like to thank the J. Paul Getty Museum for making various items available for my inspection.

Suzanne Lang helped with logistics and bibliographical support. Sam Mogelonsky redesigned my website and Larry Mogelonsky hosts it.

At Simon & Schuster, I thank my editor, Bob Bender, whose wisdom, judgment, and good sense are matched only by his support, generosity, and sense of humor. I am also grateful to his assistant, Johanna Li, for once again shepherding a project through to completion. My literary agent, Cathy Hemming, has been there every step of the way, with sound counsel, expert knowledge, and friendship.

As always, I thank my family for their help and support. I appreciate their patience over the years measured by successive Ides of March.

And finally, I thank my wife, Marcia. At every point along the way she has shared the journey so completely that this seems to me as much her book as mine.

A Note on Sources

I include the main works in English as well as a few essential foreign-language texts. Additional bibliography is available on my website, barrystrauss.com.

INTRODUCTORY

Students of classics and ancient history should have *The Oxford Classical Dictionary*, 3rd ed. (Oxford: Oxford University Press, 1999) by their side. Excellent maps of the ancient world can be found in Richard J. A. Talbert, ed., *The Barrington Atlas of the Ancient Greco-Roman World* (Princeton, NJ: Princeton University Press, 2000). Another exceptionally valuable source is Hubert Cancik and Helmut Schneider, eds., *Brill's New Pauly: Encyclopaedia of the Ancient World*, English ed., managing editor, Christine F. Salazar; assistant editor, David E. Orton (Leiden and Boston: Brill, 2002–2010), with an excellent online edition.

For Roman history without tears, see Simon Baker, *Ancient Rome: The Rise and Fall of an Empire* (n.p.: BBC Books, 2007). For an introduction to the turbulent era of the Late Roman Republic, see Tom Holland, *Rubicon* (New York: Doubleday, 2003) or Mary Beard and Michael Crawford, *Rome in the Late Republic* (London: Duckworth, 2009). For a detailed account, see Christopher S. Mackay, *The Breakdown of the Roman Republic: From Oligarchy to Empire* (New York: Cambridge University Press, 2009) or J. A. Crook, Andrew Lintott, and Elizabeth Rawson, eds., *The Last Age of the Roman Republic,* vol. 9 of *The Cambridge Ancient History,* 2nd ed. (Cambridge: Cambridge University Press, 1994). P. A. Brunt offers an introduction to the societal struggles of the era in *Social Conflicts in the Roman Republic* (New York: Norton, 1971), esp. 1–41 and 112–47.

For the Roman army, see Adrian Goldsworthy, *The Complete Roman Army* (New York: Thames & Hudson, 2003); Kate Gilliver, Adrian Goldsworthy, and Michael Whitby, *Rome at War* (Oxford: Osprey, 2005); L. J. F. Keppie, *The Making of the Roman Army: From Republic to Empire* (Norman: University of Oklahoma Press, 1984).

The most influential modern book, at least in English, on the transition from the Late Republic to the Early Empire is Sir Ronald Syme, *The Roman Revolution* (Oxford: Oxford University Press, 1939). The focus is on Augustus but there are also important chapters on Caesar's last years and on the conspiracy against him. Some of Syme's themes are the use of personal politics to build power, the irresponsibility of the Late Roman nobility, the key role that Octavian played in stirring up Caesar's troops against the Senate in 44 and 43 B.C., and the reality of monarchy behind Augustus's rhetoric of restoring the Republic. For Syme, the end of the Republic was inevitable. Erich Gruen, *The Last Generation of the Roman Republic,* 2nd ed. (Berkeley: University of California Press, 1995), argues powerfully for the contrary: that the Republic was thriving and could have continued.

ANCIENT SOURCES

What we make of the conspiracy that killed Caesar depends in large part on what we make of the ancient sources. Robert Etienne brings this point out nicely in his fine book, *Les Ides de Mars: la fin de César ou de la dictature?* (The Ides of March: The End of Caesar or of the Dictatorship?) (Paris: Gallimard/Julliard, 1973). There are five main ancient sources, in chronological order: Nicolaus of Damascus, Suetonius, Plutarch, Appian, and Cassius Dio. They agree about the overall picture of events but disagree both about certain points of detail and about the motives and relative significance of the various conspirators. Plutarch, who was Shakespeare's main source, emphasizes the role of Brutus and his idealism. Nicolaus, whom Shakespeare did not read, accentuates the cold-blooded and even cynical motives of the plotters; he also makes Decimus a key character. Earlier scholars tended to discount Nicolaus because he worked for Augustus and so appeared biased. Recently, the work of scholars like Malitz and Toher has rehabilitated Nicolaus as a contemporary and shrewd source, if indeed one who sometimes offers Augustus's version of events. As Toher argues, Nicolaus was a student of the writings of Aristotle and Thucydides, two of the ancient world's finest minds when it comes to political analysis. I am convinced that Nicolaus offers information essential to making sense of the assassination.

The five major ancient sources on the conspiracy, the assassination of Julius Caesar, and the aftermath are all available in English translation. Appian, *The Civil Wars* is translated with an introduction by J. M. Carter (London and New York: Penguin Books, 1996). For the relevant books of Cassius Dio's *History of Rome*, consult the Loeb Classical Library edition, *Dio's Roman History*, with an English translation by Earnest Cary on the basis of the translation of Herbert Baldwin Foster (London: W. Heinemann; Cambridge, MA: Harvard University Press, 1914–27). Nicolaus of Damascus's *Life of Caesar Augustus* will soon be available in a new translation with scholarly commentary by Mark Toher, ΒΙΟΣ ΚΑΙΣΑΡΟΣ (*Bios Kaisaros*) (Cambridge University Press, forthcoming). Until then, the best English version is Jane Bellemore, edited with introduction, translation and commentary, *Nicolaus of Damascus, Life of Augustus* (Bristol, England: Bristol Classical Press, 1984). Plutarch's *Lives* of Pompey and Caesar can be found in Plutarch, *Fall of the Roman Republic*, rev. ed., translated with introduction and notes by Rex Warner, revised with translations of Comparisons and a preface by Robin Seager, with series preface by Christopher Pelling (Harmondsworth: Penguin, 2005); Plutarch's *Lives* of Brutus and Mark Antony can be found in Plutarch, *Makers of Rome*, translated with an introduction by Ian Scott-Kilvert (Harmondsworth: Penguin, 1965). Plutarch's *Life* of Cato the Younger can be found in Bernadotte Perrin, trans., *Plutarch Lives VIII: Sertorius and Eumenes, Phocion and Cato the Younger* (Cambridge, MA: Harvard University Press, 1919). Suetonius's *Lives* of Caesar and Augustus are available in Gaius Suetonius Tranquillus, *The Twelve Caesars*, translated by Robert Graves, revised with an introduction by Michael Grant (London and New York: Penguin, 2003).

A good collection of translated selections from the ancient sources, along with scholarly commentary, for the rise and fall of Caesar, 60–42 B.C., is found in Naphtali Lewis, *The Ides of March* (Sanibel and Toronto: Samuel Stevens, 1984). A valuable selection of the sources through the Ides of March, with commentary and bibliography, can be found in Matthew Dillon and Lynda Garland, eds., *Ancient Rome: From the Early Republic to the Assassination of Julius Caesar* (London and New York: Routledge, 2005).

I benefited greatly from scholarly commentaries on ancient texts. Mark Toher was kind enough to share with me the relevant manuscript sections of his excellent commentary on Nicolaus of Damascus, ΒΙΟΣ ΚΑΙΣΑΡΟΣ (*Bios Kaisaros*) (Cambridge University Press, forthcoming). I learned much from Bellemore, *Nicolaus of Damascus,* and from Jürgen Malitz, *Nikolaos von Damaskus, Leben des Kaisers Augustus,* edited, translated, with a commentary (Darmstadt, Germany: Wissenschaftliche Buchgesellschaft, 2003). Christopher Pelling, *Plutarch Caesar,* translated with an introduction and commentary (Oxford: Oxford University Press, 2011), is excellent and extraordinarily valuable. Also very useful is the same author's *Life of Antony/Plutarch* (Cambridge and New York: Cambridge University Press, 1988) and J. L. Moles, *The Life of Cicero/Plutarch* (Warminster, England: Aris & Phillips, 1988). For Suetonius's *Julius Caesar,* H. E. Butler, and M. Cary, *Suetoni Tranquilli Divus Iulius,* edited with an introduction and commentary (Oxford: Clarendon Press, 1927) is old but still very useful. Carlotta Scantamburlo, *Suetonio, Vita di Cesare, Introduzione, traduzione e commento* (Pisa: Edizioni Plus, Pisa University Press, 2011) is helpful.

On Asconius, see B. A. Marshall, *A Historical Commentary on Asconius* (Columbia: University of Missouri Press, 1985).

D. R. Shackleton Bailey, ed., Cicero, *Letters to Atticus,* 7 vols. (Cambridge: Cambridge University Press, 1965–70) is fundamental, as is idem, Cicero, *Epistulae ad Familiares* (Letters to His Friends), 2 vols. (Cambridge and New York: Cambridge University Press, 1977) and idem, Cicero, *Epistulae ad Quintum Fratrum et M. Brutum* (Cambridge and New York: Cambridge University Press, 1980). Two useful commentaries on Cicero's *Philippics* are W. K. Lacey, *Second Philippic Oration/Cicero* (Bristol, Avon: Bolchazy Carducci; Warminster, England: Aris & Phillips; Atlantic Highlands, NJ: Distributed in the U.S.A. and Canada by Humanities Press, 1986) and John T. Ramsey, ed.,

Philippics I–II/Cicero (Cambridge and New York: Cambridge University Press, 2003).

CAESAR

Caesar wrote concisely but his life is a huge subject inspiring many books. For the man in a nutshell, it would be hard to beat J. P. V. D. Balsdon's excellent little volume, *Julius Caesar* (New York: Atheneum, 1967). For an introduction to the many subjects in Caesar studies today that interest scholars, see the excellent essays in Miriam Griffin, ed., *A Companion to Julius Caesar* (Oxford and Malden, MA: Wiley-Blackwell, 2009). A classic of good judgment and good scholarship is Matthias Gelzer, *Caesar: Politician and Statesman*, translated by Peter Needham (Oxford: Blackwell, 1969). Christian Meier, *Caesar*, translated by David McLintock (New York: Basic Books/HarperCollins) is a great book, scholarly and gripping, but not always right. For a critical review that advances a more negative theory of Caesar's dynastic ambitions, see E. Badian, "Christian Meier: Caesar," *Gnomon* 62.1 (1990): 22–39. An outstanding, recent biography is Adrian Goldsworthy, *Caesar: Life of a Colossus* (New Haven: Yale University Press, 2006). Philip Freeman, *Julius Caesar* (New York: Simon & Schuster, 2008) is astute and succinct. W. Jeffrey Tatum, *Always I Am Caesar* (Malden, MA: Blackwell, 2008) is a lively and insightful introduction. For those with German, E. Baltrusch offers a trenchant comparison of Caesar and Pompey in *Caesar und Pompeius* (Darmstadt, Germany: Wissenschaftliche Buchgesellschaft, 2004). Two important books by Zvi Yavetz analyze Caesar's program, his propaganda, and his appeal to the ordinary Roman: *Plebs and Princeps* (Oxford: Clarendon Press, 1969) and *Julius Caesar and His Public Image* (Ithaca, NY: Cornell University Press, 1983). For more on Caesar's appeal to the poor and noncitizens, see Luciano Canfora, *Julius Caesar: The Life and Times of the People's Dictator*, translated by Marian Hill and Kevin Windle (Berkeley: University of California Press, 2007). In a similar vein, see Michael Parenti, *The Assassination of Julius Caesar* (New York: New Press, 2003).

On Caesar as commander, see J. F. C. Fuller, *Julius Caesar: Man, Soldier and Tyrant* (New Brunswick, NJ: Da Capo, 1965); Kimberly Kagan, *The Eye of Command* (Ann Arbor: University of Michigan Press, 2006). On Caesar as risk taker, see my *Masters of Command: Alexander, Hannibal, Caesar and the Genius of Leadership* (New York: Simon & Schuster, 2012), passim.

On the enduring legacy of Caesar, see three very valuable books by Maria Wyke: *Caesar: A Life in Western Culture* (Chicago: University of Chicago Press, 2008); idem, *Caesar in the USA* (Berkeley: University of California Press, 2012); idem, ed., *Julius Caesar in Western Culture* (Oxford and Malden, MA: Blackwell, 2006).

On Caesar's early career, see: Lily Ross Taylor, "The Rise of Julius Caesar." *Greece and Rome* (Second Series) 4.1 (1957); R. T. Ridley, "The Dictator's Mistake: Caesar's Escape from Sulla," *Historia* 49.2 (2000): 211–29.

On Caesar in Gaul, see K. Gilliver, *Caesar's Gallic Wars 58–50 BC* (London: Routledge, 2003); T. R. Holmes, *Caesar's Conquest of Gaul* (Oxford: Clarendon Press, 1911); Christophe Goudineau, *César et la Gaule* (Paris: Errance, 1992); Kathryn Welch, "Caesar and His Officers in the Gallic War Commentaries," in Kathryn Welch and Anton Powell, eds., *Julius Caesar as Artful Reporter: The War Commentaries as Political Instruments* (London: Duckworth; Swansea: Classical Press of Wales, 1998), 85–110.

On the Civil War, see Adrian Goldsworthy, "Caesar's Civil War 49–44 BC," in Kate Gilliver, Adrian Goldsworthy, and Michael Whitby, with a foreword by Steven Saylor, *Rome at War* (Oxford and New York: Osprey, 2005), 106–82. I offer an analysis of Caesar's Civil War tactics and strategy in *Masters of Command*, passim.

On Caesar as propagandist, see J. H. Collins, "Caesar as a Political Propagandist," in H. Temporini, ed., *Aufstieg und Niedergang der Römischen Welt*, vol. 1.1 (Berlin and New York: DeGruyter, 1972), 922–66. On Caesar's use of Venus as propaganda, see "Caesar's Divine Heritage and the Battle for Venus," retrieved July 24, 2013, from http://www.humanities.mq.edu.au/acans/caesar /Career_Venus.htm.

On Caesar's appearance, see P. Zanker, "The Irritating Statues and Contradictory Portraits of Julius Caesar," in Griffin, ed., *Companion to Caesar*, 288–313.

The best study of Caesar as dictator is Martin Jehne, *Der Staat des Dictators Caesar* (The State of the Dictator Caesar) (Cologne, Germany: Böhlau, 1987). Important essays on the last phase of Caesar's career are found in Gianpaolo

Urso, ed., *L'ultimo Cesare: Scritti, Riforme, Progetti, Congiure: atti del Convegno Internazionale, Cividale del Friuli* (Rome: L'Erma di Bretschneider, 2000). See also John H. Collins, "Caesar and the Corruption of Power," *Historia: Zeitschrift für Alte Geschichte* 4.4 (1955): 445–65; Marta Sordi, "Caesar's Powers in His Last Phase," in Francis Cairns and Elaine Fantham, eds., *Caesar Against Liberty? Perspectives on his Autocracy,* Papers of the Langford Latin Seminar 11 (Cambridge: Francis Cairns, 2003), 190–99; J. T. Ramsey, "Did Julius Caesar Temporarily Banish Mark Antony from His Inner Circle?," *Classical Quarterly* 54.1 (2004): 161–73. On the Lupercalia, see A. K. Michels, "The Topography and Interpretation of the Lupercalia," *Transactions of the American Philological Association* 84 (1953): 35–59.

A basic work on the deification of Caesar is Stefan Weinstock, *Divus Julius* (Oxford: Clarendon Press, 1971). See the important revisions by Ittai Gradel, *Emperor Worship and Roman Religion* (Oxford: Clarendon Press, 2002).

ROMAN POLITICS: INSTITUTIONS AND PRACTICES

Two fine introductions to Roman political life in Caesar's day are Lily Ross Taylor, *Party Politics in the Age of Caesar* (Berkeley: University of California Press, 1961 [1949]) and Claude Nicolet, *The World of the Citizen in Republican Rome*, trans. P. S. Falla (London: Batsford Academic and Educational, 1980). Fergus Millar argues that Roman politics was more democratic than scholars had thought in *The Crowd in Rome in the Late Republic* (Ann Arbor: University of Michigan Press, 1988). For a skeptical view of Roman democracy, see Henrik Mouritsen, *Plebs and Politics in the Late Roman Republic* (Cambridge and New York: Cambridge University Press, 2001). Robert Morstein-Marx offers an insightful analysis of Roman political oratory, with the days after the Ides of March being an important case in point, in *Mass Oratory and Political Power in the Late Roman Republic* (Cambridge and New York: Cambridge University Press, 2004). F. Pina Polo offers a catalog of Public Meetings (*contiones*) in *Las Contiones Civiles y Militares en Roma* (Zaragoza, Spain: Universidad de Zaragoza, 1989).

On the Best Men and the Populists, see W. K. Lacey, "Boni atque Improbi," *Greece & Rome,* 2nd ser. 17.1 (1970): 3–16.

CAESAR'S RIVALS

On Pompey, two succinct biographies are Robin Seager, *Pompey the Great, A Political Biography*, 2nd ed. (Malden, MA: Blackwell, 2002) and Patricia Southern, *Pompey* (Stroud, England: Tempus, 2002). For more details, see P. A. L. Greenhalgh, *Pompey, the Roman Alexander* (Columbia: University of Missouri Press, 1981) and idem, *Pompey, the Republican Prince* (Columbia: University of Missouri Press, 1982).

A good introduction to Cato the Younger is Rob Goodman and Jimmy Soni, *Rome's Last Citizen: The Life and Legacy of Cato, Mortal Enemy of Caesar* (New York: Thomas Dunne Books, 2012).

A fine introduction to Cicero is Anthony Everitt, *Cicero: The Life and Times of Rome's Greatest Politician* (New York: Random House, 2002). Elizabeth Rawson, *Cicero: A Portrait,* rev. ed. (Ithaca, NY: Cornell University Press, 1983), is the work of an expert in the intellectual world of the Late Republic. Two good introductions to Cicero and politics are R. E. Smith, *Cicero the Statesman* (Cambridge: Cambridge University Press, 1966) and D. Stockton, *Cicero: A Political Biography* (London: Oxford University Press, 1971).

On Clodius, see W. Jeffrey Tatum, *The Patrician Tribune: Publius Clodius Pulcher* (Chapel Hill: University of North Carolina Press, 1999).

CAESAR'S MEN

Two good introductory biographies to Mark Antony are E. G. Huzar, *Mark Antony: A Biography* (Minneapolis: University of Minnesota Press, 1978) and P. Southern, *Mark Antony* (Stroud, England: Tempus, 2006). There is much of value in Adrian Goldsworthy, *Antony and Cleopatra* (New Haven, CT: Yale University Press, 2010). An important work on Antony's relationship to Caesar is J. T. Ramsey, "Did Julius Caesar Temporarily Banish Mark Antony from His Inner Circle?," *Classical Quarterly* 54.1 (2004): 161–73. A grand old account, by turns fanciful and wise, is Arthur Weigall, *The Life and Times of Marc Antony* (Garden City, NY: Garden City, 1931).

On Lepidus, see Richard D. Weigel, *Lepidus: The Tarnished Triumvir* (London and New York: Routledge, 1992); L. Hayne, "M. Lepidus and His Wife,"

Latomus 33 (1974): 76–79; L. Hayne, "M. Lepidus (cos. 78)—A Reappraisal," *Historia* 21 (1972): 661–68.

On Oppius and Balbus and the bitterness their rise inspired in the Roman nobility, see Kathryn E. Welch, "The Praefectura Urbis of 45 B.C. and the Ambitions of L. Cornelius Balbus," *Antichthon* 24 (1990): 53–69. See also Ralph Masciantonio, "Balbus the Unique," *Classical World* 61.4 (December 1967): 134–38.

THE CONSPIRATORS

The old but still fundamental discussion of the evidence for the conspirators and the conspiracy is W. Drumann, *Geschichte Roms* [History of Rome] *in seinem Übergange von der republikanischen zur monarchischen Verfassung; oder, Pompeius, Caesar, Cicero und ihre Zeitgenossen nach Geschlechtern und mit genealogischen Tabellen*, vol. 3: *Domitii–Julii*, 2nd ed., ed. P. Groebe (Leipzig: Gebrüder Borntraeger, 1906), 624–28. The commentary in Pelling, *Plutarch's Caesar* is essential for serious study of the conspirators, the assassination, and the aftermath. The best and most concise introduction to the conspiracy and the aftermath is the chapter in Greg Woolf, *Et Tu, Brute? The Murder of Caesar and Political Assassination* (London: Profile Books, 2006), 1–51; Woolf is, however, unduly diffident about the possibility of reconstructing the details of the assassination. Woolf argues that the conspirators would have gotten away with their murder if not for Caesar's soldiers, a force that insisted on revenge; the Roman nobility was probably willing to accept it. Zvi Yavetz, "Existimatio, Fama and the Ides of March," *Harvard Studies in Classical Philology* 78 (1974): 35–65, argues that the conspirators mistakenly believed that public opinion was on their side. D. F. Epstein, "Caesar's Personal Enemies on the Ides of March," *Latomus* 46, Fasc. 3 (1987): 566–70, argues that personal and not ideological motives inspired the conspirators. Andrew Lintott, "The Assassination," in Griffin, ed., *Companion to Caesar*, 72–81, takes ideological motives more seriously. Also valuable are R. E. Smith, "The Conspiracy and the Conspirators," *Greece & Rome*, 2nd Series 4.1 (1957): 58–70, and R. H. Storch, "Relative Deprivation and the Ides of March: Motive for Murder," *Ancient History Bulletin* 9 (1995): 45–52.

T. P. Wiseman, *Remembering the Roman People: Essays on Late Republican Politics and Literature* (Oxford: Oxford University Press, 2009) argues that Caesar's killers were arrogant aristocrats while Caesar followed the rule of law and had the support of the Roman people. See the valuable review by Josiah Osgood, *Classical Journal* 105.2 (2009): 180–83.

M. H. Dettenhofer offers an important insight into the generation of most of the conspirators—and for that matter, of their opponents Antony and Lepidus—who were all around the age of forty at the time of the Ides of March. See her *Perdita iuventus: zwischen den Generationen von Caesar und Augustus* (Lost Youth: Between the Generations of Caesar and Augustus) (Munich: Beck, 1992).

The most accessible book in English on Marcus Brutus is M. L. Clarke's fine work, *The Noblest Roman: Marcus Brutus and His Reputation* (Ithaca, NY: Cornell University Press, 1981), but the most penetrating analysis is in German: Hermann Bengston, *Zur Geschichte des Brutus,* Verlag der Bayerischen Akademie der Wissenschaften (Munich: Beck, 1970). Erik Wistrand offers a persuasive account of Brutus's moderation in *The Policy of Brutus the Tyrannicide* (Göteborg: Kungl. Vetenskaps-och Vitterhets-samhället, 1981). See the review essay by G. Dobesch, "Review of the Noblest Roman. Marcus Brutus and His Reputation by M.L. Clarke; The Policy of Brutus the Tyrannicide by Erik Wistrand," *Gnomon* 56.8 (1984): 708–22.

Ramsay MacMullen offers a perceptive analysis of Brutus's motives and his later reputation in *Enemies of the Roman Order: Treason, Unrest, and Alienation in The Roman Empire* (Cambridge, MA: Harvard University Press, 1966), 1–45. Sheldon Nodelman offers an insightful study of the evidence of coins and sculpture in "The Portrait of Brutus the Tyrannicide," *Occasional Papers on Antiquities 4: Ancient Portraits in the J. Paul Getty Museum* 1 (1987): 41–86. T. W. Africa puts Brutus on the couch in "The Mask of an Assassin: A Psychohistorical Study of M. Junius Brutus," *Journal of Interdisciplinary History* 8, 4 (1978): 599–626. Graham Wylie emphasizes Brutus's status as an icon and his failure as a leader in "The Ides of March and the Immovable Icon," in Carl Deroux, ed., *Studies in Latin literature and Roman history*, vol. 9 (Brussels: Latomus, 1998), 167–85. M. Radin, *Marcus Brutus* (New York and London: Oxford University Press, 1939), is highly speculative.

On Brutus as an orator see Andrea Balbo, "Marcus Junius Brutus the Orator: Between Philosophy and Rhetoric," in Catherine Steel and Henriette van Der Blom, eds., *Community and Communication: Oratory and Politics in Republican Rome* (Oxford: Oxford University Press, 2013), 315–28.

For a perceptive study of Cassius and Brutus, see Elizabeth Rawson, "Cassius and Brutus: The Memory of the Liberators," in I. S. Moxon, J.D. Smart, and A. J. Woodman, eds., *Past Perspectives: Studies in Greek and Roman Historical Writing, Papers Presented at a Conference in Leeds, 6–8 April 1983* (Cambridge and New York: Cambridge University Press, 1986), 101–19.

On Decimus Brutus, the fundamental study, with a full citation of sources, is Friedrich Münzer, s.v. *Iunius* (Brutus) (55a), in August Pauly and Georg Wissowa, eds., *Real-Encyclopädie der classischen Altertumswissenschaft, Supplementband V, Agamemnon-Statilius* (Stuttgart, 1931), cols. 369–85 (in German). Also extremely important is Bernard Camillus Bondurant, *Decimus Brutus Albinus: A Historical Study* (Chicago: University of Chicago Press, 1907). I have benefited from the short but astute analysis of Decimus in Dettenhofer, *Perdita Iuventus*, 258–62.

Syme pursued his thesis that Decimus was Caesar's bastard son in "Bastards in the Roman Aristocracy," *Proceedings of the American Philosophical Society* 104, 3 (1960): 323–27, and "No Son for Caesar?," *Historia* 29 (1980): 422–37, esp. 426–30. G. M. Duval puts forth a much more convincing thesis in "D. Junius Brutus: mari ou fils de Sempronia?," *Latomus* 50.3 (1991): 608–15. There is a good discussion of Decimus and the sea in R. Schulz, "Caesar und das Meer," *Historische Zeitschrift* 271.2 (2000): 281–309. See also John C. Rolfe, "Brutus and the Ships of the Veneti," *Classical Weekly* 11.14 (Jan. 28, 1918): 106–7.

For Decimus's behavior after Caesar's funeral, see S. Accame, "Decimo Bruto dopo i Funerali di Cesare," *Rivista di filologica e di istruzione classica* 62 (1934): 201–8. An important study of the endgame of Decimus's life is Denis van Berchem, "La Fuite de Decimus Brutus," *Les routes et l'histoire: 355 études sur les Helvètes et leurs voisins dans l'Empire romain* (Geneva: Librairie Droz, 1982), 55–65.

Although certain scholars recognize Decimus's significance in the conspiracy they argue that it is impossible to ascertain his motives; Baltrusch, *Caesar und Pompeius*, 166–67, is a good example. Syme points a way forward when he notes how much of his career Decimus spent in Gaul and how little in Rome (Syme, "No Son for Caesar?", 436). As a military man and a person with one foot in Celtic notions of honor, Decimus might not have responded kindly to his exclusion from the Parthian War and his eclipse by Octavian.

THE IDES OF MARCH

In addition to Woolf, *Et tu Brute?*, 1–18, and Lintott, "The Assassination," there are important introductions in J. V. P. D Balsdon, "The Ides of March," *Historia* 7 (1958): 80–94, and N. Horsfall, "The Ides of March: Some New Problems," *Greece and Rome* 21 (1974): 191–99. Etienne, *Ides de Mars*, offers a more detailed account. So does Stephen Dando-Collins, *The Ides: Caesar's Murder and the War for Rome* (Hoboken, NJ: Wiley, 2010). Parenti, *Assassination of Julius Caesar*, 167–86, offers a discussion. M. E. Deutsch considers an earlier, failed assassination plan in "The Plot to Murder Caesar on the Bridge," *UCP* 2 (1908/16): 267–78.

On what Caesar said to Brutus, see P. Arnaud, "Toi aussi, mons fils, tu mangeras ta part de notre pouvoir—Brutus le Tyran?," *Latomus* 57 (1998): 61–71; F. Brenk, "Caesar and the Evil Eye or What to Do with 'καὶ σύ, τέκνου'," in Gareth Schmeling and Jon D. Mikalson, eds., *Qui miscuit utile dulci: Festschrift Essays for Paul Lachlan* (Wauconda, IL: Bolchazy Carducci, 1998), 31–49; M. Dubuisson, "Toi Aussi, Mon Fils," *Latomus* 39 (1980): 881–90; J. Russell, "Julius Caesar's Last Words: A Reinterpretation," in Bruce Marshall, ed., *Vindex Humanitatis: Essays in Honor of John Huntly Bishop* (Armidale, New South Wales: University of New England, 1980), 123–28.

On Spurrina and soothsayers, see E. Rawson, "Caesar, Etruria and the Disciplina Etrusca," *Journal of Roman Studies* 68 (1978): 132–52; J. T. Ramsey, "Beware the Ides of March!: An Astrological Prediction?" *Classical Quarterly*, New Series, 50, 2 (2000): 440–54.

J. T. Ramsey offers a tour de force leading to a reevaluation of the morning's chronology in "At What Hour Did the Murderers of Julius Caesar Gather on the Ides of March 44 B.C.?," in Stephan Heilen et al., *In Pursuit of Wissenschaft: Festschrift für William M. Calder III zum 75. Geburtstag* (Hildesheim and Zurich: Olms, 2008), 351–63.

On Late Republican Roman military daggers, begin with an excellent and broader cultural history of Roman weapons, Simon James, *Rome and the Sword: How Warriors and Weapons Shaped Roman History* (London: Thames & Hudson, 2011) and then even more general considerations in G. Walker, *Battle Blades: a Professional's Guide to Combat/Fighting Knives.* (Boulder, CO: Paladin Press, 1993).

On the use of gladiators as bodyguards see A. W. Lintott, *Violence in Republican Rome,* 2nd ed. (Oxford: Oxford University Press, 1999), 83–85.

On Pompey's Portico and Senate House, the site of Caesar's assassination, see K. L. Gleason, "The Garden Portico of Pompey the Great: An Ancient Public Park Preserved in the Layers of Rome," *Expedition* 32.2 (1990): 3–13, and "Porticus Pompeiana: A New Perspective on the First Public Park of Ancient Rome," *Journal of Garden History* 14.1 (January–March 1994): 13–27.

FROM THE IDES OF MARCH TO OCTAVIAN'S TRIUMPH IN 29 B.C.

Syme, *The Roman Revolution* is a classic account of this period. Now Josiah Osgood offers an excellent narrative and analysis, with an emphasis on the experience of ordinary people, in *Caesar's Legacy: Civil War and the Emergence of the Roman Empire* (Cambridge and New York: Cambridge University Press, 2006). Adrian Goldsworthy, *Antony and Cleopatra* (New Haven: Yale University Press, 2010), is another fine introduction, prudent in its judgments and especially good on military events.

Kathryn Welch highlights the often overlooked factors of Sextus Pompey and sea power in the conflict in the decade after the Ides of March in *Magnus Pius—Sextus Pompeius and the Transformation of the Roman Republic* (Swansea: Classical Press of Wales, 2012). On the role of soldiers on the Ides of March and its aftermath, see Helga Boterman, *Die Soldaten und die roemische Politik in der Zeit von Caesars Tod bis zur Begruendung des zweiten Triumvirats* (Munich: Beck, 1968). I found much of value in Don Sutton, "The Associates of Brutus: A Prosopographical Study," (1986), Open Access Dissertations and Theses, Paper 6910, http://digitalcommons.mcmaster.ca/opendissertations/6910.

Morstein-Marx, *Mass Oratory and Political Power*, 150–58, demonstrates how Roman public opinion was up for grabs in the days following the Ides of March. Wiseman, *Remembering the Roman People*, 216–28, disagrees.

On Caesar's funeral, see Weinstock, *Divus Julius*, 346–55; G. S. Sumi,

Ceremony and Power: Performing Politics in Rome between Republic and Empire (Ann Arbor: University of Michigan Press, 2005); G. S. Sumi, "Impersonating the Dead: Mimes at Roman Funerals," *The American Journal of Philology* 123. 4 (2002): 559–85; George Kennedy, "Antony's Speech at Caesar's Funeral," *Quarterly Journal of Speech* 54.2 (1968): 99–106; D. Noy, "Half-Burnt on an Emergency Pyre: Roman Creations Which Went Wrong," *Greece & Rome*, 2nd ser. 47. 2 (2000): 186–96; Wiseman, *Remembering the Roman People,* 228–33.

There is much of value on Roman funerary customs and especially the mysterious beeswax masks in H. I. Flower, *Ancestor Masks and Aristocratic Power in Roman Culture* (Oxford: Oxford University Press), 2000.

Ulrich Gotter, *Der Diktator ist tot! Politik in Rom zwischen den Iden des März und der Begründung des Zweiten Triumvirats* (The Dictator is Dead! Politics in Rome Between the Ides of March and the Founding of the Second Triumvirate) *Historia Einzelschrift* 110 (Stuttgart, Germany: Franz Steiner, 1996), is detailed and useful on the events from March 44 B.C. to November 43 B.C. Some valuable studies on the events of 44 B.C. are L. Hayne. "Lepidus's Role After the Ides of March," *Antiquité Classique* 14 (1971): 108–17; Mark Toher, "Octavian's Arrival in Rome, 44 B.C.," *Classical Quarterly,* New Series 54. 1 (2004): 174–84; J. T. Ramsey and A. Lewis Licht, *The Comet of 44 B.C. and Caesar's Funeral Games* (Atlanta: Scholars Press, 1997); J. T. Ramsey, "Did Mark Antony Contemplate an Alliance with His Political Enemies in July 44 B.C.E.?," *Classical Philology* 96. 3 (2001): 253–68; A. E. Raubitschek, "Brutus in Athens," *Phoenix* 11 (1957): 1–11.

Good studies of Brutus and Cassius's strategy in 43–42 B.C. include Martin Drum, "Cicero's Tenth and Eleventh Philippics: The Republican Advance in the East," in Tom Stevenson and Marcus Wilson, eds., *Cicero's Philippics* (Auckland, New Zealand: Polygraphia, 2008), 82–94; Arthur Keaveney, "Cassius' Parthian Allies," *Hommages à Carl Deroux,* vol. 3 (Brussels: Latomus, 2003), 232–34.

Anthony Everitt, *The Life of Rome's First Emperor* (New York: Random House, 2003), offers a good introduction to Augustus—as Octavian was eventually known. Two fine essays by Walter Eder ("Augustus and the Power of Tradition") and Erich S. Gruen ("Augustus and the Making of the Principate") explain how he bridged the gap between Republic and Empire, in Karl Galinsky, ed., *The Cambridge Companion to the Age of Augustus* (Cambridge and New York: Cambridge University Press, 2005), 13–32, 33–51.

THE WOMEN

Richard A. Bauman, *Women and Politics in Ancient Rome* (London and New York, Routledge: 1992) is a good introduction. See also Judith Hallett, *Fathers and Daughters in Roman Society: Women and the Elite Family* (Princeton, NJ: Princeton University Press, 1984).

On Cleopatra, see Stacey Schiff, *Cleopatra: A Life* (New York: Little, Brown, 2010); Duane Roller, *Cleopatra: A Biography* (Oxford: Oxford University Press, 2010); and Diana E. E. Kleiner, *Cleopatra and Rome* (Cambridge, MA: Belknap Press of Harvard University Press, 2005).

SHAKESPEARE

S. Wells, ed., *The Oxford Shakespeare Julius Caesar* (Oxford and New York: Oxford University Press, 1984), is a fine edition with a good introduction and notes. Ernest Schanzer, ed., *Shakespeare's Appian: A Selection from the Tudor Translation of Appian's Civil Wars* (Liverpool: Liverpool University Press, 1956), includes a sensible discussion of Shakespeare's use of the ancient sources; Gary Wills, *Rome and Rhetoric: Shakespeare's Julius Caesar* (New Haven, CT: Yale University Press, 2011), is a lively introduction to the subject.

THE ANCIENT CITY OF ROME

Eva Margareta Steinby, ed., *Lexicon Topographicum Urbis Romae* [Topographical Lexicon of the City of Rome], 6 vols. (Rome: Edizioni Quasar, 1993–2000) is a fundamental encyclopedia, replacing the earlier Samuel Ball Platner, completed and revised by Thomas Ashby, *A Topographical Dictionary of Ancient Rome* (London: Oxford University Press, H. Milford, 1929). An excellent, shorter book is Lawrence Richardson, *A New Topographical Dictionary of Ancient Rome* (Baltimore: Johns Hopkins University Press, 1992). Filippo Coarelli, *Rome and Environs: An Archaeological Guide*, translated by James J. Clauss and Daniel P.

Harmon (Berkeley: University of California Press, 2007), is detailed and scholarly. Amanda Claridge, *Rome: An Oxford Archaeological Guide*, 2nd ed., rev. and
expanded ed. (Oxford and New York: Oxford University Press, 2010), is very
useful, not least as a walking guide.

Several websites are valuable, among them: "Rome Reborn: A Digital Model
of Ancient Rome," retrieved December 15, 2011, from http://www.romereborn
.virginia.edu/; "Digital Augustan Rome," retrieved December 15, 2011, from
http://digitalaugustanrome.org/; "The Theatre of Pompey," retrieved December 15, 2011, from http://www.pompey.cch.kcl.ac.uk/index.htm.

On ancient Rome as an urban space, see S. L. Dyson, *Rome: A Living Por-
trait of an Ancient City* (Baltimore: Johns Hopkins University Press, 2010); Jon
Coulston and Hazel Dodge, *Ancient Rome: The Archaeology of the Eternal City*
(Oxford: Oxford University School of Archaeology, 2000); Grant Heiken, Re-
nato Funiciello, and Donatella De Rita, *The Seven Hills of Rome: A Geological
Tour of the Eternal City* (Princeton: Princeton University Press, 2005).

On daily life in ancient Rome, see the classic by Jérôme Carcopino, *Daily
Life in Ancient Rome: The People and the City at the Height of the Empire* (New
Haven, CT: Yale University Press, 2003 [1940]). See also John E. Stambaugh,
The Ancient Roman City (Baltimore and London: Johns Hopkins University
Press, 1988); F. Dupont, *Daily Life in Ancient Rome* (Oxford: Blackwell, 1992);
and the very accessible Alberto Angela, *A Day in the Life of Ancient Rome*, trans-
lated by Gregory Conti (New York: Europa Editions, 2011).

On Roman parks and gardens, see Pierre Grimal, *Les jardins romains à la fin
de la république et aux deux premiers siècles de l'empire; essai sur le naturalisme
romain*, 3rd ed. (Paris: Fayard, 1984); Maddalena Cima and Emilia Talamo,
Gli Horti di Roma Antica (Milan: Electa, 2008); John D'Arms, "Between Public
and Private: The *epulum publicum* and Caesar's *horti trans Tiberim*," in Maddalena Cima and Eugenio La Rocca, eds., *Horti romani: atti del convegno internazionale: Roma, 4–6 maggio 1995* (Rome: "L'Erma" di Bretschneider, 1998),
33–43.

The sources for the Temple of the Deified Julius and its dedication are con-
veniently available in English translation at "Rome Reborn: The Temple of
Caesar," http://romereborn.frischerconsulting.com/ge/TS-020.html.

MISCELLANEOUS

On clothing, see L. M. Wilson, *The Roman Toga* (Baltimore: Johns Hopkins University Press, 1924).

There are many novels on the subject of this book. Allan Massie, *Caesar* (London: Hodder & Stoughton, 1993) makes Decimus the narrator, looking back on Caesar's assassination from his last days in a Gallic prison. Colleen McCullough, *The October Horse: A Novel of Caesar and Cleopatra* (New York: Simon & Schuster, 2007) gives Decimus a major role in the story of the assassination. Steven Saylor, *The Judgment of Caesar: A Novel of Ancient Rome* (New York: St. Martin's, 2004) and idem, *The Triumph of Caesar: A Novel of Ancient Rome* (New York: St. Martin's, 2008) are detective stories that marvelously evoke the conspiratorial atmosphere of Rome. Saylor's *A Murder on the Appian Way: A Novel of Ancient Rome* (New York: St. Martin's Press, 1996) is set against the backdrop of the murder of Clodius in 52 B.C. Decimus is an important character in Ben Kane's *The Road to Rome* (New York: St. Martin's Griffin, 2012). Conn Iggulden's *Emperor: The Gods of War* (New York: Delacorte Press, 2006) paints a stirring picture of the Civil War and of Caesar's assassination. Thornton Wilder's *The Ides of March* (New York: Harper Perennial, 2003 [1948]) is a subtle delight. Riccardo Bacchelli, *I tre Schiavi di Giulio Cesare* (The Three Slaves of Julius Caesar) (Milan: Mondadori, 1957) picks up on a detail in Suetonius, that after Caesar's assassination, only three slaves were left to carry his litter awkwardly back home. Margaret George, *The Memoirs of Cleopatra: A Novel* (New York: St. Martin's Press, 2004) vividly tells Cleopatra's story in a historical novel narrated by the queen herself.

Notes

CHAPTER 1. RIDING WITH CAESAR

3 *August 45 B.C.* On the chronology of Caesar's return from Hispania, see Lily Ross Taylor, "On the Chronology of Cicero's Letters to Atticus, Book XIII," *Classical Philology* 32.3 (1937): 238–40.

3 *a procession entered the city of Mediolanum* Plutarch, *Antony* 11.2. Plutarch refers only to the four men traveling "through Italy" and not any specific city but Mediolanum seems likely because it was one of the major cities of Italian Gaul.

3 *The four men had met in southern Gaul and traveled together* See Matthias Gelzer, *Caesar, Politician and Statesman*, trans. Peter Needham (Cambridge, MA: Harvard University Press, 1968), 299; Bernard Camillus Bondurant, *Decimus Brutus Albinus: A Historical Study* (Chicago: University of Chicago Press, 1907), 36.

4 *a close friend of Caesar* Nicolaus of Damascus, *Life of Caesar Augustus* 23.84; Velleius Paterculus, *The Roman History* 2.64.2; Plutarch, *Brutus* 13; Appian, *Civil Wars* 2.111; Cassius Dio, *Roman History* 44.18.1.

5 *a great historian suggested that Decimus was Caesar's illegitimate son* Ronald Syme, "Bastards in the Roman Aristocracy," *Proceedings of the American Philosophical Society* 104.3 (1960): 323–27, and "No Son for

Caesar?," *Historia* 29 (1980): 422–37, esp. 426–30. For a convincing reply, see Georges Michel Duval, "D. Junius Brutus: mari ou fils de Sempronia?," *Latomus* 50.3 (1991): 608–15.

5 *young Decimus found his way to Caesar's staff* Although we first hear of him in Gaul in 56 B.C. there is good reason to think that he had already served with Caesar in Hispania in 61 B.C. See the arguments in R. Schulz, "Caesar und das Meer," *Historische Zeitschrift* 271.2 (2000): 288–90.

6 *In 50 B.C. Decimus was back in Rome for his first elective office* G. V. Sumner, "The Lex Annalis Under Caesar (Continued)," *Phoenix* 24.4 (1971): 358–59.

6 *she divorced her previous husband, a prominent man* His name is unknown. Cicero, *Letters to Friends* 8.7.2.

6 *Sewer of Romulus faex Romuli,* Cicero, *Letters to Atticus* 2.1.8.

7 *Decimus issued coins* The coins also commemorated Decimus's adoptive family, the Postumii Albini. See M. H. Crawford, *Roman Republican Coinage* (London and New York: Cambridge University Press, 2001), vol. 1: 92, 466, 547, 711; vol. 2: 736.

7 *He gave Caesar's cause a propaganda boost* As a Roman poet later wrote, Decimus was the first man to add victory at sea to Caesar's honors in the Civil War. Lucan (A.D. 39–65), *Pharsalia* 3.761–62.

7 *Bellovaci* Livy, *Periochae* 114.9; Caesar, *Gallic War* 2.4.5; Strabo, *Geography* 4.4.3. They lived in Picardy in northern France.

8 *Italian Gaul* That is, Cisalpine Gaul.

10 *"Venus's Girl"* Plutarch, *Antony* 9; Cicero, *Letters to Atticus* 10.10.5; Cicero, *Philippics* 2.58.

10 *She alone once wore a sword and recruited an army* In the Perusine War in 41 B.C.

11 *her enemy's sling bullets* From the siege of Perusia (modern Perugia) in 40 B.C. See Corey Brennan, "Perceptions of Women's Power in the Late Republic: Terentia, Fulvia, and the Generation of 63 BCE," in Sharon L. James and Sheila Dillon James, eds., *A Companion to Women in the Ancient World* (Malden, MA: Wiley-Blackwell, 2012), 358; Judith P. Hallett, "Perusinae Glandes and the Changing Image of Augustus," *American Journal of Ancient History* 2 (1977): 151–71.

11 *Octavian was a short-statured Apollo* Suetonius, *Augustus* 79.

11 *the honor of sharing his carriage.* Velleius Paterculus, *History of Rome* 2.59.3.

12 *wearing an officer's insignia, even though Octavian* Nicolaus of Damascus, *Life of Caesar* 18.17.

13 *an assassination attempt on Caesar in 46 B.C.* Cicero, *Philippics* 2.74.

13 *According to Cicero* Cicero, *Philippics* 2.34; Plutarch, *Antony* 13.

CHAPTER 2. THE BEST MEN

15 *Caesar met in the city of Mediolanum with Marcus Junius Brutus* The sources say only that they met in Italian Gaul, without citing the city (Cicero, *Letters to Atticus* 13.40.1; Plutarch, *Brutus* 6.12) but Mediolanum is likely enough since it was a regional center and the town that later put up a statue to Brutus (see below). Although Plutarch, *Brutus* 6.12, seems to put the meeting in 46 B.C., he sometimes compresses chronology and 45 B.C. is a more likely date. See Taylor, "On the Chronology of Cicero's Letters," 239 n. 24.

15 *his chosen governor of Italian Gaul* Cicero, *Letters to Friends* 6.6.10.

15 *possibly a symptom of the epilepsy* Plutarch, *Caesar* 17.2, 53.5–6, 60.7; Suetonius, *Julius Caesar* 45.2; Appian, *Civil Wars* 2.110; Cassius Dio, *Roman History* 43.32.6. Since Caesar's friends and enemies both used reports of his health to their advantage, the ancient evidence has to be treated with caution.

15 *He personified talent, strategy, memory* Cicero, *Second Philippic* 2.116.

16 *Brutus had leading-man looks* Sheldon Nodelman, "The Portrait of Brutus the Tyrannicide," *Occasional Papers on Antiquities 4: Ancient Portraits in the J. Paul Getty Museum* 1 (1987): 41–86.

16 *they put up a statue of him in Mediolanum* Plutarch, *Brutus* 6.11, *Comparison of Dion and Brutus* 5.

17 *Caesar and Brutus traveled together through Italian Gaul* Plutarch, *Brutus* 6.12; cf. Taylor, "On the Chronology of Cicero's Letters," 238–39.

17 *The alternative to the* optimates *or "Best Men" was the* populares *or "Populists"* Such terms were imprecise and fluid. See W. K. Lacey, *"Boni atque Improbi," Greece & Rome,* 2nd ser., 17.1 (1970): 3–16.

18 *In private, he called him a king* Cicero, *Letters to Atticus* 13.37.2.

18 *"Where would he find them?"* Cicero, *Letters to Atticus* 13.40.1.

18 *"he knows on which side his bread is buttered"* Cicero, *Letters to Atticus* 13.40.1. This translation of this difficult sentence is suggested as a possibility by D. R. Shackleton Bailey, ed. and trans., *Cicero, Letters to Atticus* (Cambridge: Cambridge University Press, 1996), vol. 5: 241, and note ad loc., 388 (with discussion of another relevant comment of Cicero on Brutus at 13.41.2).

19 *"speaks Latin the most eloquently of nearly all the orators"* The speaker is Cicero's friend Atticus at Cicero, *Brutus* 252.

19 *"almost the pioneer and inventor of eloquence"* Cicero, *Brutus* 253, translated by G. L. Hendrickson in *Brutus / Cicero*; with an English translation by G. L.Hendrickson. *Orator / Cicero*, with an English translation by H. M. Hubbell, rev. ed. (Cambridge, MA: Harvard University Press, 1962), 219.

19 *"it was a greater thing to have advanced"* Pliny, *Natural History* 7.117, translated by Elizabeth Rawson, *Cicero: A Portrait*, rev. ed. (Ithaca, NY: Cornell University Press, 1983), 254.

19 *"Liberty," wrote Cicero, "has been lost"* Cicero, *Letters to Friends* 9.16.3.

19 *"some sort of a constitutional system"* "aliquam rem publicam," Cicero, *Letters to Friends* 13.68.2, maybe October 46 B.C.; cf. 6.10b.2.

19 *"What else can he do?"* Cicero, *Letters to Atticus* 13.40.4.

19 *"immortal fame" achieved by his "godlike courage"* Cicero, *For Marcellus* 26, 28.

19 *he caught a glimpse of a reviving republic* Cicero, *Letters to Friends* 4.4.3.

19 *how wise men bore* regna (*singular,* regnum) Cicero, *Letters to Friends* 9.16.6.

20 *In Roman eyes, monarchy had a suggestion* Andrew Erskine, "Hellenistic Monarchy and Roman Political Invective," *Classical Quarterly* n.s. 41.1 (1991): 106–20.

20 *So Cicero complained* Cicero, *Letters to Atticus* 13.40.1.

20 *"But before all other women"* Suetonius, *Julius Caesar* 50.2.

21 *the equivalent of hundreds of millions of dollars in today's terms* Today the average active-duty service member in the U.S. Army receives an annual

benefits and pay compensation package worth $99,000, http://www
.goarmy.com/benefits/total-compensation.html. The Hope Diamond, one
of the world's most expensive diamonds, is valued perhaps at $250 million,
http://en.wikipedia.org/wiki/Hope_Diamond, accessed June 25, 2014.

21 *financiers and political operators* Like Titus Pomponius Atticus (110–
32 B.C.), a Roman knight who was wealthy, well connected, and
powerful.

21 *"very knowing and careful lady"* Cicero, *Letters to Brutus* 1.18.1.

21 *sometimes found herself at home surrounded by eminent men* Cicero, *Letters
to Atticus* 15.11.1–3. On Servilia as Caesar's confidante and agent, see
Richard A. Bauman, *Women and Politics in Ancient Rome* (London and
New York: Routledge, 1992), 73.

21 *"every care begins and ends with you"* Cicero, *Letters to Brutus* 1.18, in
D. R. Shackleton Bailey, ed. and trans., *Cicero: Letters to Quintus and
Brutus* (Cambridge, MA: Harvard University Press, 2002), 283.

22 *a serious, pensive, and faraway look* See the bust of Cato the Younger from
the Archaeological Museum of Rabat, Morocco. Found in the House of
Venus, Volubilis. Frederick Poulsen, "Caton et le Jeune Prince," *Acta Ar-
chaeologica* 18 (1947) 117–139.

22 *"the only man to try to overturn the Republic while sober"* Suetonius, *Julius
Caesar* 53.1; Plutarch, *Cato the Younger* 24.1, *Brutus* 5.2, *Caesar* 17.9–10;
Velleius Paterculus, *The Roman History* 41.2.

22 *a passionate note from his half sister Servilia* Plutarch, *Cato the Younger*
24.1–2, *Brutus* 5.2.

23 *a favor to Servilia* Plutarch, *Brutus* 5.1.

24 *Caesar's supposed fear that Brutus was his son* Appian, *Civil War* 2.112.

24 *"What this man wants, is a major problem"* Cicero, *Letters to Atticus*
14.1.2, trans. A. W. Lintott, in *Cicero as Evidence: A Historian's Companion* (Oxford: Oxford University Press, 2008), 341.

24 *dropped everything and headed to Egypt* Plutarch, *Brutus* 6.3–5.

24 *Caesar tells a different story in the* Commentaries Caesar, *Civil War* 3.105–6.

25 *He considered Caesar a tyrant* Plutarch, *Cato the Younger* 66.2.

25 *He told his son that he had been raised in liberty* Cassius Dio, *Roman History* 43.10.4–5.

25 *Cato took a dagger* Plutarch, *Cato the Younger* 70.1; Appian, *Civil Wars* 2.98; Cassius Dio, *Roman History* 43.11.4.

25 *"O Cato, I begrudge you your death"* Plutarch, *Cato the Younger* 72.2; cf. Appian, *Civil Wars* 2.99.

25 *Brutus disapproved of his uncle Cato's act* Plutarch, *Brutus* 40.7.

25 *"Romans, watch your wives, see the bald adulterer's back home"* Suetonius, *Julius Caesar* 51, trans. Mary Beard, in *The Roman Triumph* (Cambridge, MA: Belknap Press of Harvard University, 2007), 247.

26 *"tearing himself apart like a wild animal"* Appian, *Civil Wars* 2.101

26 *He considered Cato a great man* Cicero, *Letters to Atticus* 12.4.2.

26 *"first in manly courage among all peoples"* Cicero, *Philippics* 13.30.

26 *Elite opinion followed* For example, Papirius Paetus in Cicero, *Letters to Friends* 9.18.2.

26 *she had a new estate near Naples to enjoy* Cicero, *Letters to Atticus* 14.21.3; Suetonius, *Julius Caesar* 50.2.

26 *Porcia once stabbed herself deeply in the thigh* Plutarch, *Brutus* 13.

26 *Servilia and Porcia were not getting along* Cicero, *Letters to Atticus* 13.22.4.

CHAPTER 3. DECISION IN A VILLA

29 *He didn't enter the city until October* Velleius Paterculus, *History of Rome* 2.56.3.

29 *Labici* The remains of a Republican villa found at modern San Cesareo about eighteen miles southeast of Rome might possibly belong to Caesar's villa. It is plausible but not certain that Caesar stayed there. See "San Cesareo (RM). Scavi in località Colle Noci (c.d. Villa di Massenzio)," http://www.archeologia.beniculturali.it/index.php?it/142/scavi_/scaviarcheologici_4e048966cfa3a/356, accessed July 28, 2014; Carlo Alberto Bucci, "Vandali e incuria salviamo la villa di Cesare," *La Repubblica Roma.it*, June 10, 2011, http://roma.repubblica.it/cronaca/2011/06/10/news/vandali_e_incuria_salviamo_la_villa_di_cesare-17479575/, accessed July 28, 2014.

30 *tranquility of Italy* Caesar, *Civil War* 3.57.

31 *nothing in the world was comparable to it* Cicero, *Republic* 1.70.

32 *"strengthen the Republic for the future"* Pseudo-Sallust, "Letter to Caesar," translation modified from John C. Rolfe, *Sallust* (Cambridge, MA: Harvard University Press, 1985), p. 447, 1.8.

32 *because he paid too much attention to his hairstyle* Plutarch, *Life of Caesar*, 4.9. On the date see Pelling, *Plutarch Caesar* 148–49. On the joke, see Anthony Corbeill, *Nature Embodied: Gesture in Ancient Rome* (Princeton, NJ: Princeton University Press, 2004), 134–35.

32 *"a nothing, a mere name without form or substance"* Suetonius, *Julius Caesar* 77.

32 *a pamphlet by an enemy of Caesar* Suetonius, *Julius Caesar* 77.

32 *VENI VIDI VICI, "I came, I saw, I conquered"* Suetonius, *Caesar* 37.2; Plutarch, *Caesar* 50.3; Appian, *Civil Wars* 2.91.

33 *what Aristotle called a great-souled man* Nicomachean Ethics 4.3.

33 *"the imperator Gaius Caesar deserved well of the republic"* Caesar, *Civil War* 1.13.

33 *his mother's knee* Aurelia Cotta, Caesar's mother, was later held up as a model of good parenting. Tacitus, *Dialogue on Oratory* 28.

33 *the first man in Rome* Plutarch, *Caesar* 11.3–4.

34 *a refuge for the poor* Sallust, *War with Catiline* 54.3.

34 *if it took thugs and murderers* Suetonius, *Julius Caesar* 72.

34 *a dangerous crossing of the Adriatic in a small boat* Velleius Paterculus, *History of Rome* 2.43.2. This incident took place in 73 B.C.

34 *a trap on the River Sabis* Caesar, *Gallic War* 2.15–28; Plutarch, *Caesar* 20.4–10; Appian, *Gallic Wars* Epitome 4; Cassius Dio, *Roman History* 39.3.1–2. The Battle of the River Sabis took place in 57 B.C.

35 *he said that his enemies were in charge of the Senate* Caesar, *Civil War* 1.7.

35 *surrender of Vercingetorix at Alesia* Caesar, *Gallic War* 7.89.5; Florus *Epitome of Roman History* 1.45.26; Plutarch, *Caesar* 27.9–10; Cassius Dio, *Roman History* 40.41.

35 *Cleopatra had great physical presence* Duane Roller, *Cleopatra: A Biography* (Oxford: Oxford University Press, 2010), 3; Plutarch, *Antony* 27.2.

36 *"certain Greek writers"* Suetonius, *Julius Caesar* 52.2.

37 *lamented the fact that Alexander* Suetonius, *Julius Caesar* 7.1; Cassius Dio, *Roman History* 37.52.2; Plutarch, *Caesar* 11.5–6.

38 *Power, he once said, depended on only two things* Cassius Dio, *Roman History* 42.29.4.

38 *he sent the officers' horses away* Caesar, *Gallic War* 1.25.

38 *leaving his hair and beard unshaven* Caesar, *Gallic War* 7.88.1.

38 *"absolutely attached to him and absolutely steadfast"* Suetonius, *Julius Caesar* 68.1.

38 *"He was more pleasing to the masses than to the Senate"* Livy, *History of Rome* 1.15.8; Zvi Yavetz, *Plebs and Princeps* (Oxford: Clarendon Press, 1969), 58, n. 4.

38 *"If you do right, you will be punished"* Cassius Dio, *Roman History* 43.20.3.

39 *"Make the soldiers rich"* Cassius Dio, *Roman History Epitome* 77.15.2.

39 *usually tight-lipped* Cicero, *Letters to Atticus* 14.21.2.

40 *Balbus was drawing up decrees* Cicero, *Letters to Friends* 9.15.4.

40 *helmsman on the Republic's ship of state* Cicero, *Letters to Friends* 9.15.4.

40 *if a man like Cicero had to wait to see him* Cicero, *Letters to Atticus* 14.1.2.

43 *The real estate alone cost a fortune* The land cost over 100 million sesterces (=25 million denarii). Suetonius, *Julius Caesar* 26.2. A legionary's annual wage was 225 denarii.

44 *"I have lived long enough for nature or glory"* "satis diu vel naturae vixi vel gloriae," Cicero, *For Marcellus* 25.

44 *Some of his friends thought* Suetonius, *Julius Caesar* 86.1.

44 *fainting spells and night terrors* Suetonius, *Julius Caesar* 45.1.

44 *Caesar was an epileptic* Plutarch, *Caesar* 17.2, 53.5–6, 60.7; Suetonius *Julius Caesar* 45.2, Appian *Civil Wars* 2.110; Cassius Dio, *Roman History* 43.32.6. Since Caesar's friends and enemies both used reports of his health to their advantage, the ancient evidence has to be treated with caution.

45 *the Ides of September—September 13, 45* B.C. Suetonius, *Julius Caesar* 83.1. According to the traditional Roman calendar, the Ides fell on the 13th of the month except for March, May, July, and October, when it fell on the 15th.

45 *The key to the document was* Suetonius, *Julius Caesar* 83.1; Nicolaus, *Life of Caesar Augustus* 17.48; Appian, *Civil Wars* 2.143; Cassius Dio, *Roman History* 44.35.2–3.

45 *rumor that Antony hoped to be adopted by Caesar* Cicero, *Philippics* 2.71; Nicolaus of Damascus, *Life of Caesar Augustus* 21.74.

45 *Antony's charge that Octavian sold his body to Caesar* Suetonius, *Augustus* 68.

CHAPTER 4. CAESAR'S LAST TRIUMPH

47 *lost his estate near Naples* Cicero, *Letters to Atticus* 14.21.3.

47 *"Ask me for the Republic back, Tribune Aquila!"* Suetonius, *Julius Caesar* 78.2.

48 *"That is, if Pontius Aquila will let me"* Suetonius, *Julius Caesar* 78.2.

48 *Herophilus* Valerius Maximus, *Memorable Deeds and Sayings* 9.15.1, cf. Appian, *Civil Wars* 3.2.

49 *Apollo* Wolfgang Helbig, *Fuehrer durch die oeffentlichen Sammlungen klassischer Altertuemer in Rom*, 4th ed., vol. 2 (Tuebingen: E. Wasmuth, 1963), 614, no. 1846.

49 *son of Niobe* MC Inv 3027; Helbig, *Fuehrer durch die oeffentlichen Sammlungen klassischer Altertuemer in Rom*, 553, no. 1783. See Marina Bertoletti, Maddalena Cima, and Emilia Talamo, *Centrale Montemartini. Musei Capitolini* (Electa: Milano, 2007), 75, fig. 70 for a color illustration.

49 *"They say he [Caesar] wouldn't go against the Parthians"* Cicero, *Letters to Atticus* 13.31.3.

50 *as the historian Tacitus wrote many years later* Tacitus, *Histories* 3.37.

50 *Cicero also wrote that it was hard to hold back the tears* Cicero, *Letters to Atticus* 7.30.2; Cassius Dio, *Roman History* 43.46.4.

50 *the Senate named Caesar DICTATOR IN PERPETUO* Plutarch, *Caesar* 57.1.

50 *"We should actually call King the man whom we in fact had as king"* Cicero, *On Divination* 2.110: "quem re vera regem habebamus appellandum quoque esse regem."

50 *Asinius Pollio* Cicero, *Letters to Friends* 10.31.3; possible echo in Appian, *Civil Wars* 2.111.1.

51 *"Sulla didn't know his ABCs when he laid down his dictatorship"* Suetonius, *Julius Caesar* 77—from T. Ampius Balbus, an enemy of Caesar.

51 *Every senator promised to maintain Caesar's safety* Suetonius, *Julius Caesar* 84.2, 86.1; Livy, *Periochae* 116; Appian, *Civil Wars* 2.144; Cassius Dio, *Roman History* 44.5.3.

51 *Caesar named him as the Dictator's formal second-in-command* Cassius Dio, *Roman History* 43.51.7; Appian, *Civil Wars* 3.9.30.

51 *"Father of the Fatherland"* Cassius Dio, *Roman History* 44.4.4.

52	*People joked that this was Caesar's favorite honor* Suetonius, *Julius Caesar* 45.2.

52	*share a temple with the god* Cicero, *Letters to Atticus* 12.45.2, cf. 12.48; Cassius Dio, *Roman History* 43.45.3.

52	*tradition stated that the senators killed* Livy, *History of Rome* 1.16; Cassius Dio, *Roman History* 43.45.2–4.

52	*he erased the inscription calling him a "demigod"* Cassius Dio, *Roman History* 43.14.6, 43.21.1–2; Suetonius, *Julius Caesar* 37.2.

53	*the "odious" procession, as he called it* Cicero, *Letters to Atticus* 13.44.1.

53	*"I hate the Queen"* Cicero, *Letters to Atticus* 15.15.2.

54	*They also said he would take the wealth* Nicolaus of Damascus, *Life of Caesar Augustus* 20.68; Suetonius, *Julius Caesar* 79.3.

54	*Caesar wanted to settle things in Rome first* Cicero, *Letters to Atticus* 13.31.3.

54	*He said he was concerned about his laws being disregarded* Cicero, *Letters to Atticus* 13.7.

54	*In fact, if the men he left behind fell short of his standards* Martin Jehne, *Der Staat des Dictators Caesar* (The State of the Dictator Caesar) (Cologne, Germany: Böhlau, 1987), 457–61.

55	*Caesar claimed that he already had enough glory* "satis diu vel naturae vixi vel gloriae," Cicero, *For Marcellus* 25.

56	*He complained about his rich and apathetic neighbor, Lucius Marcius Philippus* According to Macrobius [*Satires* 3.15.6], Philippus was one of the unnamed wealthy men of leisure who, complains Cicero, cared more about fishponds than the republic, Cicero, *Letters to Atticus* 1.19.6; 1.20.3.

56	*Cicero describes the whole thing in a breathless letter* Cicero, *Letters to Atticus* 13.52.

57	*Caesar wrote from Hispania* Cicero, *Letters to Atticus* 13.20.1.

57	*A friend wrote archly* Servius Sulpicius; see Cicero, *Letters to Friends* 4.5.6.

57	*Cicero thought better of it and gave up the idea* Cicero, *Letters to Atticus* 13.26.2, 12.51.2, 52.2.

57	*"Once was enough"* Cicero, *Letters to Atticus* 13.52.2.

58 *three incidents* Livy, *Periochae* 6.2–3. There is some doubt about the order of the incidents. What follows is what, on balance, appears to me to be the likeliest order.

59 *he also made a joke about their news* Cassius Dio, *Roman History* 44.8; Plutarch, *Caesar* 60.3–4; Appian, *Civil Wars* 2.107; Suetonius, *Julius Caesar* 78.1; Nicolaus of Damascus, *Life of Caesar Augustus* 78; Livy, *Periochae* 116.

59 *The sources are full of commentary* Suetonius, *Julius Caesar* 78.1; Plutarch, *Caesar* 60.4–5; Cassius Dio, *Roman History* 44.8.2; Appian, *Civil Wars* 2.107.

60 *"I am Caesar, not Rex"* Suetonius, *Julius Caesar* 6.1.

60 *He wanted to grant his usual clemency but* Velleius Paterculus, *History of Rome* 2.68.3.

60 *Caesar demanded that the tribune Caesetius's father disinherit his son* Valerius Maximus, *Memorable Deeds and Sayings* 5.7.2.

60 *some people accused Caesar of blaming the messengers* Nicolaus of Damascus, *Life of Caesar Augustus* 20.69, 22.76; Livy, *Periochae* 116.2; Suetonius, *Julius Caesar* 79.2, 80.3; Appian, *Civil Wars* 2.108–9; Plutarch, *Caesar* 61.10; Cassius Dio, *Roman History* 44.10.1–4, 11.4.

61 *In 49 B.C., he said that one of the main reasons* Caesar, *Civil War* 1.7–8.

61 *The result was to generate invidia—ill will* Livy, *Periochae* 116.2.

61 *But Caesar actually indulged in the finery of Rome's ancient kings* Cassius Dio, *Roman History* 43.43.2; Gelzer, *Caesar: Politician and Statesman*, 316, n.1.

62 *"The People give this to you through me"* Cassius Dio, *Roman History* 44.11.2.

62 *a groan and gloomy look* Cicero, *Philippics* 5.38.

62 *"Jupiter alone of the Romans is King"* Cassius Dio, *Roman History* 44.11.2–3.

62 *"the Consul Mark Antony had offered the Kingship"* Cicero, *Philippics* 2.85–87.

62 *The sources buzz with speculation* See, for example, Nicolaus of Damascus, *Life of Caesar Augustus* 21.71–74; Cicero, *Philippics* 2.85; Cassius Dio, *Roman History* 44.11.3.

63 *Later on it was claimed that Antony* Cassius Dio, *Roman History* 46.19.1–8.

63 *two opponents of Caesar* They were Cassius and Publius Casca, Nicolaus of Damascus, *Life of Caesar Augustus* 21.72. Nicolaus is not credible. See Jane Bellemore, edited with introduction, translation and commentary, *Nicolaus of Damascus, Life of Augustus* (Bristol: Bristol Classical Press, 1984) comm. ad loc., 106.

63 vir clarissimus—*a man of extraordinary brilliance* E.g., Cicero, *Letters to Atticus* 14.22.1.

63 *called Caesar a great man* "tanto viro," Cicero, *Letters to Atticus* 14.11.1; Velleius Paterculus, *History of Rome* 2.56.3.

63 *"with claims to power"... "unbearable"... "gloried in his many great victories"... "admired someone who they thought was more than just a man"* Nicolaus of Damascus, *Life of Caesar Augustus* 19.64.

63 *trying to see if there was support* Plutarch, *Caesar* 61.6; Cassius Dio, *Roman History* 44.11.3; Nicolaus of Damascus, *Life of Caesar Augustus* 21.73.

63 *Hatred is one of a ruler's greatest dangers* Machiavelli, *The Prince*, ch. 19.

CHAPTER 5. THE BIRTH OF A PLOT

67 *Or so the best-known source tells the story* Plutarch, *Caesar* 62.8, *Brutus* 10.3–7.

67 *"Our earliest in-depth source for the conspiracy even names Decimus first* See p. 82.

68 *Although Decimus said later that he acted to save the Republic* Cicero, *Letters to Friends* 11.10.4.

69 *Cicero's correspondence includes a few dozen precious letters* There are letters between Cicero and the following conspirators: Brutus (*Letters to Brutus*, two books of twenty-six letters, most of them genuine), Cassius (e.g., *Letters to Friends* 12.12), Decimus (e.g., *Letters to Friends* 11.5), Galba (*Letters to Friends* 10.30), Trebonius (e.g., *Letters to Friends* 12.16), Minucius Basilus (*Letters to Friends* 6.5).

69 *Cicero wrote one of those accounts in 44 B.C.* Cicero, *On Divination* 2.23.

71 *"old easygoing master"* Cicero, *Letters to Friends* 15.19.4. Cicero, *Letters*

to Friends, vol. 2, ed. and trans. by D. R. Shackleton Bailey (Cambridge, MA, and London, England: Harvard University Press, 2001): 287.

71 *Brutus underwent a similar conversion, perhaps independently* Cassius Dio, *Roman History* 44.14.2.

71 *perhaps Cassius was the spark* Plutarch, *Brutus* 7.4, 8.2, 10.1; Appian, *Civil Wars* 2.113; cf. Suetonius, *Julius Caesar* 80.3–4.

72 *Yon Cassius has a lean and hungry look* Shakespeare, *Julius Caesar* 1.2.194–195.

72 *a Roman portrait bust that has plausibly been identified as Cassius* The bust in question is the "pseudo-Corbulo" type. A good example, dated to the second half of the first century A.D., is found in the Montreal Museum of Fine Arts. See also Sheldon Nodelman, "The Portrait of Brutus the Tyrannicide," *Occasional Papers on Antiquities 4: Ancient Portraits in the J. Paul Getty Museum* 1 (1987): 57–59 and 59 n. 59.

73 *"the bravest of men"* Cicero, *Letters to Friends* 15.16.3.

74 *"the date"* Pseudo-Aurelus Victor, *De Virus Illustribus* 83.3.

74 *Caesar describes the two campaigns* Caesar, *Civil War* 3.5.3, 3.101.

74 *"I will die of anxiety"* Cicero, *Letters to Friends* 15.19.4.

75 *even merely the concentration of power* Cicero, *Philippics* 2.26.

75 *against awarding a long list of special honors to Caesar* Cassius Dio, *Roman History* 44.8.1.

75 *Cassius had a stronger case* Plutarch, *Brutus* 7.1–5, *Caesar* 62.4–5; Appian, *Civil Wars* 2.112; Velleius Paterculus, *History of Rome* 2.56.3; Cicero, *Philippics* 8.27. I have relied on the commentary by Pelling, Plutarch, *Caesar,* 460–61.

76 *a story that Cicero made fun of* Suetonius, *Julius Caesar* 50.2.

76 *lions of Megara* Plutarch, *Brutus* 8.6–7; *Caesar* 43.1–2, 62.8.

76 *the single-mindedness of a gladiator* Appian, *Civil Wars* 4.133.

76 *all his life Cassius drank only water* Seneca, *Letters to Lucilius* 83.12.

77 *Brutus issued coins* See "*Libertas*: The Coins of Brutus," http://www .humanities.mq.edu.au/acans/caesar/CivilWars_Libertas.htm, accessed July 27, 2014; M. H. Crawford, *Roman Republican Coinage*, vol. 1, 455–56, no. 433.

77 *spoke against a proposed dictatorship for Pompey* Quintilian, *Institutes* 9.3.95.

77 *a man who committed murder for the good of the Republic was innocent* Quintilian, *Institutes* 3.6.93.

77 *"Marcus Brutus . . . was respected"* Nicolaus of Damascus, *Life of Caesar Augustus* 26a.100, Bellemore translation modified.

77 *Brutus learned to recognize tyranny, to despise it and to rise against it* He was a member of the Academic, that is, Platonist school.

79 *"What then? Don't you think Brutus will wait for this bit of flesh?"* Plutarch, *Brutus* 8.3, *Caesar* 62.6.

79 *Plutarch added that Brutus could count on* Plutarch, *Brutus* 8.4.

80 *"If only now you were Brutus," "If only Brutus were alive," "Brutus, wake up!" "You aren't really Brutus!"* Plutarch, *Brutus* 9.5–9; Appian, *Civil Wars* 2.112; Cassius Dio, *Roman History* 44.12.3.

80 *"that Republic in which you could not only renew"* Cicero, *Brutus* 331.

80 *These men didn't want Brutus to die, said Cassius* Plutarch, *Brutus* 10.1–7.

81 *Porcia was said to be the only woman* Cassius Dio, *Roman History* 44.13.1.

81 *Still, the sources ask what anyone might wonder* Appian, *Civil Wars* 2.112.

81 *Brutus, who wrote on the theme of duties within the family* Seneca, *Letters to Lucilius* 95.45.

81 *Brutus and Cassius now recruited Decimus to the conspiracy* Plutarch, *Brutus* 12.5–6.

82 *"a close friend of Caesar"* Nicolaus of Damascus, *Life of Caesar Augustus* 23.84; Velleius Paterculus, *History of Rome* 2.64.2; Plutarch, *Brutus* 13; Appian, *Civil Wars* 2.111; Cassius Dio, *Roman History* 44.18.1.

82 *Nicolaus actually names Decimus first* Nicolaus of Damascus, *Life of Caesar Augustus* 19.59.

82 *Appian makes him next after Brutus and Cassius* Appian, *Civil Wars* 2.111.

82 *Velleius Paterculus, a Roman soldier-statesman* Velleius Paterculus, *History of Rome* 2.58.1–2.

82 *Other sources name Decimus* Cassius Dio, *Roman History* 44.13.3–4; Eutropius, *Abridgement of Roman History* 6.7.497; Suetonius, *Julius Caesar* 80.4.

82 *"neither active nor daring"* Plutarch, *Brutus* 12.5.

82 *one of Caesar's confidants* Appian, *Civil Wars* 2.111; Velleius Paterculus, *History of Rome* 64.2.

83 *Caesar named him in his will as heir in the second degree* Plutarch, *Caesar* 64.1; Suetonius, *Julius Caesar* 83.2.

83 *Caesar unwittingly named other conspirators as guardians as well* Suetonius, *Julius Caesar* 83.2; Cassius Dio, *Roman History* 44.35.2; Plutarch, *Caesar* 64.1; Appian, *Civil Wars* 2.143.

83 *Cicero portrayed him as part of a cause* Cicero, *Letters to Friends* 11.7.3.

83 *claimed descent from the founder of the Republic* Cicero, *Philippics* 2.26.

83 *Decimus's father and his grandfather* Orosius, *History Against the Pagans* 5.12; Cicero, *Letters to Atticus* 12.22.2.

83 *his eleven surviving single-authored letters* They are: Cicero, *Letters to Friends* 10.13, 11.1, 11.4, 11.7, 11.9, 11.10, 11.13, 11.13b, 11.20, 11.23, 11.26. Part of a joint letter by Decimus and Plancus to the Magistrates, Senate and People survives; it contains one reference to the Republic (11.13a.2).

84 *"liberating the Republic"* Cicero, *Letters to Friends* 11.10.5.

84 *admirably brief as a writer* Cicero, *Letters to Friends* 11.25.1–2.

84 *thirteen letters by Cicero to Decimus survive* Cicero, *Letters to Friends* 11.5, 11.6, 11.6a, 11.7, 11.8, 11.12, 11.14, 11.15, 11.16, 11.21, 11.22, 11.24, 11.25.

84 *five of them refer to liberty, tyranny, the assassination of Caesar, or the Republic* 11.5.2–3, 11.7.2, 11.6a.1, 11.8.1–2, 11.12.1–2.

84 *Decimus was ambitious, competitive, proud, and violent* Nicolaus of Damascus, *Life of Caesar Augustus* 26a.98.

84 *dignitas, a subject that comes up frequently in his correspondence* Cicero, *Letters to Friends* 11.4.2, 11.6a.1–2, 11.8.1.

84 *Decimus wanted fame and greatness* Cicero, *Letters to Friends* 11.4.3.

85 *Decimus was a very brave man* Cicero, *Letters to Atticus* 11.22.1. Note also Decimus's pride in being fearless: Cicero, *Letters to Friends* 11.20.1.

85 *Decimus could sneer at Octavian* Suetonius, *Augustus* 2.3.

85 *Gaius Fuficius Fango* Cassius Dio, *Roman History* 48.22.3; Cicero, *Letters to Atticus* 14.10.2.

85 *Paula Valeria* On her brother, Gaius Valerius Triarius, see Bondurant, *Decimus* 29 and n. 77; Franklin H. Potter, "Political Alliance by Marriage," *Classical World* 29.9 (1934): 673–74; Karl-Ludwig Elvers (Bochum), "Vale-

rius, [I 53–54]," *Brill's New Pauly*, antiquity volumes edited by Hubert Cancik and Helmuth Schneider, Brill Online, accessed April 20, 2014.

CHAPTER 6. WANTED: ASSASSINS

88 *more of Caesar's friends than his enemies* Seneca, *On Anger* 3.30.4.

88 *The policy earned gratitude and stirred anger* Nicolaus of Damascus, *Life of Caesar Augustus* 19.61–63.

88 *Nicolaus makes Caesar's policy of clemency a central grievance* Nicolaus of Damascus, *Life of Caesar Augustus* 19.62–63.

88 *it annoyed the former Pompey supporters* Nicolaus of Damascus, *Life of Caesar Augustus* 19.62.

88 *Cato protested Caesar's arrogance* Plutarch, *Cato the Younger* 66.2.

88 *"His very power of granting favors"* Florus, *Epitome of Roman History* 2.13.92; cf. Nicolaus of Damascus, *Life of Caesar Augustus* 19.63; Velleius Paterculus, *History of Rome* 2.57.1.

89 *the conspiracy was more a matter of court intrigue* Nicolaus of Damascus, *Life of Caesar Augustus* 19.58–65, esp. 60.

89 *petty jealousy* Several ancient sources cite jealousy of Caesar as a factor in the conspirators' motivation: Appian, *Civil Wars* 2.111.1; Cassius Dio, *Roman History* 44.1.1; Vellerius Paterculus, *History of Rome* 2.60.01.

90 *began to insist that Caesar treat him as an equal* Caesar, *Gallic War* 8.52.2; Cicero, *Letters to Atticus* 7.7.6, 7.13.1; Cassius Dio, *Roman History* 41.4.3.

90 *"an ardent patriot"* Cicero, *Letters to Friends* 10.28.1.

90 *"a little gift"* Cicero, *Letters to Friends* 12.16.3.

90 *Cicero said that the Republic owed Trebonius* Cicero, *Philippics* 2.27.

91 *Trebonius was the man who, said Cicero* Cicero, *Philippics* 2.34; Plutarch, *Antony* 13.

91 *he expressed pride in his role in the events of the Ides* Cicero, *Letters to Atticus* 12.16.3–4.

91 *We can't be sure of either brother's motives* Appian, *Civil Wars* 2.113 (which confuses the two brothers), 115; Plutarch, *Brutus* 15; Cicero, *Philippics* 2.27, cf. Suetonius, *Julius Caesar* 82; Plutarch, *Caesar* 66; Plutarch, *Brutus* 17.45; Cassius Dio, Roman History 44.52.2, 46.49.1

91 *as Caesar claims in his* Commentaries Caesar, *Gallic Wars* 3.1–6.

91 *enough, according to one ancient theory, to drive Galba* Suetonius, *Galba* 3.2.

91 *Galba objected in public* Suetonius, *Galba* 3.2; Valerius Maximus, *Memorable Deeds and Sayings* 6.2.11; Cicero, *Letters to Atticus* 6.18.3.

91 *his one surviving letter* Cicero, *Letters to Friends* 10.30.

92 *his moment in the Ardennes Forest* Caesar, *Gallic Wars* 6.29–30.

92 *perhaps he was the same man* Orosius, *History Against the Pagans* 6.15.8.

92 *he made him settle for a sum of money* Cassius Dio, *Roman History* 43.47.5.

92 *It was this, we are told, that made him join* Appian, *Civil Wars* 2.113; Cicero, *Letters to Friends* 6.15; Cassius Dio, *Roman History* 43.47.5.

92 *calls Cimber one of Caesar's "fellow soldiers"* Cicero, *Letters to Atticus* 6.12.2; Seneca, *On Anger* 3.30.5; Appian, *Civil Wars* 3.2; Plutarch, *Brutus* 19.2.

92 *Cicero said afterward that Cimber* Cicero, *Philippics* 2.27.

93 *"Would I, who cannot tolerate my wine"* Seneca, *Letters to Lucilius* 83.12.

93 *the sources report a total of more than sixty or even more than eighty* Suetonius, *Julius Caesar* 80.4; Orosius, *History Against the Pagans* 6.17.2; Eutropius, *Abridgement of Roman History* 6.25, 80; Nicolaus of Damascus, *Life of Caesar Augustus* 19.59.

93 *"many people were angry at him because they had been saved by him"* Nicolaus of Damascus, *Life of Caesar Augustus* 19.62.

93 *Cicero successfully pleaded his case* Cicero, *For Ligarius.*

94 *Although Caesar personally disliked Ligarius* Plutarch, *Cicero* 39.6.

94 *warnings to be careful who he pardoned* Cicero, *For Ligarius* 16.

94 *Ligarius was so eager for revenge* Plutarch, *Brutus* 11.

94 *potentially represented a huge transfer of wealth* Cassius Dio, *Roman History*, 42.51.2. On Caesar's property confiscations, see Gelzer, *Caesar*, 283–84, n. 1; Zvi Yavetz, *Julius Caesar and His Public Image* (Ithaca, NY: Cornell University Press, 1983), 140–41; Elizabeth Rawson, "Caesar: Civil War and Dictatorship," in J. A. Crook, Andrew Lintott, and Elizabeth Rawson, eds., *The Cambridge Ancient History*, 2nd ed., vol. 9, *The Last Age of the Roman Republic, 146–43 B.C.* (Cambridge: Cambridge University Press, 1994), 449–50.

94 *Brutus later complained bitterly* Appian, *Civil Wars* 2.139–41.

94 *The other Pompey supporters among the conspirators* Rubrius Ruga might possibly be the Lucius Rubrius who was People's Tribune in 49 B.C., but also possibly the Marcus Rubrius who was with Cato at Utica. Two other senators were Caecilius Bucilianus and his brother (name unknown). Then there were two men who might be either senators or knights, Sextius Naso and Marcus Spurius.

94 *They included Gaius Cassius of Parma* Another conspirator who cannot be assigned to any group is one Petronius—a mere name to us.

94 *Now he told Brutus that he thought civil war was even worse* Plutarch, *Brutus* 12.3, trans. D. Sedley, "The Ethics of Brutus and Cassius," *Journal of Roman Studies* 87 (1997): 44.

95 *In the same conversation, Brutus engaged one Statilius* Plutarch, *Brutus* 12.3–4; trans. Sedley, "Ethics of Brutus and Cassius," 44, modified.

95 *He denied the charge* Cicero, *Philippics* 2.25.

95 *Caesar had no fear of him* Cicero, *Letters to Atticus* 13.37.2.

95 *for trust and goodwill by both Brutus and Cassius* Plutarch, *Brutus* 12.1.

95 *In their judgment, Cicero lacked daring* Plutarch, *Brutus* 12.2.

96 *Antony, they said, was a supporter of monarchy* Plutarch, *Antony* 13.1, *Brutus* 18.3; Appian, *Civil Wars* 2.114.

97 *never swore an oath* Plutarch, *Brutus* 12.8; Appian, *Civil Wars* 2.114, 139; Nicolaus of Damascus, *Life of Caesar Augustus* 23.81.

97 *every conspirator revealed his own grudge* Nicolaus of Damascus, *Life of Caesar Augustus* 19.65–66.

98 *Brutus hoped for a change of heart on Antony's part* Plutarch, *Antony* 13.2, *Brutus* 18.4–5; Appian, *Civil Wars* 2.113.

98 *So he alone of the conspirators opposed killing Antony* Plutarch, *Brutus* 18.3–6.

99 *Lucius Junius Brutus, did more than drive out the king* Livy, *History of Rome* 1.59–60.

99 *"No friend ever served me and no enemy ever wronged me"* Plutarch, *Sulla* 38.4.

99 *They considered other venues for the assassination* Nicolaus of Damascus, *Life of Caesar Augustus* 80.4; Suetonius, *Julius Caesar* 80.4.

100 *Caesar formally dismissed his Spanish bodyguard* Suetonius, *Julius Caesar*

86.1; Appian, *Civil Wars* 2.107 and 114; Cassius Dio, *Roman History* 44.7.4.

100 *senators and the knights* Appian, *Civil Wars* 2.107, 109; Suetonius, *Julius Caesar* 86.1; Plutarch, *Caesar* 57.3; Cassius Dio, *Roman History* 44.7.4, 44.15.2; Velleius Paterculus, *History of Rome* 2.57.1.

100 *Cicero worried publicly about assassination plots against Caesar* Cicero, *For Marcellus* 21.

100 *Caesar showed mercy by sparing Philemon from torture* Suetonius, *Julius Caesar* 74.1.

101 *Cicero, who defended Deiotarus* The speech still exists: Cicero, *On Behalf of King Deiotarus.*

101 *Aulus Caecina published a pamphlet* Suetonius, *Julius Caesar* 75.4–5.

101 *Caesar's sources in Rome denounced conspiracies* Plutarch, *Caesar* 62.6; Suetonius, *Julius Caesar* 75.5.

101 *Caesar refused to hear information about the conspiracy* Cassius Dio, *Roman History* 44.15.1.

101 *he sometimes acted in the absence of reliable intelligence* For example, when Caesar invaded Britain, Caesar, *Gallic War* 6.20–21.

102 *"I am not much in fear of these fat, long-haired fellows"* Plutarch, *Caesar* 62.9; cf. Plutarch, *Brutus* 8.2; *Antony* 11.3; *Sayings of Kings and Generals* 206e.

102 *He had too much faith in Brutus's character* Plutarch, *Brutus* 8.1.

102 *Caesar complained to his friends about Cassius* Plutarch, *Caesar* 62.69.

102 *He brushed off Brutus's accusers* Plutarch, *Caesar* 62.6; Plutarch, *Brutus* 8.3.

102 *He put too much trust in the oath, some said* Suetonius, *Julius Caesar* 86.1.

102 *wasn't so much in his interest as in the Republic's* Suetonius, *Julius Caesar* 86.2.

102 *"the pleasure of deception"* Roberta Wohlstetter, "Slow Pearl Harbours and the Pleasures of Deception," in Robert L. Pfaltzgraff Jr., Uri Ra'anan, and Warren Milberg, eds., *Intelligence Policy and National Security.* (Hamden, CT: Archon Books, 1981), 23–34.

102 *Caesar was so depressed* Suetonius, *Julius Caesar* 86.1.

103 *a Roman senator was supposed to be easy to approach* Cicero, *On the Command of Cnaeus Pompey* 41; Tacitus, *Annals* 2.2.4.

103 *he was attacked in Rome by men with hidden daggers* Appian, *Civil Wars* 1.55–56; Plutarch, *Sulla* 8–9, *Marius* 35.

103 *give up his bodyguard even while he was still dictator* Appian, *Civil Wars* 1.3, 103–4.

103 *"straightforward by nature"* Nicolaus of Damascus, *Life of Caesar Augustus* 67; my translation, with help from Toher.

104 *But when they in turn asked him to reestablish his bodyguard* Appian, *Civil Wars* 2.107, 109; Suetonius, *Julius Caesar* 86.1; Plutarch, *Caesar* 57.3; Cassius Dio, *Roman History* 44.7.4, 44.15.2; Velleius Paterculus, *The History of Rome* 2.57.1.

104 *"even though he had no bodyguard"* Cassius Dio, *Roman History* 44.15.2.

105 *dinner with his Master of the Horse* Suetonius, *Julius Caesar* 87; Plutarch, *Caesar* 63.4; Appian, *Civil Wars* 2.115. On dining customs in Rome see M. B. Roller, *Dining Posture in Ancient Rome: Bodies, Values and Status* (Princeton, NJ: Princeton University Press, 2006).

105 *While reclining, Caesar added personal greetings* Plutarch, *Caesar* 63.4; Suetonius, *Augustus* 45.12.

106 *Caesar's answer, according to Plutarch, was an unexpected death* Plutarch, *Caesar* 63.7.

106 *a sudden one, says Appian* Appian, *Civil Wars* 2.115.

106 *sudden and unexpected, says Suetonius* Suetonius, *Julius Caesar*, 87.

106 *Suetonius adds that Caesar had discussed the subject* Suetonius, *Julius Caesar* 87.

CHAPTER 7. CAESAR LEAVES HOME

107 *Not long after five in the morning* Based on calculations for March 15, 2014, http://www.timeanddate.com/worldclock/astronomy.html?n=215 &month=3&year=2014&obj=sun&afl=-13&day=1, accessed on April 18, 2014.

107 *all the doors and windows* Or perhaps it was just the doors or only Calpurnia who was awakened—the sources disagree. Plutarch, *Caesar* 63.8; Suetonius, *Julius Caesar* 81.3; Cassius Dio, *Roman History* 44.17.2; Julius Obsequens, *Book of Prodigies* (based on Livy) 67.

107 *she dreamt she was holding a murdered Caesar in her arms* Plutarch, *Caesar* 63.9.

107 *the front pediment of their house collapsed* Plutarch, *Caesar* 63.9.

107 *In one version, his body was streaming* Appian, *Civil Wars* 2.115.

107 *The Senate had given Caesar the right to put up this pediment* Plutarch, *Caesar* 63.8–9; Valerius Maximus, *Memorable Deeds and Sayings* 1.7.2; Suetonius, *Julius Caesar* 81.3; Cassius Dio, *Roman History* 44.17.1.

108 *Even the horses that Caesar had used to cross the Rubicon* Cassius Dio, *Roman History* 44.17.2; Plutarch, *Caesar* 63.1–3; Suetonius, *Julius Caesar* 81.1–2.

109 *Spurinna was trying to warn Caesar not to go too far* Cicero, *On Divination* 1.119.

109 *Spurinna warned Caesar that his life would be in danger* Valerius Maximus, *Memorable Deeds and Sayings* 8.11.2; Suetonius, *Julius Caesar* 81.2; Plutarch, *Caesar* 63.5.

109 *"beware the Ides of March"* Shakespeare, *Julius Caesar* 1.2.18.

109 *she begged Caesar not to go to the Senate meeting* Plutarch, *Caesar* 63.10.

109 *As for Caesar, one source says that he too had a bad dream* Suetonius, *Julius Caesar* 81.3.

109 *the meal did not sit well with him and his body felt sluggish* Appian, *Civil Wars* 2.115.

110 *The next morning, he felt poorly* Suetonius, *Julius Caesar* 8.4.

110 *In particular, he is said to have suffered from vertigo* Nicolaus of Damascus, *Life of Caesar Augustus* 23.83.

110 *symptoms of an undetected epileptic seizure* This and the following medical speculations come from a personal communication with Dr. Carl Bazil, M.D., Ph.D., director, Division of Epilepsy and Sleep, Columbia University.

110 *One source says that Caesar experienced fainting and night terrors* Suetonius, *Julius Caesar* 45.1.

110 *Some in the ancient world said that Caesar was merely pretending* Plutarch, *Brutus* 16.1.

110 *about three hundred yards away* Andrea Carandini and Paolo Carafa, eds. *Atlante di Roma antica: biografia e ritratti della città* (Milano: Electa, 2012), I:290.

110 *famous exchange* Valerius Maximus, *Memorable Deeds and Sayings* 8.11.2;

Appian, *Civil Wars* 2.149; Plutarch, *Caesar* 63.5–6; Suetonius, *Julius Caesar* 81.4; J. T. Ramsey, "At What Hour Did the Murderers of Julius Caesar Gather on the Ides of March 44 B.C.?" in Stephan Heilen et al., *In Pursuit of Wissenschaft: Festschrift für William M. Calder III zum 75. Geburtstag* (Zurich: Olms, 2008), 353.

110 *"The Ides of March have come"* Shakespeare, *Julius Caesar* 3.1–2; Plutarch, *Caesar* 63.6; Suetonius, *Julius Caesar* 81.4; Appian, *Civil Wars* 2.149; Cassius Dio, *Roman History* 44.18.4; Florus, *Epitome of Roman History* 2.13.94; Valerius Maximus, *Memorable Deeds and Sayings* 8.11.2.

110 *According to some sources he ordered new sacrifices* Plutarch, *Caesar* 63.7, *Brutus* 16.1; Appian, *Civil Wars* 2.115; Cassius Dio, *Roman History* 44.17.3.

111 *Caesar decided to send the consul, Antony, to dismiss the Senate* Plutarch, *Caesar* 63.12; Appian, *Civil Wars* 2.115.

111 *Caesar would have missed the scheduled Senate meeting* Suetonius, *Julius Caesar* 81.4; Florus, *Epitome of Roman History* 2.13.94.

111 *"Mother of Aeneas"* Lucretius, *On the Nature of Things*, I.1–2, 10–16.

112 *still dark out* Cicero, *For Murena* 69.

112 *average mid-March temperatures* http://weatherspark.com/averages/32307 /3/Rome-Lazio-Italy, accessed August 1, 2014.

113 *they could carry weapons under their togas* Nicolaus of Damascus, *Life of Caesar Augustus* 23.81; cf. Suetonius, *Julius Caesar*; Cassius Dio, *Roman History* 44.16.1.

113 *It was here, at the site of the Senate meeting* Cassius Dio, *Roman History* 44.16.2.

113 *Sybilline Books* Cicero, *On Divination* 2.110; Suetonius, *Julius Caesar* 79.4–80.1; Plutarch, *Caesar* 60.2, *Brutus* 10.2; Cassius Dio, *Roman History* 44.15.3; Appian, *Civil Wars* 2.110.

113 *Shakespeare writes that Caesar was murdered* *Julius Caesar* 3.1.12.

114 *There were gladiatorial games in the Theater of Pompey that day* Appian, *Civil Wars* 2.115.

114 *"It seemed as if some god was leading the man to the justice of Pompey"* Plutarch, *Brutus*, 14.3.

115 *"They thought that the act,"* Appian, *Civil Wars* 2.114.

115 *It was believed that the senators assassinated the legendary Romulus* Plutarch

Pompey 25.4; Appian, *Civil Wars* 2.114; cf. Cassius Dio, *Roman History* 43.45.3.

115 *Plutarch cites a story that Romulus was killed in a Senate meeting* Plutarch, *Romulus* 5.

115 *According to Appian, the conspirators of 44 B.C.* Appian, *Civil Wars* 2.114.

115 *The assembly supposedly took place, like the Senate meeting* Plutarch, *Romulus* 27.6–8.

115 *was a godsend* Plutarch, *Brutus* 14.2.

116 *not one of those posers* "Dedit gladiatores sestertiarios iam decrepitos, quos si sufflasses, cecidissent," Petronius, *Satyricon* 45.

116 *the story told only by Nicolaus of Damascus* Nicolaus of Damascus, *Life of Caesar Augustus* 26a.98.

116 *Others say that the gladiators were there to take part in the games* Appian, *Civil Wars* 2.118; Cassius Dio, *Roman History* 44.16.

116 *Many elite Romans, their names a roll call of republican glory* On these cases see A. W. Lintott, *Violence in Republican Rome,* 2nd ed. (Oxford: Oxford University Press, 1999), 83–85. Another example is the Pompeian general Gaius Considius Longus: Caesar, *Civil War* 2.23; Pseudo-Caesar, *African War* 76, 9.

116 *Birria* Asconius, *Commentary on Cicero's "For Milo"* 32c.

117 *rhomphaia* Asconius, *Commentary on Cicero's "For Milo"* 32C. See Chris Christoff, "Gladiators Outside of the Arena: The Use of Gladiators as Bodyguards and Soldiers ca. 100 BCE–100 CE," Senior Honors Thesis, Department of History, Cornell University, April 14, 2014, 12–14.

117 *We don't know how many gladiators Decimus had* Nicolaus of Damascus, *Life of Caesar Augustus* 25.94, 26a.98; Plutarch, *Brutus* 12. 5.

117 *Caesar himself might have given these gladiators to Decimus* Pseudo-Cicero, *Letter to Octavian* 9; Appian, *Civil Wars* 2.122; cited in Lintott, *Violence,* 84 and n. 4.

118 *"popular shallowness"* Cicero, *Philippics* 5.49.

118 *he devoted several hours to watching gladiators training* Plutarch, *Caesar* 32.4.

118 *a very large number of gladiators in Capua* Cicero, *Letters to Atticus* 7.14.2, with discussion in K.-W. Welwei, *Unfreie im antiken Kriegsdienst,* vol. 3, *Rom* (Wiesbaden, Germany: Steiner, 1988), 137. I follow the

translation of D. R. Shackleton Bailey, *Cicero, Letters to Atticus*, vol. 4
49 B.C. 133–210 (Books 7.10–10), (Cambridge: University Press, 1968)
19, 308–9.

118 *out on maneuvers in the suburbs of Rome that morning* Cassius Dio,
Roman History 44.19.2; Zonaras, *Epitome of Histories* 10.12.

119 *no bigger than an average city block* 886 feet (270 meters) long by 220 feet
(67 meters) wide.

119 *up to fifteen thousand were settled on land in Italy* L. J. F. Keppie, *Colonisa-
tion and Veteran Settlement in Italy, 47–14 B.C.* (London: British School at
Rome, 1983), 50.

119 *Like the men on the Tiber Island, they were armed* Appian, *Civil Wars*
2.133.

119 *"country folk but very brave men and excellent citizens"* Cicero, *Letters to
Friends* 11.7.2.

120 *could not be taken before sunrise* That is, 6:23 a.m. Actually, that was apparent sunrise, a few minutes earlier than actual sunrise: http://www.esrl
.noaa.gov/gmd/grad/solcalc/, accessed July 14, 2014. J. T. Ramsey, "Beware the Ides of March!: An Astrological Prediction?" *Classical Quarterly*,
new ser. 50.2 (2000): 444, cites sunrise on March 15, 44 B.C. as 6:17
a.m. LMT.

120 *that Caesar neither did nor would prevent Brutus* Plutarch, *Brutus* 14.7.

120 *Brutus too endured sleepless nights* Plutarch, *Brutus* 13.2.

120 *Casca was unnecessarily frightened* Plutarch, *Brutus* 15.2–3; Appian, *Civil
Wars* 2.115.

120 *Popilius Laenas,* Plutarch, *Brutus* 15.4; Appian, *Civil Wars* 2.115.

120 *he soldiered on* Plutarch, *Brutus* 15.5–9.

120 *that seemed like a bad omen* Cassius Dio, *Roman History* 44.17.3.

121 *they decided to send Decimus to Caesar's house* Cassius Dio, *Roman History*
44.18.1.

121 *he was such a close friend* Nicolaus of Damascus, *Life of Caesar Augustus*
23.84; Velleius Paterculus, *History of Rome* 2.64.2; Plutarch, *Brutus* 13;
Cassius Dio, *Roman History* 44.18.1.

121 *"Like mother, like son"* Eccentricity evidently ran in this family. Sempronia's brother was a quirky character who used to mount the Speaker's

Platform in the Roman Forum in an actor's robe and boots, tossing money to the people as he went. Cicero, *Philippics* 3.16.

121 *"masculine audacity"* Sallust, *Catiline* 25.1.

121 *she opened their home to Catiline's Gallic allies—Allobroges* Sallust, *Catiline* 40.5.

122 *seeming to insult* Nicolaus of Damascus, *Life of Caesar Augustus* 23.84.

122 *or mock it* Plutarch, *Caesar* 64.2.

122 *Caesar himself had called the meeting* Suetonius, *Julius Caesar* 81.4; Nicolaus of Damascus, *Life of Caesar Augustus* 23.84; Plutarch, *Caesar* 64.3.

122 *the senators would consider him a tyrant* Plutarch, *Caesar* 64.4.

122 *Decimus ridiculed the soothsayers* Nicolaus of Damascus, *Life of Caesar Augustus* 23.84.

122 *declare Caesar king outside of Italy* Plutarch, *Caesar* 64.3; Suetonius, *Julius Caesar* 79.4; Appian, *Civil Wars* 2.110. Cicero, who should have known, declares this a mere rumor, *On Divination* 2.110.

122 *"What do you say, Caesar?"* Nicolaus of Damascus, *Life of Caesar Augustus* 23.84.

122 *He would postpone the meeting* Nicolaus of Damascus, *Life of Caesar Augustus* 24.87; Plutarch, *Brutus* 16.1.

122 *Decimus led Caesar out by the hand* Plutarch, *Caesar* 64.6; Nicolaus of Damascus, *Life of Caesar Augustus* 24.87.

122 *a Caesar who is gullible* Nicolaus of Damascus, *Life of Caesar Augustus* 23.84, 24.87.

122 *a Caesar who is passive* Plutarch, *Caesar* 64.6.

122 *a Caesar who cares about appearances* Appian, *Civil Wars* 2.116.

122 *a Caesar who is arrogant* Suetonius, *Julius Caesar* 81.4, or Cassius Dio, *Roman History* 44.18.4.

123 *another Caesar, a man who was a risk taker* Appian, *Civil Wars* 2.115.

123 *It was almost at the end of the fifth hour* Suetonius, *Julius Caesar* 81.4.

123 *A litter carried by slaves* Plutarch, *Brutus* 16.1–2; Appian, *Civil Wars* 2.116.

123 *Caesar was thronged along the way* Appian, *Civil Wars* 2.118.

123 *Artemidorus of Cnidus* Plutarch, *Caesar* 65; Appian, *Civil Wars* 2.116; Suetonius, *Julius Caesar* 81.4; Cassius Dio, *Roman History* 44.18.3.

124 *"a friend of the deified Caesar, a man of great influence with him"*

Strabo 14.2.15, Loeb, http://penelope.uchicago.edu/Thayer/E/Roman/Texts /Strabo/14B*.html.

124 *Plutarch calls him a teacher of Greek philosophy* Plutarch, *Brutus* 65.1. See Christopher Pelling, *Plutarch Caesar*, translated with an introduction and commentary (Oxford: Oxford University Press, 2011) commentary ad loc., 476, and on 48.1, 377.

124 *Popilius Laenas hurried up to speak to him* Plutarch, *Brutus* 16.2–4; Appian, *Civil Wars* 2.116.

125 *Nicolaus paints a dark picture* Nicolaus of Damascus, *Life of Caesar Augustus* 24.86.

125 *"make your own manly excellence an auspicious omen."* Nicolaus of Damascus, *Life of Caesar Augustus* 24.87.

125 *The other sources leave out Decimus and emphasize Caesar's hubris instead* Appian, *Civil Wars* 2.116; Suetonius 81.4, Cassius Dio, *Roman History* 44.18.4.

125 *Appian says that Caesar reminded the soothsayers* Appian, *Civil Wars* 2.116.

125 *the* capsae, *containers holding scrolls* Based on Cassius Dio, *Roman History* 44.16.1, where he uses the word Κιβώτια, which I translate as *capsae*.

125 *around noon* see Christopher Pelling, *Plutarch Caesar*, translated with an Introduction and Commentary (Oxford: Oxford University Press, 2011), 477.

CHAPTER 8. MURDER

127 *he laughed* Suetonius, *Julius Caesar* 81. 4; Appian, *Civil Wars* 2.116.

127 *When it comes to the details of Pompey's Senate House* Carandini and Carafa, eds. *Atlante di Roma antica* offer a hypothetical reconstruction, vol. 2: table 220, section c–c[1].

128 *That, said the Roman scholar Pliny the Elder, was open to question* Pliny, *Natural History* 35.59. Carandini and Carafa, eds. *Atlante di Roma antica*, vol. 1:505, say the painting was originally inside the Senate House but was moved by Augustus.

128 *It was somewhat smaller than Caesar's Senate House* M. Bonnefond-Coudry, *Le Senat de la République Romaine* (Rome: École Française de

Rome, 1989), 183, estimates that the interior of Pompey's Senate House at about 4000 square feet (374 sq. m), about 72 feet (22 m) long by 56 feet (17 m) wide, measured on internal lines. On another, more recent set of estimates, Caesar's Senate House had an interior surface of 494 sq. m (5317 sq. ft.) and Pompey's only 303 sq. m (3247 sq. ft.), making it only 61 percent as big as Caesar's Senate House. On this estimate, the interior of Pompey's Senate House covered only about 3200 sq. ft., with internal lines of 58 feet (17.8 m) long by 56 feet (17 m) wide; the building stood only 57 feet (17.4 m) tall. Roman archaeologist James E. Packer, personal communication, based on plans to appear in his forthcoming book on the Theater of Pompey.

128 *roof rose to a height* http://dlib.etc.ucla.edu/projects/Forum/reconstructions/CuriaIulia_1, accessed August 1, 2014.

128 *low, raised platform* The tribunal in Caesar's Senate House, for example, stood about 16 inches (40 cm) high.

128 *the latest fashion for Roman generals* See the statues from Casinum (modern Cassino) and Foruli (modern Scoppito), both in Italy. See Eugenio La Rocca, Claudio Parisi Presicce, and Annalisia Lo Monaco, eds. *I giorni di Roma: l'età della conquista* (Milan: Skira, 2010), 291–92, ills. II.23 and II.24. The colossal statue in Rome's Palazzo Spada sometimes identified as Pompey is most likely one of the Roman emperors. See Wolfgang Helbig, *Führer durch die Öffentlichen Sammlungen klassischer Altertümer in Rom,* vol. 2: (Tübingen: Ernst Wasmuth, 1966) 768–69, no. 2008.

129 *Hence, a quorum was needed* Francis X. Ryan, *Rank and Participation in the Republican Senate* (Stuttgart, Germany: Franz Steiner, 1998), 14, 26.

129 *By the time they met under the Portico* Cassius Dio, *Roman History* 44.19.1–3; Cicero, *Philippics* 2.34. For different versions see Plutarch, *Antony* 13.2 (where he says "some" detained Antony) and *Caesar* 66.4 (where he wrongly names Decimus instead of Trebonius).

129 *As Caesar entered the room, the senators rose* Plutarch, *Caesar* 66.5, *Brutus* 17.1–2; Nicolaus of Damascus, *Life of Caesar Augustus* 24.88.

130 *The great orator planned to attack Antony* Cicero, *Philippics* 2.88.

130 *used daggers, not swords.* Suetonius refers only to *pugio* (dagger). The Greek sources refer both to *egkheiridia* (daggers) and *ksiphea* (a word that can mean either sword or dagger). Daggers: Nicolaus of Damascus, *Life*

of Caesar Augustus, 23.81, 24.88; Suetonius, *Julius Caesar* 82.2; Plutarch, *Caesar* 69.3; *Brutus* 14.4; Appian, *Civil Wars* 2.117. Swords: Nicolaus of Damascus, *Life of Caesar Augustus,* 24.89; Plutarch, *Caesar* 66. 10, 67.3; *Brutus* 17.4–7; Appian, *Civil Wars* 2.117; Cassius Dio, *Roman History* 44.16.1. Same weapon called both dagger and sword: Plutarch, *Caesar* 66.7.

131 *A martial artist who works with replicas of Roman weapons* Personal communication, Dwight McElmore.

131 *A coin issued by Brutus* Cassius Dio, *Roman History* 25.3; M. H. Crawford, *Roman Republican Coinage* (London and New York: Cambridge University Press, 2001) 1: 518, no. 508/3; cf. 100; 2:741.

132 *supposedly glanced at the statue of Pompey* Plutarch, *Caesar* 66.2.

132 *The five main ancient sources are in general agreement* I pick and choose details from the ancient sources. Although this technique is not without problems, it is justified in this case because the five accounts are so similar. The differences are minor, and I note them.

132 *advance planning* stated explicitly at Nicolaus of Damascus, *Life of Caesar Augustus* 26a.99.

132 *Centurions* Cicero, *On Divination* 2.23.

133 *clasping Caesar's hands and kissing his breast and his head* Plutarch, *Brutus* 17.3.

133 *assassination attempt in 47 B.C.* Pseudo-Caesar, *Alexandrian War* 48–55, esp. 52.2; Valerius Maximus, *Memorable Deeds and Sayings* 9.4.2.

133 *Cimber disrespected Caesar* Nicolaus of Damascus, *Life of Caesar Augustus* 24.88, cf. T. P. Wiseman, *Remembering the Roman People: Essays on Late Republican Politics and Literature* (Oxford: Oxford University Press, 2009), 211 and n.1.

133 *Caesar was angry* Nicolaus of Damascus, *Life of Caesar Augustus* 24.88.

133 *"Why, this is violence!"* Suetonius, *Julius Caesar* 82.1.

133 *pulling down Caesar's toga was the signal to start the attack* Cassius Dio, *Roman History* 44.19.4.

134 *Nicolaus, Plutarch, and Appian say that Casca had a sword* Nicolaus of Damascus, *Life of Caesar Augustus* 24.89; Appian, *Civil Wars* 2.117; Plutarch, *Brutus* 17.4. Plutarch, *Caesar* 66.7, calls it both a *ksiphos* and an *egkheiridion.*

134 *Nicolaus says that Casca was nervous* Nicolaus of Damascus, *Life of Caesar Augustus* 24.89.

134 *Dio says that there were too many attackers for Caesar* Cassius Dio, *Roman History* 44.19.5.

134 *Nicolaus simply says that Caesar stood up to defend himself* Nicolaus of Damascus, *Life of Caesar Augustus* 24.89.

134 *Plutarch says Caesar turned around and grabbed Casca's dagger* Plutarch, *Caesar* 66.7; handle: Plutarch, *Brutus* 17.5.

134 *Appian adds that he hurled Casca away with great violence* Appian, *Civil Wars* 2.117.

134 *Suetonius says that Caesar caught Casca's arm and stabbed him with his stylus* Suetonius, *Julius Caesar* 82.2.

134 *"anger and shouting"* Appian, *Civil Wars* 2.117.

134 *"Impious Casca!"—or, in another version, "Accursed Casca! What are you doing?"* Plutarch, *Caesar* 66.8; Cassius Dio, *Roman History* 44.19.5.

134 *Suetonius claims that Caesar merely groaned* Suetonius, *Julius Caesar* 82.2.

134 *Dio says that Caesar was unable to say anything* Cassius Dio, *Roman History* 44.19.5.

135 *Plutarch and Nicolaus say that Casca shouted in Greek* Plutarch, *Caesar* 66.8, *Brutus* 17.5; Nicolaus of Damascus, *Life of Caesar Augustus* 24.89.

135 *According to Nicolaus, Gaius Casca* Nicolaus of Damascus, *Life of Caesar Augustus* 24.89.

135 *in a circle* Plutarch, *Caesar* 66.10.

135 *Plutarch's description of Caesar being driven* Plutarch, *Caesar* 66.10.

135 *Two ancient sources use the language of a sacrifice* Plutarch, *Caesar* 66.11, cf. *Brutus* 10.1; Florus, *Epitome of Roman History* 2.13.92.

135 *Nicolaus mentions three besides Casca* Nicolaus of Damascus, *Life of Caesar Augustus* 24.89.

135 *Nicolaus also says that Cassius tried for a second blow* Nicolaus of Damascus, *Life of Caesar Augustus* 24.89.

135 *Appian agrees that Cassius struck Caesar in the face* Appian, *Civil Wars* 2.117.

135 *Plutarch says that Brutus struck Caesar in the groin* Plutarch, *Caesar* 66.11.

136 *"Et tu, Brute?" or "You too, Brutus?"* Shakespeare, *Julius Caesar* 3.1.77.

136 "kai su, teknon" *which means, "you too, child"* Suetonius, *Julius Caesar* 82.2; Cassius Dio, *Roman History* 44.19.5

136 *he might have been quoting Caesar* Pelling, *Plutarch Caesar* 482–83.

136 *of modesty* Valerius Maximus, *Memorable Deeds and Sayings* 4.5.6.

136 *Suetonius states, and Dio implies* Suetonius, *Julius Caesar* 82.2; Cassius Dio, *Roman History* 44.19.5.

136 *According to Plutarch, it was only when he saw Brutus approach him* Plutarch, *Caesar* 66.12, *Brutus* 17.6.

136 *Less probable, Appian has Caesar do so after Brutus strikes him* Appian, *Civil Wars* 2.117.

136 *Suetonius adds that Caesar also drew his toga over his legs* Suetonius, *Julius Caesar* 82.2; Cassius Dio, *Roman History* 44.19.5.

137 *Valerius Maximus, a Roman writer of the first century A.D.* Valerius Maximus, *Memorable Deeds and Sayings* 4.5.6.

137 *Brutus, for example, had a wound in his hand* Nicolaus of Damascus, *Life of Caesar Augustus* 24.89.

137 *No fewer than eight ancient sources say that* Livy, *Periochae* 116; Plutarch, *Caesar* 66.7; Suetonius, *Julius Caesar* 82.3; Appian, *Civil Wars* 2.117 and 147; Valerius Maximus, *Memorable Deeds and Sayings* 4.5.6; Florus, *Epitome of Roman History* 2.13.95; Eutropius, *Abridgement of Roman History* 6.25; Zonaras, *Epitome of Histories* 10.11.

137 *Nicolaus explicitly says otherwise* Nicolaus of Damascus, *Life of Caesar Augustus* 24.90.

137 *He also says, alone of the sources, that Caesar received thirty-fve wounds* Nicolaus of Damascus, *Life of Caesar Augustus* 24.90.

138 *there were more than eighty conspirators in total* Nicolaus of Damascus, *Life of Caesar Augustus* 19.59.

138 *but it sounds like a poetic touch, echoing the mistreatment of Hector's corpse* Homer, *Iliad* 22.371, Toher, commentary ad loc.

138 *great joy from seeing with his own eyes the just death of a tyrant* Cicero, *Letters to Atticus* 14.14.4.

139 *why Censorinus took on the undesirable role of a seller of public property* J. T. Ramsey, "Did Julius Caesar Temporarily Banish Mark Antony from His Inner Circle?," *Classical Quarterly* 54. 1 (2004): 168–69.

139 *too shocked and horrified* Plutarch, *Caesar* 66.9.

139 *Nicolaus tells us only that the conspirators bore down on them* Nicolaus of Damascus, *Life of Caesar Augustus* 26.96.

140 *Antistius* Suetonius, *Julius Caesar* 82.2.

140 *Assuming that this was Gaius Casca's wound* Wolfgang Klemm, *Caesar, Biografie*, vol. 2 (Vienna and Munich: Neckenmarkt, 2009), 185, 209.

140 *"Thus he who had filled the whole world with the blood"* Florus, *Epitome of Roman History* 2.13.95.

141 *Caesar fell at the foot of the statue* Professor Antonio Monterroso, University of Córdoba and Spanish National Research Council (CSIC), an archaeologist who resurveyed the ruins of Pompey's Senate House, announced in 2012 that he had found evidence of a monument to mark the precise spot where Caesar fell, at the eastern end of the building where the tribunal would have stood. But other scholars responded with skepticism and the debate continues. See "Spanish researchers find the exact spot where Julius Caesar was stabbed," *ScienceDaily* www.sciencedaily .com/releases/2012/10/121010102158.htm (accessed February 2, 2014).

141 *blood flowed from his woolen garments to the statue base* Plutarch, *Caesar* 66.13.

141 *"in that Senate, the greater part of which he had chosen"* Cicero, *On Divination* 2.23. Cicero exaggerates. On a more sober estimate Caesar had handpicked more than a third of the members of the Roman Senate. Martin Jehne, *Der Staat des Dictators Caesar* (Cologne, Germany: Böhlau, 1987), 393, 404; Ronald Syme, *Roman Papers*, vol. 1, ed. E. Badian (Oxford: Clarendon Press, New York: Oxford University Press, 1979), 98–99.

CHAPTER 9. A REPUBLIC IN THE BALANCE

143 *They folded their togas around their left arms like shields* Appian, *Civil Wars* 2.119; Plutarch, *Tiberius Gracchus* 19.4.

143 *Cretan archers* Plutarch, *Gaius Gracchus* 16.3.

143 *vengeance of Caesar's soldiers* Appian, *Civil Wars* 2.119; Florus, *Epitome of Roman History* 2.17.2.

144 *"with manly spirit but childish judgment"* Cicero, *Letters to Atticus* 14.21.3.

145 *The story that he exchanged his consul's toga for slave's clothes* Plutarch, *Antony* 14.1.

145 *Still, some Romans hid themselves in their homes* Nicolaus of Damascus, *Life of Caesar Augustus* 26.95; Plutarch, *Caesar* 67.1–2, *Brutus* 18.3, *Antony* 19.1. Appian, *Civil Wars* 2.118; Cassius Dio, *Roman History* 44.22.2; Cicero, *Philippics* 2.88.

145 *Some say that earlier he tried to address the senators* Plutarch, *Caesar* 67.1, *Brutus* 18.1; Appian, *Civil Wars* 2.119.

145 *Appian says the conspirators expected the other senators* Appian, *Civil Wars* 2.115.

146 *This was not murder, said Brutus* Nicolaus of Damascus, *Life of Caesar Augustus* 25.92.

146 *They had planned this move in advance* Nicolaus of Damascus, *Life of Caesar Augustus* 25.94.

146 *Cassius, Brutus, and Decimus led them, along with Decimus's gladiators* Velleius Paterculus, *Roman History* 2.58.1–2.

146 *daggers drawn—"naked," as the ancient expression says* Nicolaus of Damascus, *Life of Caesar Augustus* 25.94, cf. 25.91; Plutarch, *Brutus* 18.3.

146 *Nicolaus says they ran in flight; Plutarch says* Nicolaus of Damascus, *Life of Caesar Augustus* 25.94; Plutarch, *Caesar* 67.3, cf. *Brutus* 18.7.

146 *They agree that the men cried out* Nicolaus of Damascus, *Life of Caesar Augustus* 25.94; Plutarch, *Caesar* 67.3, cf. *Brutus* 18.7.

146 *Appian claims that one assassin carried a freedman's felt cap* Appian, *Civil Wars* 2.119.

146 *Cicero claims that some of them called out his name* Cicero, *Philippics* 2.28 and 30; Cassius Dio, *Roman History* 44.20.4.

146 *Between them, Appian and Plutarch name some half-dozen men* Plutarch, *Caesar* 67.4; Appian, *Civil Wars* 2.119.

146 *Lentulus Spinther* Cicero, *Letters to Friends* 12.14.

146 *Gaius Octavius* T. P. Wiseman, "Some Republican Senators and their Tribes," *Classical Quarterly* 14 (1964): 124.

147 *Marcus Aquinus* On Marcus Aquinus, Patiscus, L. Staius Murcus, and Dolabella, see Pelling commentary on *Plutarch Caesar* 67.4, 487–88.

147 *Still the sources report looting and frightened people* Appian, *Civil Wars* 2.118; Cassius Dio, *Roman History* 44.20.2–3.

147 *it was not much bigger than today's St. Peter's Square* The square is about 20 acres or 8 hectares. The highest point of the Capitoline Hill stands about 160 feet (49 m) above sea level.

147 *the conspirators divided the terrain into sectors* Nicolaus of Damascus, *Life of Caesar Augustus* 25.94.

147 *"occupied the Capitol"* Velleius Paterculus, *History of Rome* 2.58.2, cf. Livy, *Periochae* 116.

148 *Some thought the killing of Caesar was the fairest of deeds* Tacitus, *Annals* 1.8; Nicolaus of Damascus, *Life of Caesar Augustus* 26a.99.

148 *"justly slain"*—iure caesus Suetonius, *Julius Caesar* 76.1; Cicero, *Philippics* 13.2.

148 *"the wickedest man ever killed"* Cicero, *Letters to Atticus* 12.2, trans D. R. Shackleton Bailey, *Cicero: Epistulae ad Familiares: vol. 2, 47–43 BC* (Cambridge and New York: Cambridge University Press, 1977), 481.

148 *To Cicero, the conspirators were liberators* Cicero, *Letters to Friends* 11.27.8.

148 *To Caesar's dear friend Gaius Matius, Caesar was a very great man* Cicero, *Letters to Atticus* 11.28.

148 *As Caesar's friends saw things* Velleius Paterculus, *History of Rome* 2.57.1; cf. Cicero, *Letters to Atticus* 14.22.2.

148 *"jealousy of his fortune and power"* Appian, *Civil Wars* 2.111.1; Cassius Dio, *Roman History* 44.1.1; Florus, *Epitome of Roman History* 2.13.92.

149 *"Congratulations!"* Cicero, *Letters to Friends* 6.15.

149 *To Decimus he called it the greatest deed in history* Cicero, *Letters to Friends* 11.5.1.

149 *"Has anything greater ever been done, by holy Jupiter"* Cicero, *Philippics* 2.32.

149 *When Brutus addressed his visitors* Plutarch, *Brutus* 18.9–11.

150 *Nicolaus of Damascus says that gladiators and slaves protected them* Nicolaus of Damascus, *Life of Caesar Augustus* 26a.99.

150 *Nicolaus scoffed at Brutus's "supposed reasonableness"* Nicolaus of Damascus, *Life of Caesar Augustus* 26a.99.

150 *Plutarch, who saw Brutus as a hero* Plutarch, *Brutus* 18.11.

150 *Just a month earlier, Caesar had sat on the same platform* Nicolaus of Damascus, *Life of Caesar Augustus* 26a.99; Plutarch, *Brutus* 18.11, *Caesar* 61.4.

150 *his hand was still injured* Appian, *Civil Wars* 2.122.

150 *As he came forward* Plutarch, *Brutus* 18.12; Nicolaus of Damascus, *Life of Caesar Augustus* 26a.100; Appian, *Civil Wars* 2.122.

150 *he had what the Romans called* gravitas Tacitus, *Dialogue on Oratory* 25.5.

150 *tedious and lax* Tacitus, *Dialogue on Oratory* 18.5.

150 *dull and cold* Tacitus, *Dialogue on Oratory* 21.5, referring to Brutus's speech for King Deiotarus.

150 *accuses them of boastfulness and self-congratulation* Appian, *Civil Wars* 2.122, cf. Cassius Dio, *Roman History* 44.21.

151 *Nicolaus is probably referring to Cassius* Nicolaus of Damascus, *Life of Caesar Augustus* 26a.99.

151 *"burning with enthusiasm" for Brutus and Cassius* Cicero, *Letters to Atticus* 15.11.2.

151 *Nicolaus says that many people came to join the men on the Capitoline* Nicolaus of Damascus, *Life of Caesar Augustus* 17.49.

151 *Appian maintains just the opposite—the people hated the assassins* Appian, *Civil Wars* 2.122.

151 *Plutarch says that the crowd was silent* Plutarch, *Caesar* 67.7, *Brutus* 13.

151 *Nicolaus says that the people were confused and anxious* Nicolaus of Damascus, *Life of Caesar Augustus* 27.100.

151 *that his goal was liberty and peace* Cicero, *Letters to Friends* 11.2.2.

152 *Plutarch says this showed how much the people objected* Plutarch, *Brutus* 18.12–13, cf. Appian, *Civil Wars* 2.121, 126.

152 *a kinship relationship by marriage* For an example, see Eutropius, *Abridgement of Roman History* 10.5—Constantine's attack on his sister's husband Licinius as an example of misuse of this kinship relationship.

152 *Some sources say that Dolabella* As reported by Appian, *Civil Wars* 2.122.

152 *Public opinion was still up for grabs.* Robert Morstein-Marx, *Mass Ora-*

tory and Political Power in the Late Roman Republic (Cambridge and New York: Cambridge University Press, 2004), 150–58, esp. 157, is groundbreaking on this subject.

152 *Cicero, who reports the news* Cicero, *Philippics* 2.89.

152 *"first day on the Capitoline"* Cicero, Letters to Atticus 14.10.1.

153 *"By the immortal gods"* Cicero, *Letters to Atticus* 14.10.1.

153 *"the two Brutuses* [that is, Brutus and Decimus] *and Cassius"* Cornelius Nepos, *Life of Atticus* 8.1. See also Tacitus, *Annals* 1.10. On Nepos and his politics, see Cynthia Damon, *Nepos, Life of Atticus* (Bryn Mawr, PA: Thomas Library, Bryn Mawr College, 1993), 1–2.

153 *"the whole state moved towards them"* Cornelius Nepos, *Life of Atticus* 8.1.

153 *If Appian is right, most of the senators sympathized* Appian, *Civil Wars* 2.127.

153 *"Enough service to a tyrant"* Nicolaus of Damascus, *Life of Caesar Augustus* 26.95.

153 *These three ordinary slaves carried Caesar's litter home* Suetonius, *Julius Caesar* 82.3, 47.

153 *Since it took four slaves to carry a litter* Suetonius, *Julius Caesar* 82.3; Appian, *Civil Wars* 2.118.

154 *The curtains of the litter were raised and people could see* Suetonius, *Julius Caesar* 82.3; Appian, *Civil Wars* 2.118.

154 *According to Nicolaus, they cried at the sight* Nicolaus of Damascus, *Life of Caesar Augustus* 26.97.

154 *Remembering her warning that morning, she called Caesar's name* Nicolaus of Damascus, *Life of Caesar Augustus* 26.97.

154 *Suetonius says that the conspirators planned to drag Caesar's body* Suetonius, *Julius Caesar* 82.4.

154 *Sometime before the day ended, a storm hit Rome* Cassius Dio, *Roman History* 44.52.1. Pseudo-Aurelius Victor, *De viris illustribus* 78.10, says that on the day of Caesar's funeral the sun hid its orb.

154 *As the sun set* Actually, apparent sunset (slightly later than actual sunset). See http://www.esrl.noaa.gov/gmd/grad/solcalc/; Nicolaus of Damascus, *Life of Caesar Augustus* 27.101–2.

155 *a paradox* Elizabeth Rawson, "The Aftermath of the Ides," in J. A. Crook,

Andrew Lintott, and Elizabeth Rawson, eds., *The Cambridge Ancient History*, 2nd ed., vol. 9, *The Last Age of the Roman Republic* (Cambridge: Cambridge University Press, 1994), 468.

155 *The men who seized and defended the Capitoline Hill* Nicolaus of Damascus, *Life of Caesar Augustus* 25.94; Florus, *Epitome of Roman History* 2.17.2.

155 *Lepidus moved his soldiers* Nicolaus of Damascus, *Life of Caesar Augustus* 27.106; Zonaras, *Epitome of Histories* 10.12 (492C).

155 *Lepidus called a Public Meeting and delivered a speech* Cassius Dio, *Roman History* 44.22.2.

155 *Lepidus was ready* Nicolaus of Damascus, *Life of Caesar Augustus* 27.103, 106.

155 *a gathering of Caesar's close supporters in Mark Antony's house* Nicolaus of Damascus, *Life of Caesar Augustus* 26.106.

156 Carinae, *or the Keels* Located northeast of the Forum on the saddle of land between the Oppian and Velian Hills, the Carinae lay roughly between the modern Colosseo metro station and the church of San Pietro in Vincoli.

156 *because certain buildings* Or possibly because the lay of the land looked like a row of upturned boats. See Lawrence Richardson, *A New Topographical Dictionary of Ancient Rome* (Baltimore: Johns Hopkins University Press, 1992), 71.

156 *The meeting lasted until evening* Appian, *Civil Wars* 2.124. On the details of the meeting see also Nicolaus of Damascus, *Life of Caesar Augustus* 27.106.

156 *Matius feared an uprising in Belgian Gaul* Cicero, *Letters to Atticus* 14.1.1, 14.9.3.

156 *Sextus Pompey* Cicero, *Letters to Atticus* 16.4.2.

156 *Antony had no troops of his own* Cassius Dio, *Roman History* 44.34.5–6.

157 *The conferees at Antony's house decided to negotiate* Appian, *Civil Wars* 2.124.

157 *What followed was a long night in Rome* Appian, *Civil Wars* 2.125, 134.

157 *Antony got control both of Caesar's private fortune and his state papers* Appian, *Civil Wars* 2.125.

157 *According to Plutarch, Caesar's fortune amounted to 4,000 talents* Plutarch,

Antony 15; probably equivalent to 25 million denarii or 100 million sesterces. See Plutarch, *Cicero* 43.8; Appian, *Civil Wars* 3.17; Christopher Pelling, *Life of Antony/Plutarch* (Cambridge and New York: Cambridge University Press, 1988), commentary ad loc., 155.

158 *Cinna appeared for the meeting* Appian, *Civil Wars* 2.126; Cicero, *Letters to Atticus* 14.14.2, *Philippics* 2.89.

158 *By now, March 17, more of Caesar's veterans were starting to arrive* Nicolaus of Damascus, *Life of Caesar Augustus* 17.49, 27.103.

158 *Nicolaus claims that most of the conspirators' supporters melted away* Nicolaus of Damascus, *Life of Caesar Augustus* 17.49.

158 *leader of the Early Republic* Spurius Cassius Vicellinus, executed 485 B.C.

159 *map of Italy* Or possibly an allegorical representation. Varro, *On Agriculture* 1.2.1; Lawrence Richardson, *A New Topographical Dictionary of Ancient Rome* (Baltimore: Johns Hopkins University Press, 1992), 379.

159 *The details of the debate come largely from Appian and Cassius Dio* For the points in the following paragraphs see Appian, *Civil Wars* 2.126–35; Cassius Dio, *Roman History* 44.22–34.

159 *Transalpine Gaul* Unlike the previous situation, the province now comprised central and northern France as well as Belgium but not Provence or Marseille, which were now separate.

159 *would later father a son who became Emperor Tiberius* Suetonius, *Tiberius* 4.1.

160 *"Peace!" called some and "vengeance!" cried others* Appian, *Civil Wars* 2.131.

160 *Cicero gave a long speech* Cicero, *Philippics* 1.1; Cassius Dio, *Roman History* 44.22–34; Plutarch, *Cicero* 42.3; Livy, *Periochae* 116.4.

160 *Cicero called Caesar a king in private* Cicero, *Letters to Atticus* 13.37.2.

161 *"since it is advantageous to the state"* Appian, *Civil Wars* 2.135.

161 *Antony moved to abolish the dictatorship* Cicero, *Philippics* 1.3, 2.91.

161 *considered this merely a tactical retreat* Cicero, *Philippics* 2.90–92.

161 *Cicero later said in private* Cicero, *Letters to Atticus* 14.10.1, 14.14.2; *Philippics* 1.1.

162 *Temple of Jupiter* Appian, *Civil Wars* 2.141.

162 *Appian reports what Brutus is supposed to have said* Appian, *Civil Wars* 2.137–42.

162 *Cicero wanted thunderbolts* Cicero, *Letters to Atticus* 15.1a.2.

162 *He understood their anxiety* Cassius Dio, *Roman History* 44.34.5.

164 *In addition to Antony and Dolabella, Cicero spoke* Appian, *Civil Wars* 2.142.

164 *Dio says that the conspirators sent a letter down the hill* Cassius Dio, *Roman History* 44.34.3.

164 *and even, says Dio, swore the strongest oaths* Cassius Dio, *Roman History* 44.34.3.

164 *hostages* Appian, *Civil Wars* 2.142; Joel Allen, *Hostages and Hostage-Taking in the Roman Empire* (Cambridge: Cambridge University Press, 2006), 47–48.

164 *Perhaps, as Appian says, Antony and Dolabella fretted* Appian, *Civil Wars* 2.142.

164 *To some, it looked like the majority of Romans were glad* Cassius Dio, *Roman History* 44.35.1; Livy, *Periochae* 116.4.

165 *He asked Cassius if he had a dagger under his armpit* Cassius Dio, *Roman History* 44.34.7.

CHAPTER 10. A FUNERAL TO REMEMBER

167 *The Senate was meeting again* Plutarch, *Brutus* 20.1; Appian, *Civil Wars* 2.135–36; Suetonius, *Julius Caesar* 83.1.

167 *So, in private, did Cicero's friend Atticus* Cicero, *Letters to Atticus* 14.10.1, 14.14.3.

168 *as Appian has Antony say, Caesar's soldiers would never tolerate it* Appian, *Civil Wars* 2.134.

168 *Caesar's will* Suetonius, *Julius Caesar* 83.2; Nicolaus of Damascus, *Life of Caesar Augustus* 17.48; Appian, *Civil Wars* 2.143; Cassius Dio, *Roman History* 44.35.2.

170 *"in vast numbers"* Nicolaus of Damascus, *Life of Caesar Augustus* 17.49.

171 *Antony was now the natural leader of a large force* Nicolaus of Damascus, *Life of Caesar Augustus* 17.50.

171 *Gallic chieftain's* Caesar, *Gallic War* 6.19.4.

171 *Caesar had left instructions for his funeral with his niece, Atia* Nicolaus of Damascus, *Life of Caesar Augustus* 17.48.

171 *public funeral for Sulla the Dictator* Appian, *Civil Wars* 1.105–6; Plutarch, *Sulla* 36–38. On Sulla's funeral, see Arthur Keaveney, *Sulla: the Last Republican*, 2nd ed. (London and New York: Routledge, 2005), 174–76; on Sulla as a "Perfumed Corpse," see Adrienne Mayor, *The Poison King: The Life and Legend of Mithradates, Rome's Deadliest Enemy* (Princeton, NJ: Princeton University Press, 2010), 256.

172 *funeral for his aunt Julia* Suetonius, *Julius Caesar* 6.

172 *Clodius's funeral in 52 B.C.* Cicero, *For Milo* 33, 90; Asconius, *Commentary on Cicero's "For Milo"* 33, 42C; Cassius Dio, *Roman History* 40.49.3; Geoffrey S. Sumi, "Power and Ritual: The Crowd at Clodius' Funeral," *Historia: Zeitschrift für Alte Geschichte* 46.1 (1997): 80–102; W. Jeffrey Tatum, *The Patrician Tribune: Publius Clodius Pulcher* (Chapel Hill: University of North Carolina Press, 1999), 241.

173 *Modern experiments with beeswax funeral masks* http://www.archaeology .org/news/1694–140106-roman-wax-masks-funeral, http://news.yahoo .com/uncannily-lifelike-roman-masks-recreated-wax-180427165.html.

173 *ran to escort it as a kind of bodyguard* Appian, *Civil Wars* 2.143.

174 *If Appian is right, the armed men began to regret* Appian, *Civil Wars* 2.143.

174 *Cicero, Appian, Plutarch, and Dio* Cicero, *Philippics* 2.91; Appian, *Civil Wars* 2.143–46; Plutarch, *Antony* 13.3; Cassius Dio, *Roman History* 44.35.4–50.

174 *Suetonius says that Antony did not give a proper funeral oration at all* Suetonius, *Julius Caesar* 84.2.

174 *Appian gives a generally plausible, if overly dramatic, account* Appian, *Civil Wars* 2.143–46.

175 *The audience chanted to the sound of a flute* Appian, *Civil Wars* 2.146; H. I. Flower, *Ancestor Masks and Aristocratic Power in Roman Culture* (Oxford: Oxford University Press, 2000), 125–26.

175 *"Did I save them just so that they could destroy me?"* Suetonius, *Julius Caesar* 84.2.

175 *"honorable men"* Shakespeare, *Julius Caesar* 3.28.83, 124, 151, 153.

176 *Dio says that Lepidus's soldiers prevented them* Cassius Dio, *Roman History* 44.50.2–3; Appian, *Civil Wars* 2.148, says it was the priests of Jupiter who stopped them.

176 *two "beings" bearing swords* Suetonius, *Julius Caesar* 84.3.

176 *Cicero says that rioters consisted of slaves and poor people* Cicero, *Letters to Atticus* 14.10.2.

176 *"ruffians, mostly slaves"* Cicero, *Philippics* 2.91.5.

176 *The crowd surged to the homes of Brutus and Cassius* Plutarch, *Caesar* 68.2–3, *Brutus* 20.5–6; Suetonius, *Julius Caesar* 85; Cassius Dio, *Roman History* 44.50.4; Appian, *Civil Wars* 2.147; Valerius Maximus, *Memorable Deeds and Sayings* 9.9.1.

177 *Publius Servilius Casca—was strongly guarded* Cassius Dio, *Roman History* 44.52.3.

177 *Cicero claims that the same torches* Cicero, *Philippics* 2.91.4.

177 *"The pretty funeral oration was yours"* Cicero, *Philippics* 2.91.2.

177 cui bono? Cicero, *For Sextus Roscius Amerinus* 84; *For Milo* 32.

178 *"especially the Jews"* Suetonius, *Julius Caesar* 84.5, following the translation into Italian and commentary by Carlotta Scantamburlo, *Suetonio, Vita di Cesare, Introduzione, traduzione e commento* (Pisa: Edizioni Plus, Pisa University Press, 2011).

179 *Afterward, the consuls ruled* Cassius Dio, *Roman History* 44.51.1.

179 *he called Decimus a poisoner* Cicero, *Philippics* 13.11.25.

179 *"Et tu, Decime?"* Appian, *Civil Wars* 2.143, 146.

179 *letter survives from Decimus to Brutus and Cassius* Cicero, *Letters to Friends* 11.1.

179 *"moderate boost in dignitas"?* Cicero, *Letters to Friends* 11.1.1.

179 *"we must give in to fortune"* Cicero, *Letters to Friends* 11.1.3.

180 *He now told Hirtius that he wanted to stay in Rome* Cicero, *Letters to Friends* 11.1.6.

180 *In several letters written over the next year* Cicero, *Letters to Friends* 11.10.1, 11.11.2, 11.14.2 (where Cicero cites a reference in one of Decimus's letters to his detractors); cf. 11.4.1.

180 *"a most wicked conspiracy"* Cicero, *Letters to Friends* 11.13a.2.

180 *Revolution, as Mao said, is not a dinner party* Mao Zedong, "Report on an Investigation of the Peasant Movement in Hunan" (March 1927), in *Selected Readings from the Works of Mao Tse-tung* (Peking: Foreign Languages Press, 1967), 22.

180 *Emerson said that when you strike at a king, you must kill him* See Liva

Baker, *The Justice from Beacon Hill: The Life and Times of Oliver Wendell Holmes* (New York: HarperCollins, 1991), 90–91.

CHAPTER 11. THE STRUGGLE FOR ITALY

185 *By the time the messenger got to Apollonia* On Octavian's movements from Apollonia to Brundisium, see Nicolaus of Damascus, *Life of Caesar Augustus* 16.38–18.57.

185 *With the future uncertain, Atia recommended* Nicolaus of Damascus, *Life of Caesar Augustus* 16.38–39.

186 *There were six legions* Appian, *Civil Wars* 3.24.

186 *Meanwhile, some officers went to Octavian* Nicolaus of Damascus, *Life of Caesar Augustus* 16.41, 17.46; Velleius Paterculus, *History of Rome* 2.59.5.

186 *About the soldiers, though, he had no doubts* Nicolaus of Damascus, *Life of Caesar Augustus* 16.42.

186 *Octavian cried* Nicolaus of Damscus, *Life of Caesar Augustus* 18.51.

189 *Cicero always believed the assassins made a mistake* Cicero, *Letters to Atticus* 15.11.2; *Philippics* 2.34.

189 *Antony had his daughter engaged to Lepidus's son* It seems unlikely that the marriage ever took place. See Richard D. Weigel, *Lepidus: The Tarnished Triumvir* (London: Routledge, 1992), 47–48.

190 *men wanted to consecrate the spot* On the column and altar, I follow the arguments of Geoffrey S. Sumi, "Topography and Ideology: Caesar's Monument and the Aedes Divi Iulii in Augustan Rome," *Classical Quarterly* 61.1 (2011): 205–19. The main ancient sources are: Cassius Dio, *Roman History* 44.55.1; Suetonius, *Julius Caesar* 84.5, 85; Cicero, *Philippics* 1.5.

191 *Cicero had mixed feelings* Cicero, *Letters to Atticus* 16.8.1, 16.14.1, 16.15.3.

191 *Octavian later claimed that the urban plebs* Nicolaus of Damascus, *Life of Augustus* 28.108, cf. Appian, *Civil Wars* 3.28; Cassius Dio, *Roman History* 45.6.5.

193 *where Brutus and Cassius withdrew after leaving the capital* Plutarch, *Brutus* 21.1.

193 *"a delightful place, right by the sea"* Cicero, *Letters to Atticus* 12.19.

194 *Rather than take a chance, Atticus had declined* Nepos, *Atticus* 8.1–3.

194 *said they had dismissed their friends from the cities of Italy* Cicero, *Letters to Atticus* 11.2.1, end of May.

194 *a scene later described by Cicero in a letter to Atticus* Cicero, *Letters to Atticus* 15.11; see also 15.12.

195 *They heaped the most blame on Decimus* Cicero, *Letters to Atticus* 15.16.

195 *"I've really never heard anyone say that!"* Cicero, *Letters to Atticus* 15.11.2.

195 *Cicero calls Brutus depressed* For example, Cicero, *Letters to Atticus* 15.10–12.

195 *Brutus and Cicero met a very important envoy* Cicero, *Letters to Atticus* 16.4.1–2.

196 *On August 4, Brutus and Cassius wrote a letter* Cicero, *Letters to Friends* 11.3.1.

196 *They cattily added that they were amazed* Cicero, *Letters to Friends* 11.3.2.

196 *"Bear in mind not only how long Caesar lived"* Cicero, *Letters to Friends* 11.3.4.

196 *he and Cassius issued edicts* Velleius Paterculus, *History of Rome* 2.62.3.

196 *He and Porcia had a tearful farewell* Plutarch, *Brutus* 23.

197 *Decimus had two legions* Appian, *Civil Wars* 3.49; Cicero, *Letters to Friends* 10.24.3, which describes the second legion as having two years' experience in 43 B.C.

197 *He claimed to have fought* Cicero, *Letters to Friends* 11.4.

197 *Decimus wrote to Cicero* Cicero, *Letters to Friends* 11.4, 6.

197 *Cicero promised to take care of Decimus's dignitas* Cicero, *Letters to Friends* 11.6.

197 *He refers in other letters as well to Decimus's dignitas* Cicero, *Letters to Friends* 11.6a.1–2, 11.8.1.

198 *how much the Roman people love him* Cicero, *Letters to Friends* 11.8.1.

198 *the greatest and most famous man of all* Cicero, *Letters to Friends* 11.4.3.

198 *Myrtilus* Cicero, *Letters to Atticus* 15.13.2, 16.11.5.

198 *He hailed Decimus as a defender of the Republic* Cicero, *Philippics* 4.8–9.

199 *"At the age of nineteen"* Res gestae divi Augusti (The Exploits of the Deified Augustus) 1.1.

199 *He promptly paid each man 500 denarii and promised* Appian, *Civil Wars* 3.48.

199 *Both Antony and Octavian knew it* Cassius Dio, *Roman History,* 45.14–15.

200 *he feared Octavian* Cicero, *Letters to Brutus* 1.4a.2–3.

200 *Cicero's requests to come to Decimus's aid* Cicero, *Letters to Brutus* 1.10.1,5; 1.12.2; 1.14.2.

200 *he didn't want "to offend" Caesar's veterans* Cicero, *Philippics* 13.13.

200 *"a large number of gladiators"* Appian, *Civil Wars* 3.49; Jürgen Malitz, *Nikolaos von Damaskus, Leben des Kaisers Augustus,* edited, translated, with a commentary (Darmstadt, Germany: Wissenschaftliche Buchgesellschaft, 2003) 172, n. 327.

201 *Valeria Paula* Cicero, *Letters to Friends* 11.8.

201 *He knew that the Senate was using him* Appian, *Civil Wars* 3.64.

201 *Trebonius had told Cicero that he was proud* Cicero, *Letters to Friends* 12.16.4.

201 *He and his allies carried out several grand gestures* Cassius Dio, *Roman History* 46.36.1–5, 37.3–5; cf. Cicero, *Philippics* 8.7.20; Frontinus, *Strategems* 3. 13.7–8; Pliny, *Natural History* 10.110.

202 *managed to float salt and sheep* Frontinus, *Strategems* 3.14.3–4.

202 *Conditions in Mutina were, in general, dreadful* Cicero, *Letters to Brutus* 2.1; *Letters to Friends* 12.6.2.

202 *the battle of Forum Gallorum* The sources for the battle are Cicero, *Letters to Friends* 10.30; Appian, *Civil Wars* 3.66–70; Cassius Dio, *Roman History* 46.37.1–7.

202 *If Appian is right about the battle, the veterans* Appian, *Civil Wars* 3.68.

202 *Galba sent Cicero a memorable account* Cicero, *Letters to Friends* 10.30.

202 *chronicle Galba's military missteps in Gaul* Caesar, *Gallic War* 3.1–6.

202 *a second battle took place outside Mutina* The sources for the battle are Appian, *Civil Wars* 3.71–72; Cassius Dio, *Roman History* 46.38; Suetonius, *Augustus* 10.4; Plutarch, *Antony* 17.1.

203 *Antony claimed that Octavian* Suetonius, *Augustus* 10.4.

203 Octavian Caesar was a hero at Mutina: Suetonius, *Augutus* 10.4.

203 *a statue be erected in Pontius's honor* Cicero, *Letters to Brutus* 1.15.8.

204 *according to Appian, Decimus tried to smooth the way* Appian, *Civil Wars* 3.73.

204 *In a letter to Cicero on May 9, 43 B.C.* Cicero, *Letters to Friends* 11.13.1.

204 *Decimus told Octavian* Cicero, *Letters to Friends* 11.10.4.

204 *it served Octavian's purpose to wound Antony* Cassius Dio, *Roman History*, 45.14–15.

205 *"If Caesar [Octavian] had listened to me"* Cicero, *Letters to Friends* 11.10.4.

205 *"the young man should be complimented"* "laudandum adulescentem, ornandum, tollendum," Cicero, *Letters to Friends* 11.20.1.

206 *to feed his troops he spent not only his own fortune* Cicero, *Letters to Friends* 11.10.5. See Crawford, *Roman Republican Coinage*, vol. 2: 697.

206 *He criticized Decimus for failing* Cicero, *Letters to Brutus* 1.10.2.

206 *Lepidus was unreliable* Cicero, *Letters to Friends* 11.9.1.

207 *Decimus was in contact with the Allobroges* Cicero, *Letters to Friends* 11.11.2.

207 *Cicero asked Brutus and Cassius to send help* Cicero, *Letters to Brutus* 1.14.2; Cassius, *Letters to Friends* 12.9.2.

CHAPTER 12. VENGEANCE

209 *"villainy and madness"* Cicero, *Letters to Atticus* 15.13.4.

210 *"I only wish you could see how much I fear him!"* Cicero, *Letters to Brutus* 1.4a.3.

211 *Porcia died after an illness* The version in Plutarch, *Brutus* 53.5–7 is preferable to the lurid suicide account in Valerius Maximus, *Memorable Deeds and Sayings* 4.6.5 and Appian, *Civil Wars* 4.136.

211 *"Not only your army but all citizens"* Cicero, *Letters to Brutus* 1.9.2.

212 *Servilia asked if they should send for Brutus now* Cicero, *Letters to Brutus* 1.18.1–2.

212 *Now that Lepidus had defected to Antony, Brutus worried* Cicero, *Letters to Brutus* 1.13.1.

213 *"This will make him consul, if you won't"* Suetonius, *Augustus* 26.1, cf. Cassius Dio, *Roman History* 46.43.4.

213 *the judge who had voted to acquit Brutus* He was Silicius Corona: Cassius Dio, *Roman History* 46.49.5; Appian, *Civil Wars* 3.95.

214 *She found asylum with Atticus* Cicero, *Letters to Atticus* 15.11.2; Nepos, *Atticus* 11.

214 *One source claims that Antony's wife, Fulvia* Cassius Dio, *Roman History* 47.8.4.

215 *Censorinus* Velleius Paterculus, *History of Rome* 2.14.3.

216 *They disagree as to how Decimus died* Appian, *Civil Wars* 3.98; Livy, *Periochae* 120; Velleius Paterculus, *History of Rome* 2.64.1; Valerius Maximus, *Memorable Deeds and Sayings* 4.7.6, 9.13.3; Cassius Dio, *Roman History* 46.53.3, cf. Seneca, *Letters to Lucilius* 82.12.

217 *"the sinews of war"* Cicero, *Philippics* 5.5; Appian claims that Cassius echoed this comment, Appian, *Civil Wars* 4.99.

217 *They committed themselves to fighting for the freedom* Cassius Dio, *Roman History* 47.32.2.

217 *the latter his kinsman, said Brutus* Plutarch, *Brutus* 28.1.

217 *he said that he felt more shame* Plutarch, *Brutus* 28.2.

218 *For his part, Brutus assaulted the cities of Lycia* The account of Appian, *Civil Wars* 4.76–82 is more persuasive than the pro-Brutus public relations version in Plutarch, *Brutus* 30–32.

218 *a massive number of legionaries* Appian, *Civil Wars* 4.88, 108; see the discussion by Adrian Goldsworthy, *Antony and Cleopatra* (New Haven, CT: Yale University Press, 2010), 252.

219 *According to Appian, Cassius addressed* Appian, *Civil Wars* 4.98.

219 *Every legionary got 1,500* Appian, *Civil Wars* 4.100.

219 *They didn't match the amount that Antony and Octavian* Cassius Dio, *Roman History* 47.42.5.

219 *they didn't have it yet* Appian, *Civil Wars* 4.99.

219 *according to Appian, Cassius emphasized* Appian, *Civil Wars* 4.99.

219 *The gorgeous array of money* See M. H. Crawford, *Roman Republican Coinage* (London and New York: Cambridge University Press, 2001), vol. 1: 513–18, nos. 498–508; cf. 100; vol. 2: 741.

219 *One coin, issued by Brutus and Casca* Crawford, *Roman Republican Coinage,* vol. 1: 518, no. 507/2; cf. 100; vol. 2: 741.

220 *One coin, however, stands out from the rest* Crawford, *Roman Republican Coinage,* vol. 1: 518, no. 508/3; cf.100; vol. 2: 741.

220 *"In addition to these activities"* Cassius Dio, *Roman History* 47.25.3, Loeb translation.

221 *Caesar's friends claimed* Cicero, *Philippics* 13.23; 2.31; on sicarii see also Suetonius, *Julius Caesar* 72.

221 *"you will see me at Philippi"* Plutarch, *Brutus* 36 and, on the vision's second appearance, 48.1. Shakespeare, *Julius Caesar* 4.2.325–36, has Brutus see Caesar's ghost on the night before the battle but the sources tell a different story.

221 *Cassius supposedly saw Caesar's ghost* Valerius Maximus, *Memorable Deeds and Sayings* 1.8.8.

221 *Brutus wrote with courage and acceptance to Atticus* Plutarch, *Brutus* 29.9.

222 *The odds were good for Brutus and Cassius at Philippi* The sources on the battle are Appian, *Civil Wars* 4.109–31; Cassius Dio, *Roman History* 47.42.1–49.4; Plutarch, *Brutus* 40–52.

222 *a veritable roll call of Roman nobles* Velleius Paterculus, *History of Rome* 2.71.1–2.

222 *Afterward, reports credited him with paying careful attention* Cassius Dio, *Roman History* 47.41.3.

223 *Some ancient writers said* On Cassius's death see Plutarch, *Brutus* 43; Appian, *Civil Wars* 4.113–14; Cassius Dio, *Roman History* 47.46.2–5.

223 *Cassius's birthday* Although the date of the first battle of Philippi is debatable, the sources state that it was his birthday. Plutarch, *Brutus* 40.4; Appian, *Civil Wars* 4.113.

223 *"the last of the Romans"* Appian, *Civil Wars* 4.114.

223 *Brutus was no general* Plutarch, *Comparison of Dion and Brutus* 3.1–2; Velleius Paterculus, *History of Rome* 2.72.2.

224 *For once, Plutarch is more credible* Plutarch, *Brutus* 50–52; Appian, *Civil Wars* 4.131; Cassius Dio, *Roman History,* 47.49.1–2; see Clarke, *The Noblest Roman,* 70–72.

224 *Other nobles joined the ranks of the fallen* Velleius Paterculus, *History of Rome,* 2.71.1–2.

224 *"when virtue broke"* Horace, *Odes* 7.2.11. On Horace and Brutus's vir-

tue more generally, see John Moles, "Politics, Philosophy, and Friendship in Horace: Odes 2,7," in William S. Anderson, ed., *Why Horace? A Collection of Interpretations* (Wauconda, IL: Bolchazy-Carducci, 1999), 130–42.

224 *As Plutarch says, even those who hated him for killing Caesar* Plutarch, *Brutus* 1.2–3.

225 *the story goes that when Antony found Brutus's dead body* Plutarch, *Brutus* 53.4.

225 *all, that is, except his head* Appian, *Civil Wars* 4.135; Suetonius, *Augustus* 13.1; Cassius Dio, *Roman History* 47.49.2.

225 *"This was the noblest Roman of them all"* Shakespeare, *Julius Caesar* 5.5.69.

225 *sentiments about Brutus that Plutarch ascribes to him* Plutarch, *Brutus* 29.7.

226 *Brutus said that Antony would pay* Plutarch, *Brutus* 29.10–11.

226 *Military gravestones . . . contemporary poetry* See Josiah Osgood, *Caesar's Legacy: Civil War and the Emergence of the Roman Empire* (Cambridge and New York: Cambridge University Press), 108–51.

227 *massacred a large number of enemy senators* Suetonius, *Augustus* 15.

227 *Suetonius writes that within three years* Suetonius, *Julius Caesar* 89.

228 *Decimus Turullius* Cassius Dio, *Roman History* 51.8.2–3; Valerius Maximus, *Memorable Deeds and Sayings* 1.1.19.

228 *Turullius's colleague Cassius of Parma* Velleius Paterculus, *History of Rome* 2.87.3; Valerius Maximus, *Memorable Deeds and Sayings* 1.7.7.

228 *"little works"* Horace, *Epistles* 1.4.3.

228 *Cassius of Parma wrote satire* Suetonius, *Augustus* 4.2; Kenneth Scott, "The Political Propaganda of 44–30 B.C.," *Memoirs of the American Academy in Rome* 11 (1933): 13–16.

228 *Cassius of Parma was the last of Caesar's assassins to die* Velleius Paterculus, *History of Rome* 2.87.3.

CHAPTER 13. AUGUSTUS

230 *Octavian held a triple triumph* Cassius Dio, *Roman History* 51.21.

230 *two of her children by Antony* Cleopatra Selene and Alexander Helios. The

third child, Ptolemy Philadelphus, is not mentioned, and presumably he was already dead. Cassius Dio, *Roman History* 51.21.8.

230 *"too many Caesars is not a good thing"* Arius in Plutarch, *Antony* 81.2.

230 *On the eighteenth of the month Sextilis* Cassius Dio, *Roman History* 51.22; Augustus, *Res Gestae* 19.

230 *Caesar's birthday* Cassius Dio, *Roman History* 47.18.6. Caesar was actually born on July 13 but that day conflicted with an annual Apollo festival.

231 *After Antony's death: Cassius Dio,* Roman History 51.19.3. See Jerzy Linderski, "The Augural Law," in Hildegarde Temporini, ed., *Aufstieg und Niedergang der römischen Welt* 2.16 (1986): 2187–88.

231 *Parricide Day* Suetonius, *Julius Caesar* 88; Cassius Dio, *Roman History* 47.19.1.

231 *Pompey's Senate House* Suetonius, *Julius Caesar* 88, *Augustus* 31; Cassius Dio, *Roman History* 47.19; Eva Margareta Steinby, ed., *Lexicon Topographicum Urbis Romae* (Rome: Edizioni Quasar, 1993), vol. 1: 334–35.

233 *"The evil that men do"* Shakespeare, *Julius Caesar*, 3.2.75–76.

234 *"If we want everything to stay the same"* "Se vogliamo che tutto rimanga come è, bisogna che tutto cambi," Giuseppe Tomasi di Lampedusa, *Il Gattopardo*, 1. ed. in "Le comete."

234 *Augustus portrayed Decimus as an archvillain* So we can judge by Decimus's prominence in Nicolaus of Damascus, who was influenced by Augustus's memoirs.

234 *"I'll do it but only if I live"* Seneca, *Letters to Lucilius* 10.82.12.

235 *At least three or four friends of Brutus* Publius Volumnius, Empylus, Asinius Pollio, Lucius Sestius, and Bibulus. See Ramsay MacMullen, *Enemies of the Roman Order*, 18 and, on Bibulus, Plutarch, *Brutus* 13.

235 *The story goes that when Augustus saw a statue* Plutarch, *Comparison of Dion and Brutus* 5.

236 *magnificent funeral* Tacitus, *Annals* 3.76.

236 *lived into her eighties* On her age, see L. Hayne, "M. Lepidus and His Wife," *Latomus* 33 (1974): 76 and n. 4.

Index